Early African Entertainments Abroad

AFRICA AND THE DIASPORA

History, Politics, Culture

SERIES EDITORS

Thomas Spear
Neil Kodesh
Tejumola Olaniyan
Michael G. Schatzberg
James H. Sweet

Early African Entertainments Abroad

From the Hottentot Venus to Africa's First Olympians

Bernth Lindfors

The University of Wisconsin Press

Publication of this book has been aided by
a College of Liberal Arts Subvention Grant awarded by
The University of Texas at Austin.

The University of Wisconsin Press
1930 Monroe Street, 3rd Floor
Madison, Wisconsin 53711-2059
uwpress.wisc.edu

3 Henrietta Street, Covent Garden
London WC2E 8LU, United Kingdom
eurospanbookstore.com

Library of Congress Cataloging-in-Publication Data

Lindfors, Bernth, author.
Early African entertainments abroad: from the Hottentot Venus
to Africa's first Olympians / Bernth Lindfors.
pages   cm — (Africa and the diaspora: history, politics, culture)
Includes bibliographical references and index.
ISBN 978-0-299-30164-4 (pbk.: alk. paper)
ISBN 978-0-299-30163-7 (e-book)
1. Africans—Europe—Public opinion—History.
2. Africa—In popular culture.
3. Blacks in popular culture—History.
4. Racism in popular culture—History.
5. Sideshows.
I. Title.   II. Series: Africa and the diaspora.
DT16.5.L57   2014
791.089′9604—dc23
2014007282

Contents

List of Illustrations   vii

Acknowledgments   xi

Introduction   3

1   Courting the Hottentot Venus   10

2   The Bottom Line: African Caricature in Georgian England   34

3   Ira Aldridge at Covent Garden   47

4   Clicks and Clucks: Victorian Reactions to San Speech   75

5   Charles Dickens and the Zulus   89

6   A Zulu View of Victorian London   111

7   Dr. Kahn and the Niam-Niams   123

8   The United African Twins on Tour: A Captivity Narrative   131

9   Circus Africans   158

10   Africa's First Olympians   176

Conclusion   185

Notes   197

Bibliography   221

Index   239

Illustrations

1	Poster of the exhibition of the Hottentot Venus in London	12
2	Aquatint of Sartjee, the Hottentot Venus	13
3	Aquatint of Sartjee, the Hottentot Venus	18
4	Painting of the Hottentot Venus	29
5	Illustration of the Venus de Medici and the Hottentot Venus	30
6	Cast of the body of the Hottentot Venus	32
7	Caricature of the Hottentot Venus and Lord William Wyndham Grenville	38
8	Caricature of the Hottentot Venus, Miss Harvey, and Miss Ridsdale	39
9	Caricature of the Hottentot Venus and the Duke of Clarence	41
10	Playing card featuring the Hottentot Venus	43
11	Caricature of a naval officer, the King of Tombuctoo, and his daughters	44
12	French caricature of the Hottentot Venus and Scots guards	45
13	French caricature of the Hottentot Venus and spectators	45
14	Playbill for Ira Aldridge's first appearance at the Theatre Royal Covent Garden	54
15	Sketch of Ira Aldridge as Othello at the Theatre Royal Covent Garden	59
16	Engraving of Ira Aldridge as Mungo in *The Padlock*	69

17 Playbill for an exhibition of the Bosjesmans at Egyptian Hall, London 77
18 Sketch of the Bosjesmans in the *Pictorial Times* 79
19 Sketch of the Bosjesmans in the *Illustrated London News* 79
20 Illustrated poster for an exhibition of the Bosjesmans at Egyptian Hall, London 80
21 Cover of a booklet titled *The Bosjesmans, or Bush People* 84
22 Sketch of the Earthmen in the *Illustrated London News* 86
23 Sketch of the Earthmen on a British song cover 87
24 Cover of a booklet by C. H. Caldecott titled *Descriptive History of the Zulu Kafirs, Their Customs and Their Country* 92
25 Playbill for the Zulu Kaffirs at St. George's Gallery, Hyde Park Corner, London 94
26 Sketch of the Zulu Kaffirs in the *Illustrated London News* 96
27 Poster of the Zulu Kaffirs, the Aztec Lilliputians, and the Earthmen at Cremorne Gardens, London 105
28 Sketch of a later troupe of Zulus in the *Illustrated London News* 108
29 Cover of a booklet titled *The Niam-Niams or the Tailed Family of Central Africa* 129
30 Sketch of the African Twins 136
31 Playbill for the African Twins at the Theatre Royal Liverpool 139
32 Sketch of the African Twins at Egyptian Hall, Piccadilly 145
33 Poster of the African Twins and their mother 153
34 Cover of a biographical sketch of Millie-Christine 155
35 Song cover of the Two-Headed Nightingale 156
36 Postcard of Clicko, the Wild Dancing South African Bushman 160
37 Photo of Congress of Freaks with the Ringling Bros. and Barnum & Bailey Circus 160
38 Poster of the Ubangi Savages 161
39 Photo of Ubangi women with circus showgirls 161
40 German postcard showing pseudo-Africans 163
41 American circus troupe with pseudo-Zulus 163
42 Poster of Amazulu Princess and companions 165
43 Poster of Wild Kaffirs in Chester, England 166
44 Carte de visite of Zip, the What-Is-It? 168
45 Poster of Zip, the What-Is-It? 169
46 Photo of Zip 172
47 Photo of Zip 172
48 French biographical pamphlet on Zip 173

49 Photo of Len Tau and Jan Mashaini, South African marathon
    runners 178

50 Photo of Pygmies at the 1904 World's Fair in St. Louis 181

51 Photo of Pygmies at the 1904 World's Fair in St. Louis 182

52 Photo of Ota Benga, one of the Pygmies at the 1904 World's
    Fair in St. Louis 191

53 Death mask of Steaurma Jantjes, a Hottentot exhibited in Boston
    and New York 193

54 Cover of a farce involving the Zulu Kaffirs in Germany 194

55 Sketch of a later troupe of Zulus at the Folies-Bergère in Paris 194

56 Caricature by George Cruikshank of "Giraffes—Granny-Dears
    and Other Novelties" 195

Acknowledgments

The essays collected here originally appeared in whole or in part in the following publications and are reprinted with permission as noted.

"Courting the Hottentot Venus," *Africa* (Rome) 40 (1985): 133–48.

"The Afterlife of the Hottentot Venus," *Neohelicon* 16, no. 2 (1989): 293–301. Reprinted with permission of Springer.

"The Bottom Line: African Caricature in Georgian England," *World Literature Written in English* 24 (1984): 43–51.

"Ira Aldridge at Covent Garden, April 1833," *Theatre Notebook* 61, no. 3 (2007): 144–63. Reprinted with permission of Trevor Griffiths, editor of *Theatre Notebook*.

"Clicks and Clucks: Victorian Reactions to San Speech," *Africana Journal* 14, no. 1 (1983): 10–17. Copyright © by Africana Publishing. Reprinted with permission of Lynne Rienner Publishers on behalf of Africana Publishing.

"Seeing the Races Through Zulu Spectacles: Victorian Cultural Attitudes in Modern Times," *Anglistik & Englischunterricht* 16 (1982): 107–17.

"Charles Dickens and the Zulus," *African Literature Today* 14 (1984): 127–40, a journal edited by Eldred Jones. Reprinted with permission of James Currey, an imprint of Boydell & Brewer Ltd.

"A Zulu View of Victorian London," *Munger Africana Library Notes* 48 (1979): 1–19.

"Hottentot, Bushman, Kaffir: Taxonomic Tendencies in Nineteenth-Century Racial Iconography," *Nordic Journal of African Studies* 5, no. 2 (1996): 1–30. Reprinted with permission of Axel Fleisch, editor of *Nordic Journal of African Studies*.

"Dr. Kahn and the Niam-Niams," *Études Germano-Africaines* 6 (1988): 27–36.

"The United African Twins on Tour: A Captivity Narrative," *South African Theatre Journal* 2, no. 2 (1988): 16–41. Reprinted with permission of Petrus du Preez, editor of *South African Theatre Journal*.

"Circus Africans," *Journal of American Culture* 6, no. 2 (1983): 9–14. Reprinted with permission of John Wiley & Sons, Inc.

"P.T. Barnum and Africa," *Studies in Popular Culture* 7 (1984): 18–27. Reprinted with permission of Rhonda V. Wilcox, editor of *Studies in Popular Culture*.

"Africa's First Olympians," *West Africa*, August 6, 1984, 1575–77.

Several of these essays have been reprinted in edited volumes and in collections of my own writings. All of them have been revised and updated to some extent, and they are brought together here as contributions to the study of racial stereotypes in popular culture, particularly as manifested in characteristic verbal and visual responses to African performers in England and America in the nineteenth century. However, given the similarity of some of the individuals and groups represented as well as the circumstances in which they were originally presented to the public as related subjects in a series of discrete studies on a common theme, it has proven difficult to avoid occasional repetitions and redundancies altogether. I accept full responsibility for such infelicities.

I am grateful to the libraries and publications cited for permission to reproduce the images that illustrate the essays. I also wish to thank my daughter Susan for helping with the index and my daughter Brenda for photographing some of the images. In addition, I am grateful that publication of this book has been aided by a College of Liberal Arts Subvention Grant awarded by The University of Texas at Austin.

Early African Entertainments Abroad

Introduction

Long before Darwin, European scientists were wrestling with the question of man's relationship to other living creatures. In the "Great Chain of Being" that was presumed to link all forms of sentient life, man was thought to stand midway between the apes and the angels, a favored if somewhat ambiguous position that made him both animal and spirit. But just as there were different species in the animal world that could be arranged in a hierarchical order of supremacy, so were there different varieties of men and women who could be classified as inferior and superior types and placed accordingly on a graded scale of innate ability.[1] In the animal world Homo sapiens obviously lorded it over the rest, and in this supreme category European man was considered—at least by European men—to be at the very pinnacle of earthly creation. It may have been the scientists' preoccupation with taxonomic tidiness that led logically to the postulation of an absent transitional figure or "missing link" that was believed to have served as a direct genetic connection between men and brutes.

Some scientists, of course, were of the opinion that the link was not missing. By calling attention to the close resemblance of the lowest men and women to the highest apes, they sought to prove that the great chain was intact and un-broken. In their theories non-Western peoples, particularly Africans, were cited as examples of debased creatures sufficiently different in mind and body from European peoples to constitute a separate and unequal branch of the human family, if indeed they deserved to be called human at all. Charles White in *An*

Account of the Regular Gradation in Man and in Different Animals and Vegetables (1799) concluded that "the African, more especially in those particulars in which he differs from the European, approaches to the ape . . . [and] the characteristics which distinguish the African from the European are the same, differing only in degree, as those which distinguish the ape from the European."[2] Sir William Lawrence in his *Lectures on Physiology, Zoology and the Natural History of Man* (1819) stated that "the Negro structure approximates unequivocally to that of the Monkey. It not only differs from the Caucasian model, but is distinguished from it in two respects: the intellectual characters are reduced, the animal features enlarged and exaggerated. This inferiority of organization is attended with corresponding inferiority of faculties; which may be proved, not so much by the unfortunate beings who are degraded by slavery, as by every fact in the past history and the present condition of Africa."[3] Even Baron Georges Cuvier, widely regarded as the greatest naturalist of his day, believed that it was "not for nothing that the Caucasian race has gained domination over the world and made the most rapid progress in the sciences, while the Negroes are still sunken in slavery and the pleasures of the senses. . . . The shape of their head relates them somewhat more than us to the animals."[4] Africans, whether manlike apes or apelike men, belonged at the bottom of the ladder and were the lowest anthropomorphic link in the great chain.

These racist theories were founded less on direct observation than on an acceptance of reports from biased eyewitnesses. Travelers, missionaries, slavers, and plantation owners had told tales of their encounters with Africans, and these accounts, sometimes heavily embroidered with misconceptions, rumors, and outright lies, were accepted as truth and cited in the scientific literature of the day. Cannibalism, for instance, was reported to be rampant throughout Africa, even though few European authorities on the subject went so far as to claim having actually watched Africans eat human flesh. Hearsay and imaginative projection remained convenient substitutes for firsthand observation. One could theorize boldly, unencumbered by facts.

As Michael Pickering has noted: "Over the past two centuries, no colonial or potentially colonial continent has been more anachronistically 'othered' . . . than Africa. [Much of this 'othering'] developed out of two complementary qualities: the profound, but unquestioned sense of superiority of those who produced the stereotypes and their profound, but unrecognized depth of ignorance of those who were so stereotyped. The European approach to Africa over much of the past two centuries betrayed a huge failure of imagination and understanding."[5]

By 1833–34, when England officially abolished slavery in all its territories, London had a small but very visible black population. Black servants, soldiers, and entertainers could be seen in many parts of the city, but most of them hailed from the New World rather than directly from the "Dark Continent." Autochthonous Africans were still hard to find, and when a few of them started to turn up on stages or at fairs exhibited as anthropological curiosities, they invariably created a sensation. A steatopygous San woman, suggestively billed as the "Hottentot Venus," had made a small fortune for her managers between 1810 and 1815 before dying in Paris, whereupon her body had been handed over to the anatomists and had been dissected by the great Cuvier himself, who studied the peculiar parts with great enthusiasm.[6] In the 1840s, shortly after Tom Thumb's conquest of Europe, a family of five diminutive "Bosjesmans" (i.e., San)—two men, two women, and a child—were exhibited with enormous success all over the British Isles. They were followed in the early 1850s by a pair of young "troglodytes" or "Earthmen" (probably also San) who sang and danced their way across England, Scotland, Wales, and Ireland, sometimes in the company of two "Aztec Lilliputians" with whom they formed a popular short partnership. In 1853 a troupe of thirteen Zulus—eleven men, a woman, and a child—were a smash hit for four months in London before going on tour in the major cities of France, Belgium, Germany, and Prussia.[7]

All these shows excited the curiosity of Europeans, but the peoples exhibited could hardly be called typical Africans. Indeed, the reason they were chosen for public display was that they were abnormal in some spectacular way: the Hottentot Venus had a huge rump, the Bosjesmans and Earthmen were unusually small, the "blood-thirsty" Zulu warriors were presented as culturally exotic. Yet it was "savages" of this outlandish sort who were paraded as representative inhabitants of Africa. Freaks and anomalies were palmed off as the norm.

Naturally scientists flocked to these exhibitions and took careful measurements as well as eager mental notes. When a performer died, he or she was subjected to even closer scrutiny, the skeleton, skull, and other durable remains being preserved for posterity. The nineteenth century saw the rise of comparative anatomy and ethnography as important interrelated sciences, and African subjects, alive or dead, furnished some of the data crucial for forming and testing theories about human variation. Debates raged about how to measure intelligence, how to account for cultural differences, how to classify the various peoples of the world. Many scientists of this period agreed with the notorious anatomist Robert Knox, author of *The Races of Man* (1850), that "race or hereditary descent is everything."[8] African specimens were needed as objective proof in support of subjective notions of European racial superiority.

This quest for basic biological information had a political dimension as well. In her perceptive study of scientific racism in Great Britain, Nancy Stepan notes that "a fundamental question about the history of racism in the first half of the nineteenth century is why it was that, just as the battle against slavery was being won by abolitionists, the war against racism in European thought was being lost. The Negro was legally freed by the Emancipation Act of 1833, but in the British mind he was still mentally, morally and physically a slave."[9] Answers to this question have been sought in the intellectual climate of that period, particularly in the shifts of thought that marked the transition from a revolutionary Romantic age to an imperialistic Victorian one.[10] The tendency has been to examine the words and deeds of the leading thinkers, policy makers, religious figures, and adventurers of those times—the scientists, authors, statesmen, missionaries, explorers, and travelers—and to trace through them the evolution of a distorted image of black peoples that both attracted and repelled the fair-skinned, reinforcing irrational assumptions of fundamental racial difference. Throughout Europe (and America), native Africans were stereotyped as brutish, dimwitted, naive, emotional, undisciplined, uncultured[11]—in short, children of nature who needed to be civilized and domesticated. British abolitionists sought to protect them from gross exploitation, while the British government aimed to harness their raw energy for the development of colonial commerce, an enterprise deemed beneficial to Africans themselves, for it would give them useful employment, raise their standard of living, and thereby help to refine their ways. The paternalistic relationship between colonizer and colonized was thus perceived as a necessary symbiosis that was morally correct. At an abstract intellectual level British racism after the Enlightenment may have been largely benign, or intended as such, even while its material effects were often malignant in the extreme.

Racial stereotypes were also powerfully conveyed to the common person through the popular literature of the day, especially the adventure fiction set in various corners of the colonial empire. In a study aptly titled *The Africa That Never Was*, Dorothy Hammond and Alta Jablow documented the role imaginative literature played in disseminating far-fetched racist ideas to non-African readers.[12] Such value-laden discourse, directed at a mass audience, probably did more collective harm than the published reports of ethnologists, many of whom in the later half of the nineteenth century became increasingly preoccupied with formulating "objective" racial theories based on comparisons of quantitative data derived from precise measurements of various anatomical parts, especially the skull.[13] But the subjectivity of the pop writers and the objectivity of the social and physical scientists pointed to the same conclusions because they were based on the same premise: that Africans were by nature inferior to Europeans.

Among men and women of conscience it was believed that this inherent difference in biological status made certain moral demands upon the superior race. Clearly it was unethical to enslave an inferior, but it was considered perverse to marry one. In dealing with subnormal human beings some distance had to be achieved between enforcing total social control and allowing absolute personal freedom. Blacks had to be released from oppressive physical captivity yet kept strictly confined to their proper biological niche at the bottom of the natural human ladder. The civilized and the savage had to remain separated from one another, if only to prevent disastrous taxonomic confusion. For otherwise the neat, color-coded distinctions that marked significant gradations in varieties of mankind could become blurred and indecipherable. It would then be impossible to distinguish at a glance between the Self and the Other.

One very effective method of distancing Africans from Westerners was through visual images. Even the illiterate masses could understand a picture, and the picture didn't have to be accurate to convey a powerful impression. Indeed, before the advent of photography, hand-drawn sketches of black people functioned as a kind of ocular shorthand, reducing complex human beings to a pattern of schematic lines meant to represent their essence. Some of this racial iconography aspired to exact representation undistorted by bias or overstatement, but much of it consciously or unconsciously expressed a bigoted attitude toward the individual or group depicted, emphasizing differences that set this race apart from others. Blacks were thus made to appear less than fully human precisely at the time their basic human rights were being secured through legislation. The paradoxes of British and American racial paternalism are indelibly inscribed in the visual arts of the nineteenth century, particularly in those arts that forthrightly aided and abetted racist thinking.

Racial arguments were advanced in media ranging from careful illustrations in scientific texts to highly exaggerated political caricatures and lampoons, from picturesque portraits in travel books to grotesque images on posters and handbills advertising ethnic entertainments. What gave many of these images an aura of authenticity was the fact that they were drawn from life. The artists who produced them did not have to rely on tall tales or hearsay for their impressions but could record their own responses to living creatures they could see with their own eyes, close up, and in the flesh. The growing international trade in ethnological show business provided them with ample opportunities to record firsthand impressions of non-Western peoples. But this kind of enhanced physical intimacy did not necessarily produce an unbiased visual record. The various distancing devices these artists adopted to portray their subjects tell us something about racial attitudes in the West in the nineteenth century, a century that began with attempts at exploration of selected parts of the African interior and ended with Europe's aggressive expropriation of the entire continent.

There have been numerous attempts to record and interpret Western responses to non-Western peoples. The majority of these have been international in scope,[14] and some have dealt primarily with human oddities or freaks,[15] but only a few—such as Jan Nederveen Pieterse's *White on Black: Images of Africa and Blacks in Western Popular Culture*, Hugh Honour's *The Image of the Black in Western Art: From the American Revolution to World War I*, and Jan Marsh's *Black Victorians: Black People in British Art, 1800–1900*—have concentrated exclusively on the available archive of visual representations of black people. Recent multidisciplinary studies of slavery in the eighteenth century—particularly Simon Gikandi's *Slavery and the Culture of Taste* and Catherine Molineux's *Faces of Perfect Ebony: Encountering Atlantic Slavery in Imperial Britain*—have offered new insights into the cultural significance of common racial ideas permeating British art, literature, and theater. My project, though similar to those done earlier by such pioneers, is more narrowly focused solely on representative Africans and pseudo-Africans, especially several distinctive individuals and groups who gained notoriety in nineteenth-century Britain and elsewhere by performing in public as typical specimens of a particular ethnic group. These were some of the celebrities who gave body to Western concepts of African difference, concepts that continued to circulate in the twentieth century and still linger today as pernicious racial stereotypes. Nineteenth-century black show business in the West left a disturbing legacy of indelible phylogenetic imagery.

Yet the story wouldn't be complete without considering at least one exception, so I have included an account of the response in London to early Shakespearean performances of Ira Aldridge, a gifted African American actor who assumed an African identity in order to stage an effective argument about the humanity of black people. Unlike most of the other performers discussed, Aldridge did not have a manager or impresario who introduced him to the public; rather, he was able to speak for himself and create his own image. And he did this as an actor on the legitimate stage, not as a freak in an ethnological exhibition. Yet he too experienced racial discrimination despite his evident Westernization. There was a concerted effort among some theater critics to keep him off the stage in London, even though audiences there responded warmly to his performances. Indeed, there is evidence that his appearances as Othello had a positive influence on the racial attitudes and opinions of many of those who saw him in that role. We must not forget that in the nineteenth century there were others like him, particularly acculturated British and American blacks, who projected a more wholesome image of Africanness.[16]

The studies of particular individuals and troupes collected here are meant to provide a fuller record of modes of African show business in the West in the nineteenth and early twentieth centuries. The emphasis throughout is on how

African peoples were represented and perceived when they appeared in person, in pictures, or in parodies before audiences outside the African continent. These are graphic chapters in a long history of the reification of derogatory racial concepts in the West.

Some of these stories and images may be off-putting to a modern reader, but for that I offer no apology. I have tried my best to let the record speak for itself, only regretting that testimony from the performers themselves tends to be missing from the historical archive. It would have been interesting to know more about how these individuals and groups felt about the conditions of their employment, how they negotiated with their managers, and how they related to the spectators who came to see them perform. What did they learn from their experiences abroad? What did they think of white people? What stories did they tell their kinsmen when they returned home? We can only speculate about such matters for, except in a few rare instances, we cannot hear them speak for themselves.

1

Courting the Hottentot Venus

On Thursday, September 20, 1810, an unusual advertisement appeared in London's *Morning Post*:

> THE HOTTENTOT VENUS.———Just arrived (and may be seen between the hours of One and Five o'clock in the evening, at No. 225, Piccadilly), from the Banks of the River Gamtoos, on the Borders of Kaffraria, in the interior of South Africa, a most correct and perfect Specimen of that race of people. From this extraordinary phenomena [*sic*] of nature, the Public will have an opportunity of judging how far she exceeds any description given by historians of that tribe of the human species. She is habited in the dress of her country, with all the rude ornaments usually worn by those people. She has been seen by the principal Literati in this Metropolis, who were all greatly astonished, as well as highly gratified, with the sight of so wonderful a specimen of the human race. She has been brought to this country at a considerable expence, by Kendrick Cerar [*sic*], and their stay will be but of short duration.—To commence on Monday next, the 24th inst.—Admittance, 2s. each.

This cleverly worded announcement, implying prior endorsement by luminaries in polite society, was calculated to arouse public interest in the exhibition of a woman from one of the remotest reaches of the British Empire. The reference to "a most correct and perfect Specimen" who "exceeds any description given by historians of that tribe of the human species" suggested that this was a female remarkably well formed and good-looking, a rare beauty capable of charming all who gazed upon her. The title she bore—"The Hottentot Venus"— contributed more than a pinch of piquancy to an image of exotic, voluptuous allure.

But to anyone of that day who had heard anything at all about Hottentots and could read between the lines, the joke would have been obvious. Venus indeed! If this woman was typical of her people, she would not be a beauty queen by English standards but rather a monstrosity, an aberration of nature, a grotesque freak. Her most remarkable features would be a huge, steatopygous bottom and an elongated genital "apron," characteristics that were thought to link her more closely to baboons and monkeys than to human beings. Any "correct and perfect" specimen of Hottentot womanhood would have to exceed particular European anatomical norms to such an extent as to appear grossly misshapen, oddly malformed. Her perfection could only be spectacular imperfection, her voluptuousness a farce.

The coarse joke drew crowds. The show was not widely advertised in the weeks that followed so it may have owed its initial success to posters displaying her peculiarities as well as to word-of-mouth endorsements from customers who had paid their two shillings to see this novel creature, but when a controversy arose in the press about the decency of her display—a dispute that ultimately had to be resolved in court—her notoriety grew until she became a household word. Songs, quips, spoofs, and caricatures inspired by the "Hottentot Venus" began to circulate widely, transforming her into a phenomenon of the popular culture of her day.

She remained on the London stage for more than eight months, then toured the provinces for a while, and a few years later resurfaced for a sixteen-month run in Paris, where she made a lasting impact not only on popular culture but also on natural science. After her premature death in 1815 she was dissected by Baron Georges Cuvier, the leading naturalist in France, who published a definitive report on her anatomical peculiarities. Other scientists followed Cuvier's lead, using this rare specimen as a basis for sweeping generalizations about the physical and cultural characteristics of certain native peoples of South Africa. As a consequence, one bottom-heavy woman continued to influence the way Africans were perceived in Europe until ultimately she became reified as a biological concept, a scientifically sanctified racial cliché. Her skeleton, decanted brain, and other remains were preserved and studied at the Museé de l'Homme, where a plaster cast of her body, naked and unadorned, stood on public display until 1982. Thus, of all early nineteenth-century stage performers, the Hottentot

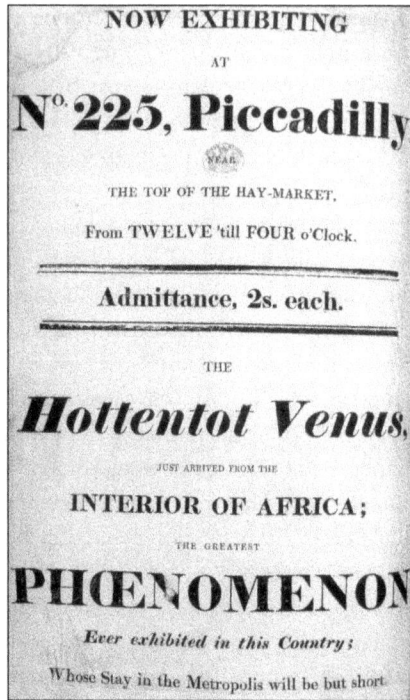

NOW EXHIBITING

AT

N°.225, Piccadilly,

NEAR

THE TOP OF THE HAY-MARKET.

From TWELVE 'till FOUR o'Clock.

Admittance, 2s. each.

THE

Hottentot Venus,

JUST ARRIVED FROM THE

INTERIOR OF AFRICA;

THE GREATEST

PHŒNOMENON

Ever exhibited in this Country;

Whose Stay in the Metropolis will be but short.

Figure 1. Poster of the exhibition of the Hottentot Venus in London, 1810. © The British Library
Board. Reprinted by permission of the British
Library (Lysons Collectanea c.103.k.11, vol. 1,
p. 100).

Venus must be recognized as the one who has had the greatest overall exposure
and the longest consecutive run.

But it is not her career in show business or science that interests us here.
Rather, it is her day in court that prompts a fresh postmortem examination, for
the controversy surrounding her exhibition and the manner in which her working conditions were investigated and her interests protected shed light on humanitarian impulses and legal constraints in the Romantic age. Let us see what
kind of justice a Hottentot could expect in Georgian England.

First, the background to her case.[1] Sartjee Baartman (for that was her
real name) had been conveyed to England by Alexander Dunlop, a British
army surgeon who had formed a show business partnership with Hendric Cezar,
a Coloured farmer at the Cape. On arriving in London, Dunlop had tried to
sell his share in her, as well as a giraffe skin, to William Bullock, a prosperous
antiquarian who owned a museum of art and natural history. Bullock had

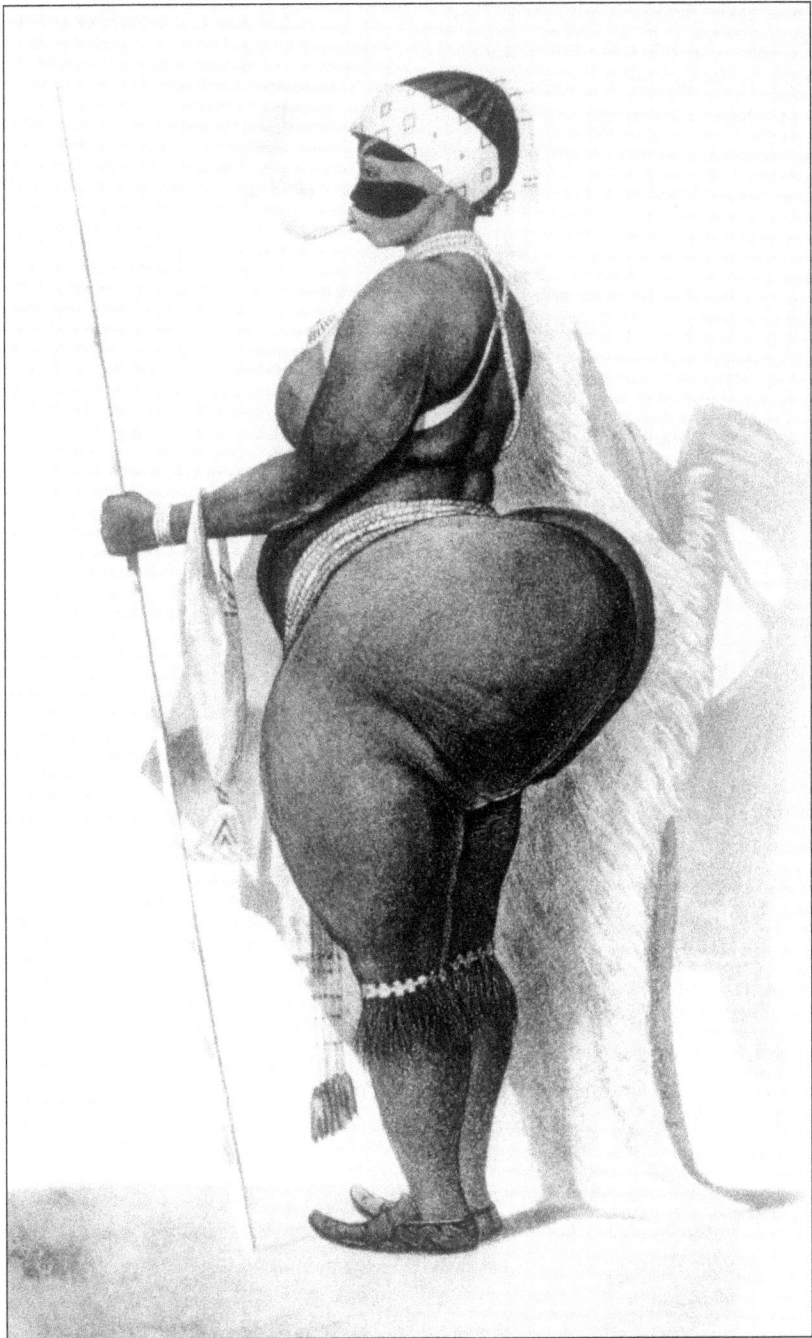

Figure 2. Aquatint of Sartjee, the Hottentot Venus, 1810. © The British Library Board. Reprinted by permission of the British Library (Lysons Collectanea c.103.k.11, vol. 1, opp. p. 101).

bought the skin but refused the Hottentot, so Dunlop had sold out to his partner Cezar, who began exhibiting her in London with such success that Dunlop soon regretted having so rashly relinquished his interest in her. Sartjee apparently had taken no part in these negotiations, even though she may have been the one most affected by the outcome.

The show itself was described in a report in the *Times* as taking place on

> a stage raised about three feet from the floor, with a cage, or enclosed place at the end of it; that the Hottentot was within the cage; that on being ordered by her keeper, she came out, and that her appearance was highly offensive to delicacy. . . . The Hottentot was produced like a wild beast, and ordered to move backwards and forwards, and come out and go into her cage, more like a bear in a chain than a human being. . . . She frequently heaved deep sighs; seemed anxious and uneasy; grew sullen, when she was ordered to play on some rude instrument of music. . . . And one time, when she refused for a moment to come out of her cage, the keeper let down the curtain, went behind, and was seen to hold up his hand to her in a menacing posture; she then came forward at his call, and was perfectly obedient. . . . She is dressed in a color as nearly resembling her skin as possible. The dress is contrived to exhibit the entire frame of her body, and the spectators are even invited to examine the peculiarities of her form.[2]

Some of the spectators accepted this invitation by touching her rump and searching for evidence of padding or some other artifice beneath her skimpy, skin-colored dress. A woman who saw the show reported: "One pinched her, another walked round her; one gentleman *poked* her with his cane; and one *lady* employed her parasol to ascertain that all was, as she called it, '*nattral*.' This inhuman baiting the poor creature bore with sullen indifference, except upon some great provocation, when she seemed inclined to resent brutality, which even a Hottentot can understand. On these occasions it required all the authority of the keeper to subdue her resentment."[3] Another spectator told a similar tale of what had transpired on the night he had seen her perform:

> She was extremely ill, and the man insisted on her dancing, this being one of the tricks which she is forced to display. The poor creature pointed to her throat and to her knees as if she felt pain in both, pleading with tears that he would not force her compliance. He declared that she was sulky, produced a long piece of bamboo, and shook it at her: she saw it, knew its power, and, though ill, delayed no longer. While she was

playing on a rude kind of guitar, a gentleman in the room chanced to
laugh: the unhappy woman, ignorant of the cause, imagined herself
the object of it, and as though the slightest addition to the woes of sickness, servitude, and involuntary banishment from her native land was
more than she could bear, her broken spirit was aroused for a moment,
and she endeavored to strike him with the musical instrument which
she held: but the sight of the long bamboo, the knowledge of its pain,
and the fear of incurring it again, calmed her. The master declared
that she was as wild as a beast, and the spectators agreed with him,
forgetting that the language of ridicule is the same, and understood
alike, in all countries, and that not one of them could bear to be the
object of derision without an attempt to revenge the insult.[4]

It is clear from these remarks that not everyone in the audience found this
kind of entertainment amusing. Within a few weeks, letters of protest began to
appear in the London press complaining not only of the degraded nature of the
exhibition but also of the state of servitude in which the woman apparently was
being kept.[5] Since the slave trade had recently been abolished in British territories, why was the keeper of this unhappy woman being allowed to profit from
her misery? Such a display was both immoral and illegal.

Hendric Cezar responded to this outcry by addressing a rejoinder to the
editor of the *Morning Chronicle*:

Sir,

Having observed in your paper of this day, a letter signed "An
Englishman," containing a malicious attack on my conduct in exhibiting
a Hottentot woman, accusing me of cruelty and ill treatment exercised
towards her, I feel myself compelled, as a stranger, to refute this asper-
sion, for the vindication of my own character, and the satisfaction of
the public. In the first place, he betrays the greatest ignorance in regard
to the Hottentot, who is as free as the English. This woman was my servant at the Cape, and not my slave, much less can she be so in England,
where all breath [*sic*] the air of freedom; she is brought here with her
own free will and consent, to be exhibited for the joint benefit of both
our families. That there may be no misapprehension on the part of the
public, any person who can make himself understood to her is at perfect
liberty to examine her, and know from herself whether she has not been
always treated, not only with humanity, but the greatest kindness and
tenderness.

HENDRIC CEZAR[6]

This response provoked more letters to the editor about the show, with some correspondents asserting that Cezar was being less than candid in his remarks and should be compelled to give more details about how he inveigled this woman away from her home and country.[7] One called upon the Missionary Society to intervene on her behalf,[8] and another, "knowing the adventurous hardihood of science," expressed prescient concern lest the woman perish during the winter and then fall into the hands of the anatomists.[9]

Cezar replied again a few days later, offering to show his passport from Lord Caledon, governor of the Cape of Good Hope, to anyone who cared to see it, and asserting once more that the Female Hottentot was "a subject well worthy the attention of the Virtuoso [*sic*], and the curious in general . . . [as] has been fully proved, by the approbation of some of the first Rank and chief Literati in the kingdom, who saw her previous to her being publicly exhibited." He went on to say that he himself no longer took an active part in the exhibition: "as my mode of proceeding at the place of public entertainment seems to have given offense to the Public, I have given the sole direction of it to an Englishman, who now attends." But he also took the opportunity to raise an important new issue by asking if the Hottentot Venus had not "as good a right to exhibit herself as an Irish Giant, or a Dwarf, &c, &c."[10] In other words, wasn't she, like other people in England, at liberty to take up whatever form of employment suited her? Didn't she have a right to work?

Cezar's letter drew a number of angry responses,[11] but only one of these addressed the new issue. Someone signing himself "Humanitas" argued in a long letter to the editor that

> yes, she has a right to *exhibit herself*, but there is no right in her *being exhibited*. The Irish Giant, Mr. Lambert, and the Polish Dwarf, were all masters and directors of their own movements; and they, moreover, *enjoyed, they themselves enjoyed, the profits of their own exhibition*: the first two were men of sound understanding, and were able to tell when *they were plundered and defrauded of these profits, and to insist on the appropriation of exhibition profits to themselves*: the money derived from personal misfortune *was their own*: it comforted them in the active moments of their existence, or supplied them with enjoyment when laid aside. Do the public believe that one shilling, nay a single farthing, of the profits arising from her exhibition will ever go into the hands of the Female Hottentot, or of her relatives or friends? Who audits the accounts? Who looks after the balance between expence and income? the avaricious speculator, or the unfeeling gaoler who have brought her here, who receive the

money, and—who will keep it. No; after having run the gauntlet
through the three capitals of England, Scotland, and Ireland, and
traversed their provincial towns, dragged through them with greater
barbarity than Achilles dragged the body of Hector at the foot of his
chariot round Troy's walls, this miserable female will be taken back to
the Cape; not enriched by European curiosity, but rendered poorer if
possible than when she left her native soil.[12]

As these letters make plain, the battle over Sartjee Baartman was shaping
up into a classic confrontation between heated humanitarianism and cold
commerce, between the abolitionist conscience and the entrepreneurial ideal,
between love and money.

The matter was taken to court by three members of the African Institution—
Zachary Macaulay, Thomas Gisborne Babington, and Peter Van Wageninge—
who filed an affidavit at Chancery Lane on October 17 after having seen performances by the Hottentot Venus a few days earlier. Macaulay, explaining
that he was secretary of the African Institution, an organization "the object of
which is the civilization of Africa," said he had gone to Piccadilly on October 11
because he had understood from public advertisements that "a native of South
Africa denominated the Hottentot Venus of a most extraordinary and unnatural
shape was publicly exhibited for Money" there, and he wanted to find out
"under what circumstances she came to England and whether she was made a
public spectacle with her own free will and consent or whether she was compelled to exhibit herself."[13] He said that if she wished to return to her own
country, the African Institution would be anxious to arrange that she be transported there.

This was no idle boast. Though formed only three years earlier, the African
Institution brought together the leaders of the abolition movement in Britain,
who collectively could exert a great deal of moral pressure on governmental
and religious bodies. Macaulay himself, in addition to his duties as secretary of
this new organization, was then serving on the governing Committee of the
Church Missionary Society, and he had been one of the first governors of the
Sierra Leone Colony, which had been formed at the end of the eighteenth
century for the purpose of repatriating blacks living in Nova Scotia to a new
settlement at Freetown. He was in a good position to marshal support for the
repatriation of Sartjee Baartman.

In his affidavit Macaulay described the stage erected in the room in which
this woman was exhibited and stated that when she appeared, she "was clothed
in a dress resembling her complexion which is very dark and her dress was so

Figure 3. Aquatint of Sartjee, the Hottentot Venus, 1810. From author's collection.

tight that her shapes above and the enormous size of her posterior parts are as visible as if the said female were naked and the dress is evidently intended to give the appearance of her being undressed."

He then went on to recount at length the conversation he entered into with Hendric Cezar, who told him that he had obtained her at the Cape of Good Hope from "Dutch Boors" who had come from the interior and that he had been given permission from the government at the Cape to take her to England. Surprised to hear this, Macaulay asked, "What, did Lord Caledon who is Governor at the Cape give permission for her being brought to England?" Cezar said he did. "Was Lord Caledon's permission in writing?" Macaulay asked. Yes, Cezar replied, it was. "Did Lord Caledon know that she was brought to this country to be exhibited?" Macaulay persisted. "Oh! Yes, Yes," Cezar answered, whereupon Macaulay asked to see the document Lord Caledon had signed, for being in the habit of corresponding with him, he believed he would be able to recognize his handwriting. "What, won't you believe my word?" Cezar responded. "I have already told you that he has signed it and I shall give you no further satisfaction." Macaulay proceeded to ask further questions about the woman, but the exhibitor refused to answer them, saying, "I do not choose to have so many questions put to me."

In the rest of his deposition Macaulay elaborated on the performance he had witnessed, noting that Cezar "sometimes would call the said female to him, and when she came would desire her to turn round and would invite the spectators to feel her posterior parts. . . . in fact she is exhibited to the public in the same manner that any animal of the brute creation would be exhibited." The woman gave clear signs of being unhappy and dejected, signs that led Macaulay to conclude that she was "under the restraint and control of her exhibitor and is deprived of her liberty." As an example of this, he told of her being ordered to play on a musical instrument "somewhat like a guitar" and displaying evident "mortification and misery at her degraded situation in being made a spectacle for the derision of the bystanders without the power of resistance."

Babington and Van Wageninge, in their part of the joint deposition, testified that at the request of Macaulay they had gone to see a performance by this woman on October 15 and had found it to be exactly as described by him. Van Wageninge, a native of Holland, on being informed by the exhibitor that she could speak imperfect Dutch, put many questions to her ("whence she came, whether she had any relations, whether she was happy and comfortable here, and whether she was desirous of returning home"), but she would not answer any of them. Babington and Van Wageninge said they had heard her utter several deep sighs such as would be given by someone whose mind was distressed, and they related the incident in which the curtain was drawn for a moment and the woman threatened with a beating by Cezar for not responding to his commands. They agreed with Macaulay that she was being kept in a condition of involuntary servitude.

On the first of November a supporting affidavit was filed by William Bullock, proprietor of the Liverpool Museum in London, who reported the offer that Alexander Dunlop had made to sell him both a Hottentot woman and a giraffe skin. Bullock, "feeling that such an exhibition would not meet the countenance of the public declined acceding to Mr. Dunlop's proposal and only purchased the skin." In later dealings with Dunlop, Bullock heard him lament being "so unfortunate as to sell and dispose of his Interest in the exhibiting of the said Hottentot Woman and that he has now next to nothing to do with her."[14]

The matter was brought before the magistrates of the Court of the King's Bench on Saturday, November 24, with the attorney general pleading on Sartjee's behalf. Since verbatim transcripts of court proceedings were not kept in those days, we must rely on "Law Intelligence" reports in newspapers for an account of what happened when this unusual case was heard. According to *Bell's Weekly Messenger*, the attorney general's motion asked the following:

> That Mr. Henry [*sic*] Cezar should shew cause why a Writ of Habeas Corpus should not be directed to him, for the three following purposes— First, to bring up the body of a Hottentot woman, whom he detains, as a public spectacle, in his custody. Secondly, And that he should permit her to be examined by persons cognizant of the language which she understands, whether she is thus detained at her own election, and that such examination should not take place in the presence of Mr. Cezar or any of his keepers. Third, To show cause why, at the discretion of the Court, the said female prisoner should not be given up to the charge and protection of the African Institution, they undertaking to give security to the Court, that they will convey her safely back to her own country.[15]

In support of this motion the attorney general presented the affidavits that had been filed by Macaulay and others representing the African Institution and by William Bullock, and he commented briefly on the disgraceful nature of the performance as well as on the woman's obvious displeasure at displaying herself in so humiliating a manner. At this point one of the magistrates, Mr. Justice Le Blanc, suggested that if the performance was indecent, it would be possible for criminal proceedings to be instituted against Cezar for a breach of public decorum. The attorney general answered that such was not his present purpose; he sought only an opportunity to ascertain whether the woman was in a state of coercion, and he felt that this could best be done by putting the pertinent questions to her in Dutch in the absence of her keeper but in the presence of court-appointed witnesses for both sides. Some discussion followed as to whether the woman had sufficient command of Dutch to be interviewed in that language, but after being reassured that she appeared to understand Low Dutch, the magistrates felt inclined to rule in favor of this part of the petition.

However, with regard to the third point raised—that the court direct that the woman be transferred from her keeper to the protection of the African Institution—the presiding magistrate, Lord Ellenborough, anticipated a possible legal snag: the court could only restore the liberty of a person held under coercion; it could not transfer this woman to the custody of some other person or group, however benevolent, unless she herself chose to be placed in such custody: "Before we can remove her from her present situation, we must be satisfied that she is an object capable of making an election; that she feels pain from the constraint in which she is at present held; and that she is desirous of being put under the care of persons who will restore her to her own country."[16] These, then, were the issues to be resolved through an interview in Low Dutch with the woman called the Hottentot Venus. The representatives of the African Institution would be given an opportunity to explain their intentions to the woman so she could make a free choice at the conclusion of the hearing. Lord Ellenborough's reference to "the constraint in which she is at present held" suggests that he may have assumed that the African Institution's assessment of her situation was accurate and would be corroborated by her own statements. Though there were a few small procedural problems remaining, such as the selection of impartial interviewers, the case seemed to he going the abolitionists' way.

The interview took place two days later with the results being reported to the court on November 28. Since the deposition made by the witnesses present contains the only testimony we have from Sartjee Baartman herself, and since it includes a number of interesting details, only a few of which were enlarged upon in court, it may be of interest to reproduce the entire document here:

> She does not know when she left her native place she being very young when she came to the Cape: the Brother of her late Master, Peter Caesar, brought her to the Cape: she came with her own consent with Peter Caesar and was taken into the service of Henrick Caesar as his nursery maid; she came by her own consent to England and was promised half of the money for exhibiting her person—she agreed to come to England for a period of six years; she went personally to the Government in Company with Henrick Caesar to ask permission to go to England: Mr. Dunlop promised to send her back after that period at his own expence and to send the money belonging to her with her— she is kindly treated and has every thing she wants; Has no complaints to make against her master or those that exhibit her: is perfectly happy in her present situation: has no desire whatever of returning to her own

country not even for the purpose of seeing her two Brothers and four sisters: wishes to stay here because she likes the Country and has money given her by her Master of a Sunday when she rides about in a Coach for a couple of hours—Her father was in the habit of going with Cattle from the interior to the Cape and was killed in one of those Journeys by the "Bosmen," her mother died twenty years ago—she has a Child by a Drummer at the Cape with whom she lived for about two years yet being always in the employ of Henrick Caesar; the child is since dead—she is to receive one half of the money received for exhibiting herself and Mr. Dunlop the other half—she is not desirous of changing her present situation—no personal violence or threats have been used by any individual against her; she has two Black Boys to wait upon her: One of the men assists her in the morning when she is nearly completely attired for the purpose of fastening the Ribbon round her waist—her dress is too cold and she has complained of this to Henrick Caesar who promised her warmer Cloathes; Her Age she says to be twenty two and that her stay at the Cape was three years—To the various questions we put to her whether if she chose at any time to discontinue her person being exhibited, she might do so, we could not draw a satisfactory answer from her—She understands very little of the Agreement made with her by Mr. Dunlop on the twenty ninth October 1810 and which Agreement she produced to us—The time of Examination lasted for about three hours—and the questions put to her were put in such a language as to be understood by her.—and these Deponents say they were informed by the said female that she could neither read or write.

S. Solly

Mr. Geo. Moojen[17]

These unexpected revelations must have astonished the magistrates and the gentlemen of the African Institution, and although there were a few points in the testimony that possibly could have been challenged in court, it was clear from Sartjee Baartman's statements that she completely understood the commercial nature of her contract with Dunlop, that she did not feel pain as a consequence of the conditions of her employment, and that she had no desire to retire from show business or to be placed under the protection of the African Institution. To head off any argument over the point that "she understands very little of the Agreement made with her by Mr. Dunlop on the twenty ninth October 1810," Dunlop had arranged for a Notary Public, Mr. Arend Jacob Guitard, to file a supplementary affidavit stating that he had translated this Agreement from English into Dutch, had read it twice "plainly and distinctly" to Sartjee Baartman, and that it had appeared to him "that she understood the contents thereof and was therewith satisfied."[18]

Mr. Gasalee, the defending attorney, then rose to refute some of the charges that had been made against his clients. First, in response to the allegation that Cezar had threatened to strike the woman on stage, Gasalee countered that Cezar no longer took any part in the exhibition, so it could not now be claimed that she was being treated cruelly by him before the public. Second, as far as the imputation of indecency was concerned, Gasalee wanted the court to know that during her performance she wore not only a thin silk dress but also a cotton one underneath it. He went on to say that if the African Institution wished to protect her financial interests, his clients would be pleased if they would appoint a trustee to take care of her share in the profits of the exhibition. But since it was evident from her own sworn testimony that the woman was under no restraint, their case against Cezar and Dunlop should be dismissed.[19]

Actually, there was no need for Gasalee to have offered these additional arguments, for the plaintiffs were ready to concede defeat. The attorney general, admitting that the case against the defendants could not he sustained after the introduction of these new affidavits, summed up by stating that, regardless of the final outcome, anyone who had heard of this action in court must certainly feel that "it was very much to the credit of this country that even a Hottentot could find friends to protect her interests."[20] He trusted that henceforth the woman would be properly taken care of and that "those Gentlemen who had so honourably to themselves taken the trouble of looking into her situation, would continue to see that her interests were protected."[21] As expected, Lord Ellenborough then declared the case dismissed but not before issuing a stern warning that if "any immodest or indecent exposure of this female stranger should take place, those who had the care of her must know that the law would direct its arm with uplifted resentment against the offending parties."[22]

The abolitionists thus lost in court but won in principle. Though they did not manage to close the show down, they do appear to have succeeded in cleaning it up, and Sartjee Baartman may have suffered fewer indignities on stage in the months that followed. Public reaction to the court case was quite positive. One journal exclaimed that "the enquiry does honour to the liberal and humane spirit of our times; to the feelings of the individuals who first instituted it, and to the benevolence of that society by which it was supported."[23] The gentlemen of the African Institution evidently had achieved a minor moral victory.

Nonetheless, what most impressed ordinary people about the case was not the high conscience of the abolitionists but the low cupidity of the Hottentot. Her insistence upon her right to make a spectacle of herself, like any profit-minded dwarf or giant in the exhibition trade, became the subject of countless jokes, cartoons, and newspaper doggerel. Here is the text of a ballad that began to circulate after the court ruled in her favor:

A Ballad
The storie of the Hottentot Ladie and her lawful Knight, who essaied to release her out of captivitie, and what my lordes the judges did therein.

Oh have you been in London towne,
Its rareties to see:
There is, 'mongst ladies of renown,
A most renowned she.
In Piccadillie Streete so faire
A mansion she has got,
On golden letters written there,
"THE VENUS HOTTENTOT."

But you may ask, and well, I ween,
For why she tarries there;
And what, in her is to be seen,
Than other folks more rare.
A rump she has, (though strange it be),
Large as a cauldron pot,
And this is why men go to see
This lovely Hottentot.

Now this was shown for many a day,
And eke for many a night;
Till sober folks began to say,
That all could not be right,
Some said, this was with her goodwill:
Some said, that it was not,
And asked why they did use so ill
This ladie HOTTENTOT.

At last a doughty Knight stood forth,
Sir Vikar was his name;
A knight of singular good worth,
Of fair and courtly fame.
With him the laws of chivalrie

Were not so much forgot;
But he would try most gallantly
To serve the HOTTENTOT.

He would not fight but *plead* the cause
Of this most injured she;
And so, appealed to the laws,
To set the lady free.
A mighty "Habeas corpus"
He hoped to have got,
Including rump and all, and thus
Release the HOTTENTOT.

Thus driving on with might and main
This Gallant Knight did say,
He wished to send her home again,
To Africa far away.
On that full pure and holy plan
To soothe her rugged lot:
[He] swore, in troth, no other man
Should *keep* his HOTTENTOT.

He went unto the Judges grave,
Whose mercies never fail;
And there, in gallant stile, and brave,
Set forth the ladie's tale.
He said, a man of cruel heart,
(Whose name is now forgot,)
Did shew, for pay, the hinder part
Of this fair HOTTENTOT.

That in this land of libertie,
Where freedom groweth still,
No one can show another's tail
Against the owner's will.
And wished my lordes to send some one,
To know whether or not
This rare exhibiting was done
To please the HOTTENTOT.

The judges did not hesitate
This piteous tale to hear,
Conceiving her full-bottom'd state,
Claimed *their* especial care;
And told the Knight that he might do
As he thought best, and what:
E'en visit privately, and view,
His ladie HOTTENTOT.

Then straight two gentlemen they set,
(One English and one Dutch)
To learn if she did money get;
And, if she did, how much.
Who, having finished their intent,
And visited the spot,
Did say t'was done with full consent
Of the fair HOTTENTOT.

When speaking free from all alarm,
The whole she does deride;
And says she thinks there is no great harm
In shewing her b—kside.
Thus ended this sad tale of woe,
Which raised well, I wot,
The fame, and the revenues too,
Of Sartjee HOTTENTOT.

And now good people all may go
To see this wondrous sight;
Both high born men, and also low,
And eke the good Sir Knight.
Not only this her state to mind,
Most anxious what she got;
But looking to her latter end
Delights the HOTTENTOT.[24]

This ballad, meant as a humorous gloss on a round, unvarnished tale, never-theless touched upon an aspect of British justice that had very serious implications for Sartjee Baartman—namely, that she could not be protected from exploitation because in ignorance she freely elected to continue working, no doubt believing that she stood to benefit from further self-exposure. Given the opportunity to quit show business, escape from the control of Cezar and Dunlop, and seek repatriation to her homeland, she chose to remain on stage in London. She was willing to collaborate in her own degradation in order to earn more money. Granted, she may never have understood exactly what the lawsuit was all about, and she may have made a fatal error in placing more trust in her managers than in the representatives of the African Institution, but she could not have failed to comprehend what the conditions of her employment were. She had agreed to allow herself to be exhibited indecently to the European public, and she persisted in this tawdry occupation for more than five years, stopping only when her health finally broke down. She may have been the victim of the cruelest kind of predatory ruthlessness, but her collusion in her own victimization seems clear. She wanted the show to go on and the profits to keep rolling in. She wanted to capitalize on Western curiosity.

The depths to which she may have been willing to descend to achieve her objective are suggested in a remark made by a French anthropologist when commemorating the one-hundredth anniversary of her death. After a brief review of the career of this notorious celebrity, he said that more than four decades earlier he had heard a scandalous report that "she did not scorn those of her admirers who had the kind of morals that made Sodom famous"; moreover, he felt "compelled to admit that the wax mouldings [of her private parts] in our possession do nothing to contradict these malicious rumors."[25] To put it plainly, she may have engaged in prostitution as well as exhibitionism. Her degradation may have been complete.

But it would be unfair to blame Sartjee Baartman for having fallen into this way of life. She did not fall; she was pushed into depravity by Western opportunists who saw in her a chance to take advantage of Africa's innocence. Promising her a fortune, they lured her into the kind of misery that leads to self-destruction. She may have hoped to become rich by working abroad, but her ultimate reward was an early death. Humanitarian intervention and British justice could not save her from this fate because she swore before witnesses that she was perfectly happy and under no restraint. Taking her at her word, the magistrate presiding over her case was compelled to rule that she could not be emancipated and repatriated because she was already free—and this included being at liberty to make tragic mistakes. Sartjee Baartman, the "Hottentot Venus," had her day in court and lost.

Shortly after her case was decided in favor of her managers, a Christmas pantomime called "The Hottentot Venus, or Harlequin in Africa" was performed in London and subsequently was carried to the provinces. Four years later, when she was performing in Paris, she was made the subject of a one-act sketch, *La Vénus hottentote, ou haine aux Françaises* (The Hottentot Venus, or Hatred of Frenchwomen),[26] at the Théâtre de Vaudeville, which became part of the regular repertoire of this theater and continued to be performed even after her death.

By the time she died in December 1815, she was already firmly established in European popular imagination as an outlandish figure, a somatic pun, and in the years that followed she remained a focus for ridicule. On Queen Victoria's coronation day in 1838 we find a second "Hottentot Venus" performing at a fair in Hyde Park, and then in the provinces.[27] A decade later, in Thackeray's *Vanity Fair*, a character named George Osborne, responding to his father's suggestion that he marry Miss Swartz, a wealthy heiress from the West Indies, exclaimed, "Marry that mulatto woman? . . . I don't like the colour, sir. Ask the black that sweeps opposite Fleet Street, sir. *I'm* not going to marry a *Hottentot Venus.*"[28] And toward the end of the century Swinburne, in a caustic essay on Walt Whitman, summoned up her image once again: "Mr. Whitman's Eve is a drunken applewoman, indecently sprawling on the slush and garbage of the gutter amid the rotten refuse of her overturned fruit-stall; but Mr. Whitman's Venus is a Hottentot wench under the influence of cantharides and adulterated rum."[29] The "Hottentot Venus" evidently had risen from the grave and taken on a life of her own, having been transformed from a real woman into a popular stereotype.

But it was in science that her career had its longest posthumous extenuation. Immediately after her death Baron Georges Cuvier, the leading naturalist in France, had dissected her, examining her peculiar parts very thoroughly and taking care to preserve her skeleton, skull, brain, and other durable remains; he also wrote a lengthy scientific report on his findings.[30] Plaster casts were made of her body, waxen molds of her genitalia, and all these natural and artificial objects became subjects of intense scrutiny in the years that followed, furnishing generations of scientists with biometric data on racial characteristics. For instance, half a century after her death, Paul Broca used her skeleton to test a theory that longer forearms were a sign of inferior intelligence in certain races, especially those thought to have evolved more slowly from our anthropoid ape ancestors, but he quickly abandoned the theory when the skeletons of the Hottentot Venus, an Australian aborigine, and an Eskimo proved to have shorter forearms than the skeletons of white Europeans.[31] Louis Pierre Gratiolet used her brain, which he called "one of the most precious pieces in our collection," as an example of a physiological extreme in his classic comparative study of human and primate intelligence;[32] so did John Marshall when he read a paper titled "On the Brain of a Bushwoman; and on the Brains of Two Idiots of European Descent" at a meeting of the Royal Society in London in 1864.[33] Her skull

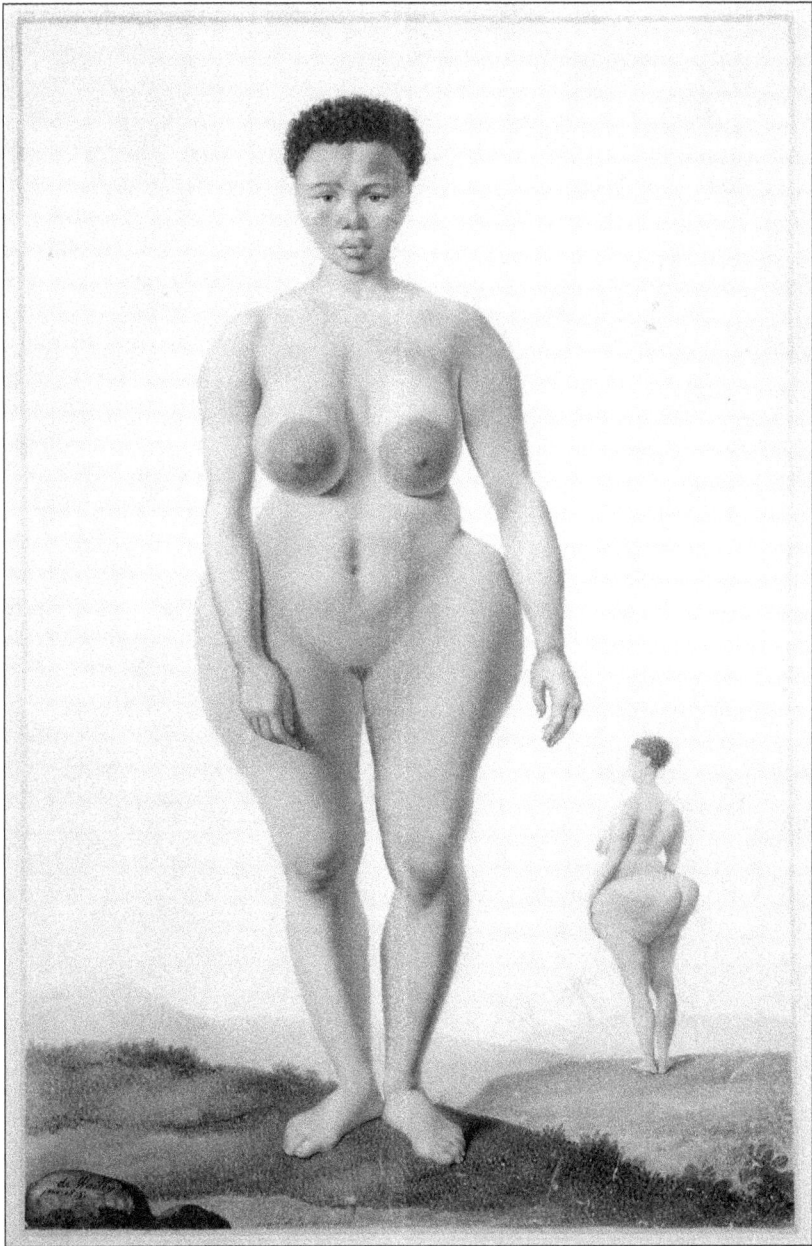

Figure 4. Painting of the Hottentot Venus by Léon de Wailly, 1815. © RMN-Grand Palais / Art Resource, NY. Reprinted by permission of the Muséum National d'Histoire Naturelle, Paris (Collection des vélins, vol. 69, no. 1).

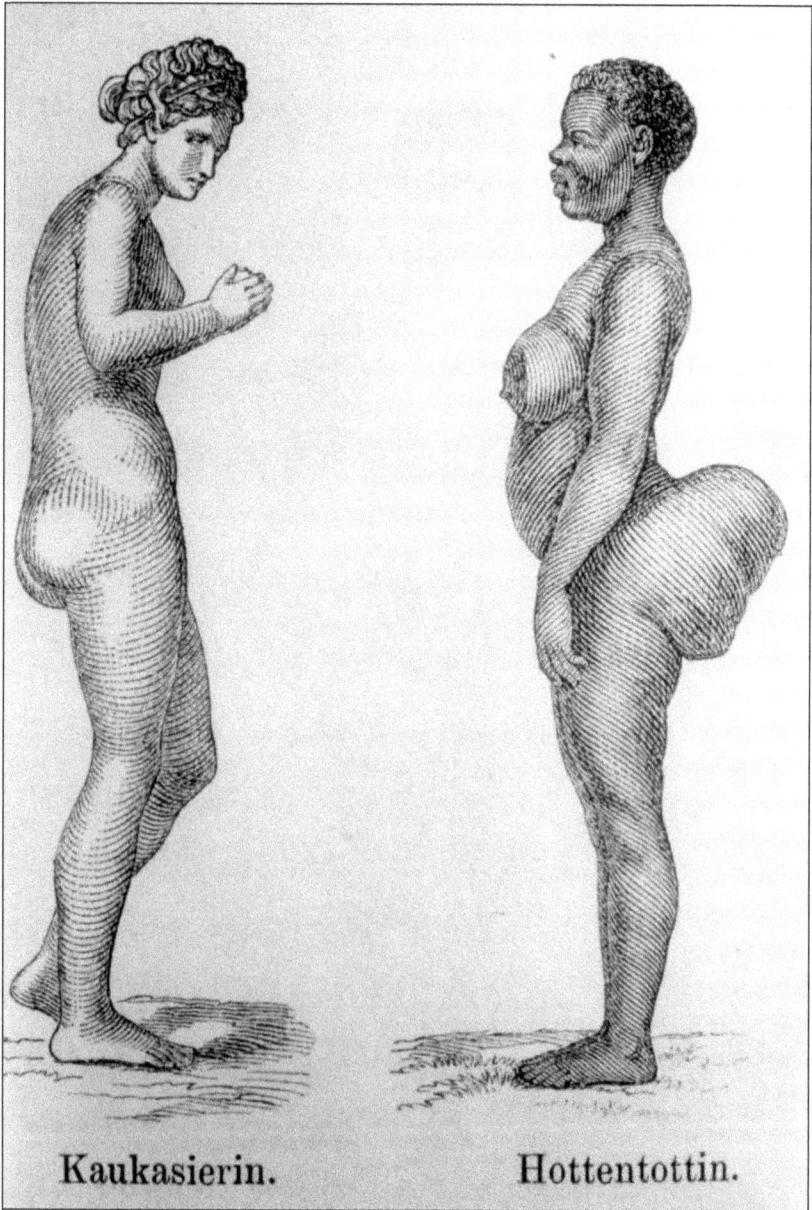

Kaukasierin. **Hottentottin.**

Figure 5. Illustration of the Venus de Medici and the Hottentot Venus. In Hubert von Luschka, *Die Anatomie des Menschen in Rücksicht auf die Bedürfnisse der praktischen Heilkunde: 2,2 Die Anatomie des menschlichen Beckens* (Tübingen: Laupp, 1864), 8. © The British Library Board. Reprinted by permission of the British Library (7421.f.15).

turned up frequently in textbooks of anatomy, usually placed between skulls of a European and an orangutan to illustrate increasing degrees of prognathism as one descended from the higher to the lower orders in the animal kingdom. Pioneers in the newly emerging discipline of craniometry, which dominated biological science in the late nineteenth and early twentieth centuries, made extensive use of data drawn from precise measurements of her cranial capacity; and proponents of phrenology, its pseudo-scientific counterpart, interpreted the shape of her forehead as a sure sign of moral and intellectual inferiority. Soon, too, her image began appearing in encyclopedias of ethnology, even in world histories of costume and fashion, though this time incorrectly clad in a white body stocking.[34] The underlying assumption in most of these so-called serious studies of the Hottentot Venus was that she and the race she represented were different from and decidedly inferior to others—not only physically but also intellectually, morally, and culturally. To European eyes she would never be the equal of a Venus de Medici (see fig. 5), never measure up to Western aesthetic or philosophical standards. Viewed in this ethnocentric manner, she has helped successive generations of Europeans to achieve a more flattering opinion of themselves.

To satisfy public curiosity about unusual African peoples, the skeleton, brain, and a plaster cast of the body (see fig. 6) of the Hottentot Venus were placed on public display in Case 33 of the Musée de l'Homme's anthropological exhibition hall, where they remained for many years a source of instruction and entertainment for visitors. These antiquated human relics were finally removed from the public eye in 1982 after protests were made by groups who found the exhibit offensive and demeaning to women as well as to Africans. Her career in show business thus can be said to have finally ended, but her career in science may continue for some time to come. In the past two centuries the Hottentot Venus has become a standard reference point in anthropometric research, living on as a fixed set of statistics in biological discourse.

In popular culture too she has remained a very durable concept, one that is not likely to die out soon. After being reincarnated as a specific ethnic type, she has achieved an independent existence as a free-floating general symbol of African exoticism. She lives on not as a notorious individual, not even as a Hottentot, and certainly not as a Venus, but as a convenient racial—and racist— cliché.

In recent years there have been efforts to change her image and restore to her some measure of human dignity. In 1994, not long after the African National Congress won the general election in South Africa, President Nelson Mandela asked France to return her remains to her homeland. The French National Assembly finally agreed to do this in March 2002, and her body was

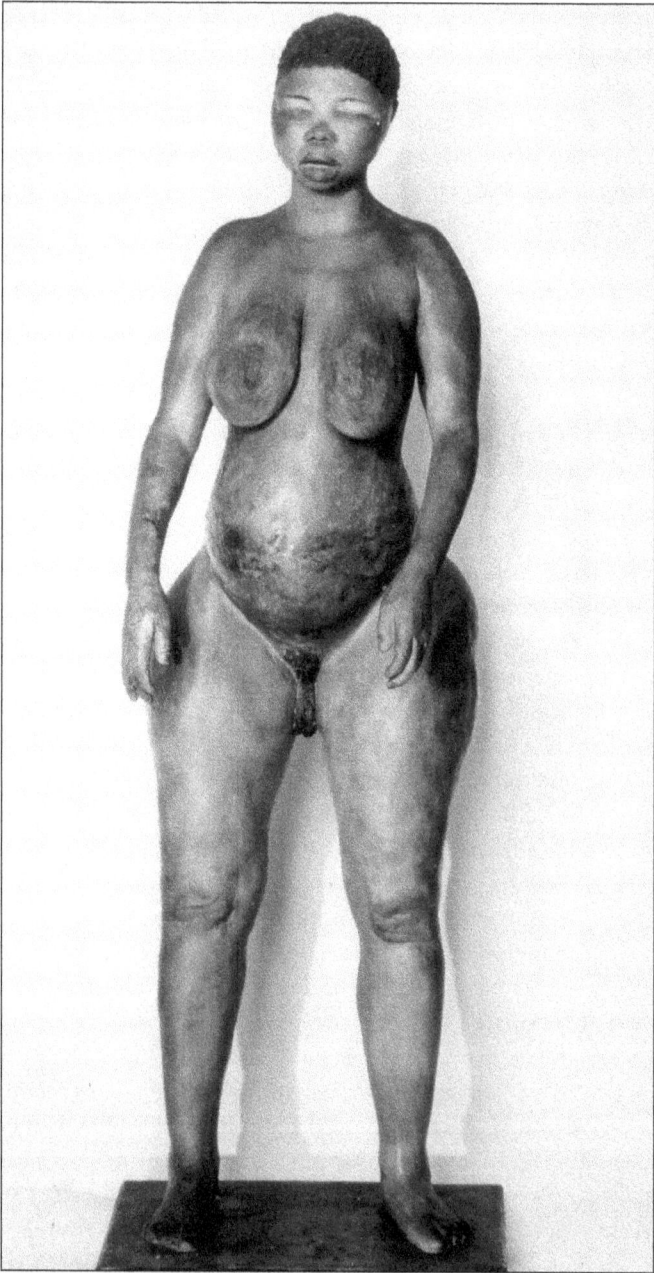

Figure 6. Cast of the body of the Hottentot Venus, 1816. © Photo SCALA, Florence, and Musée du quai Branly, 1816. Reprinted by permission of SCALA and the Musée de quai Branly, Paris (c.61.1193.493).

buried five months later in Hankey, a town in the Gamtoos River Valley that was presumed to be near her place of birth. President Thabo Mbeki gave the funeral oration, saying, "The story of Sarah Baartman is the story of the African people. . . . It is the story of the loss of our ancient freedom . . . [and] of our reduction to the state of objects who could be owned, used and discarded by others."[35] That story has now been recounted at some length in two pioneering biographies—Rachel Holmes's *The Hottentot Venus* (reissued in the United States as *African Queen: The Real Life of the Hottentot Venus*) and Clifton Crais and Pamela Scully's *Sara Baartman and the Hottentot Venus: A Ghost Story and a Biography*—that provide much new information on her life and career based on extensive field research in South Africa and Europe. In addition, a recent collection of essays titled *Representation and Black Womanhood: The Legacy of Sarah Baartman*, edited by Natasha Gordon-Chipembere, has attempted to disrupt "iconic, pop-culture narratives to seek an alternative Africanist rendering of a person whose life has left a profound impact on the ways in which Black women are displayed and represented the world over."[36] Other anthologies and sympathetic biographical narratives have appeared,[37] as well as imaginative portrayals of her in novels,[38] plays,[39] poetry,[40] and films.[41] Historians, anthropologists, sociologists, anatomists, literary critics, art historians, genealogists, and feminists have seized upon her tale as a phyletic exemplum and a telling illustration of racial and sexual domination.[42] Sartjee Baartman has thus come to represent Western man's inhumane treatment of non-Western women. She has been raised from the dead to remind us of an unsavory chapter in the ongoing history of unequal gender relations.

2

The Bottom Line

African Caricature in Georgian England

Between 1714 and 1830, Great Britain was ruled by four kings named George, descendants of the Hanoverian line to the throne. Profound changes took place during this time in the British Isles and in those parts of the world colonized by British subjects. At home, a traditional agricultural economy was gradually being transformed by greater manufacturing activity into a modern, industrial economy, a shift that was beginning to turn a rural society into an urban one. Abroad, an empire was being built to supply the raw materials needed to sustain economic growth at home. In North America and the Caribbean, this colonial enterprise was founded on human exploitation, especially the utilization of non-European peoples as slave labor. Since indigenous Indian populations in these regions could not supply the level of manpower required, millions of Africans were forcibly transported to the New World to work in fields and mines appropriated by European settlers. Indeed, it was the slave trade that made extensive British colonization in the New World not only possible but also very profitable.

Yet during the same period, an antislavery movement gathered such momentum in Great Britain that by 1833–34 slavery was formally abolished in all British territories. By then, England had already lost its colonies on the North American coast, but it continued to exert its influence on the high seas to disrupt the international traffic in slaves. Eventually, the other European nations as well as the United States followed the example of Great Britain by prohibiting slavery. The humanitarian impulse that first emerged in strength in Georgian England thus ultimately spread to the rest of the Western world.

But the abolition of slavery did not necessarily lead to more enlightened views in Europe and the United States about the nonwhite peoples of the world. The black man might have been regarded by whites as a man and a brother in one sense—that is, as someone entitled to equal political status as a human being—but he was not generally accepted as a biological equal. Old fears, prejudices, and stereotypes continued to color the notions that whites held of blacks, even after decades of close contact with them. It has been estimated that by 1772 at least fifteen to twenty thousand blacks were living in England, many of them in London.[1] Some had come directly from Africa, usually as slaves or servants; others, from the West Indies, had come as slaves, servants, runaways, or freemen. A few wrote books about their experiences in an effort to contribute to the public debate on emancipation,[2] and several made their mark in late Georgian London as popular performers—boxers, musicians, dancers, even famous prostitutes.[3] One might expect that in such circumstances relatively frequent face-to-face interactions between whites and blacks would have led to better cross-cultural understanding, or at least to less biased racial attitudes. But though this may have occurred on a small scale, there is powerful pictorial evidence to suggest that English perceptions of blacks during the Georgian era not only failed to improve markedly but may have grown even more grotesquely distorted. The evidence I refer to appears in the satirical caricatures of the day.

One must admit, of course, that caricatures are by nature distortions and that most of the humor in them derives from the gross liberties the artists take with their subjects. By exaggerating certain details, artists can create graphic jokes at the expense of whomever they depict. To achieve this satirical purpose, accuracy of portrayal is neither necessary nor desirable. But cartoons can flatter as well as abuse. The target need not be defamed even when devastatingly misrepresented. Much depends on the strategy of the satirists and the moral implications embedded in their art. Every caricaturist must determine how and where to draw a line so that it will carry an idea. If we cannot read the mind of caricaturists between their lines, their art will say nothing to us.

Anyone surveying the images of black people in eighteenth- and early nineteenth-century English caricatures will have deciphered at least three salient messages. First, blacks seldom appeared as the primary point of focus in this form of graphic humor. In fact, on the rare occasion that a black person was included in a caricature, he or she usually stood off to the side as a supernumerary figure—a servant, a cymbals player or drummer in a military band, a beggarly onlooker, a ragamuffin in a vulgar mob. Their low visibility may accurately reflect the marginality of blacks in Georgian society.

Second, even in pro-emancipation cartoons where they were centrally positioned and sympathetically portrayed as slaves under duress (for example, as victims of whipping, lynching, or other forms of physical abuse), blacks remained relatively passive participants in the drama depicted: instead of initiating action, they were acted upon. There was nothing heroic or dignified about their behavior. They were merely helpless creatures in pain. This may have been effective abolitionist propaganda, but it did nothing to raise blacks to the level of confident, assertive whites. It suggested that slaves needed to be helped because they were quite incapable of helping themselves.

Third, black people, whether supernumeraries or suffering slaves, were presented in most caricatures as a foil to whites. By including one or more blacks in a picture, artists could develop effective contrasts to white characters, thereby extending the range of their social commentary. They might also adopt the tactic of portraying blacks in a typical white role or whites in a typical black role in order to make an amusing point. Underlying such juxtapositions and role reversals was the unstated assumption that blacks and whites were fundamentally different in a number of ways, so different that they must be construed as irreconcilable opposites. The implicit message was that never the twain could meet, at least not on an equal footing. Georgian caricaturists, by playing upon imagined ethnic polarities, thus aided and abetted racist tendencies in their society. The dialectics of their art argued against the brotherhood of man.

To illustrate further uses and abuses of black subjects in Georgian caricature, it may be useful to concentrate on a single individual who gained some notoriety in London in 1810 to 1811 as a popular performer. Sartjee Baartman, a Khoi (i.e., Hottentot) woman from South Africa, was exhibited in a room at Piccadilly Circus as "a most correct and perfect Specimen of that race of people."[4] Due to her pronounced steatopygia, she rapidly became a favorite source of social and political satire. Articles appeared on her in the *Satirist, or, Monthly Meteor,* an irreverent political magazine that delighted in poking fun at Lord William Wyndham Grenville, a former Whig prime minister who at that time was thought to be jockeying for political power because King George III had fallen seriously ill and was showing symptoms of mental deterioration. In these circumstances it was anticipated that the Prince of Wales would soon be declared prince regent, Spencer Perceval's ministry would then fall, and Lord Grenville would be called upon to form a broadly based coalition government. Grenville, his relatives and associates, and all others who advocated this form of governance had come to be known popularly as "Broad Bottoms," a term that "connoted the comprehensive character of the Ministry and the bulky posteriors of the Grenvilles,"[5] and it didn't take long for political commentators to capitalize on this coinage and draw comical comparisons between such people and Sartjee Baartman.[6]

However, the medium in which the Hottentot Venus became most visible in London was comic graphic art. The early nineteenth century was a period when political caricature flourished in England, and some of the leading artists working in this genre could not resist including images of Baartman in their attacks on the political follies of their day. Whether any of them had actually seen her perform is unknown, but they certainly were aware of what was drawing people to her exhibition.

In their depictions of her, they frequently imitated a poster that had been ordered by her manager to advertise the show. This aquatint, drawn by Frederick Christian Lewis and published on September 18, 1810, shows "Sartjee, the Hottentot Venus" in profile, with her famous buttocks displayed to the best advantage (see fig. 2).[7] She is wearing a simple headscarf, a beaded belt, hairy garters around her knees, a pair of shoes, and little else. A large, fleecy garment, possibly a sheepskin, hangs from her shoulders, suggesting that she used this as a body covering until obliged to shed it during her performance. The show, then, initially may have included a rather crude form of strip-tease, with Sartjee peeling down from a formless sheepskin cloak to a form-fitting, skin-colored, silk-and-cotton body stocking. The aquatint gives the impression that she is naked but for the "rude ornaments"—beads, cloth, face paint, staff, and pipe—that the original newspaper advertisement claimed were "usually worn by those people." A second poster, published shortly before the exhibition went on tour to the provinces, shows a frontal view of "Sartjee the Hottentot Venus" (see fig. 3). Numerous imitations were made of these posters, the side view being the favorite pose. The posters reinforced the illusion that here was a splendid savage in the raw.

The first political carton based on Lewis's original aquatint to surface in London appears to have been an unsigned engraving titled "A Pair of Broad Bottoms" (see fig. 7), which Mary Dorothy George attributes to William Heath.[8] Sartjee and Grenville are standing rump to rump with the playwright Richard Brinsley Sheridan half-kneeling behind and between them and measuring the projection of Sartjee's bottom with calipers. Grenville, dressed in old-fashioned court attire and looking back over his shoulder at Sartjee, is saying, "Well I never expected Broad Bottoms from Africa! but one should never dispair! Mind *Sherry* don't let your *Fireey Nose* touch the Venus for if theres any *Conbustibls* about her we shall be Blown Up!!!" Sheridan, who was then a Member of Parliament, a good friend of Grenville, and a staunch Broad-Bottomite himself,

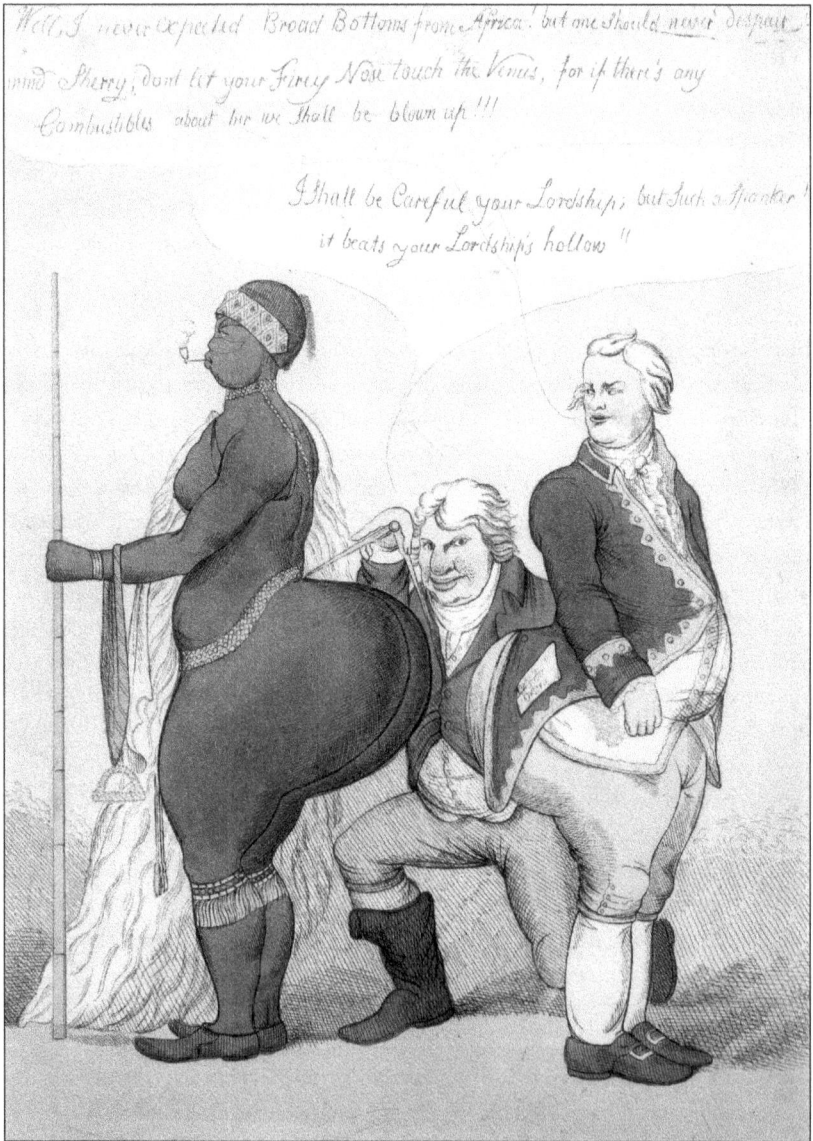

Figure 7. Caricature of the Hottentot Venus and Lord William Wyndham Grenville, 1810. From author's collection.

Figure 8. Caricature of the Hottentot Venus, Miss Harvey, and Miss Ridsdale, 1810. © The British Library Board. Reprinted by permission of the British Library (Mary Dorothy George, Catalogue of Political and Personal Satires, X.0981/776, vol. 8, no. 11602).

replies, "I shall be Carefull your Lordship! but such a Spanker it beats your Lordship's hollow." On a piece of paper in Grenville's pocket is written the word "Chanselor," a reference to Grenville's controversial appointment as chancellor of the University of Oxford in July of that year.

Heath followed this up with two more engravings featuring the Hottentot Venus. The first, titled "The Three Graces" (see fig. 8) and published by Fores on November 13, 1810, may have been aimed at three loose women of fashion known ironically in London as the "Three Graces."[9] Heath made his ad hominem assault through analogy by picturing three female freaks then on display in the city: Sartjee (who was given the central position in the portrait), "Miss Harvey the Beautiful Albiness with Silk hair perfectly white and pink Eyes!!" and "Miss Ridsdale Only 30 Inches high and 35 years Old." The latter two could be seen at Wigley's Rooms, Spring Gardens. Sartjee is represented as saying of them, "Vat Uggerly tings no like a fine Voman no Grease about dem like I."

In the other engraving, published by Fores two days later, Heath returned to political satire by lampooning "Love at First Sight or a Pair of Hottentots, With an Addition to the Broad Bottom Family!!"[10] Now Grenville was portrayed as a Hottentot wearing the same beads, garters and armlets as Sartjee, whom he faces in profile. Both are smoking small pipes, and he holds her left wrist in his right hand. They are attended by Grenville's brother, the Marquis of Buckingham, and by Buckingham's son, Lord Temple. Grenville is saying, "at Last I have met with a True Broad Bottom real Flesh no Deception!!! I wonder if Broad Bottoms would breed in this Country." Sartjee responds with, "Me hear of your *Bottom*, me Long to See it, me write to you about it!!!" Buckingham, quoting a line from a Sheridan play, exclaims, "Ah sure a Pair were never seen so Justly formed to meet by Nature," to which Temple adds, "Charming Indeed, oh I am so pappy [*sic*] the *Family* is not *Extinct*." In all three of Heath's prints, Sartjee is pictured in the same posture and garb as in the original aquatint by Lewis.

Another political cartoonist who made use of the Grenville-Sartjee equation was Charles Williams, whose engraving "Prospects of Prosperity, or Good Bottoms Going in to Business" was published shortly after the Hottentot Venus had her days in court.[11] Williams depicted Grenville and Sartjee as moving toward one another for an embrace while others look on from behind. Grenville, who has a "List of the new Admin . . ." in his pocket, is saying, "My dear Sartje, I come to congratulate you you are going to trade on your own bottom I find, I expect soon to be in the same situation myself." Her response is, "Ah! glad of dat broder Broady, good ting! me got only half my bottom belong to me no do much good wid dat." Standing to the rear of Sartjee is her manager muttering, "Curse it I'm so vexed that I have a great mind to dissolve partnership and make her purchase the other half." Behind Grenville are Perceval and three of his ministers: Foreign Secretary Wellesley, Home Secretary Ryder, and Lord Chancellor Eldon. Wellesley remarks, "If his Bottom once gets into business again we may dissolve partnership!" To this Perceval, gowned in his robe as chancellor of the exchequer, replies, "Aye and I shall be obliged to part with this comfortable cloak for all weathers." Ryder adds, "and I must turn Out Ryder," and Eldon chimes in, "To turn out in my opinion will not be wEldone." The cartoon, by commenting on both Sartjee's shrewd business sense and Grenville's suspected ambition, brought together two themes of topical interest, allowing each aspirant to reflect the ludicrous mendacity of the other. To emphasize the parallel, Grenville and Sartjee were shown in the same outstretched posture and with the same outsized posteriors.

Williams turned to the figure of the Hottentot Venus again about a year later to travesty the Duke of Clarence's sixth unsuccessful marriage proposal to Miss Tylney-Long, a wealthy heiress.[12] After this refusal the duke had proposed to several other heiresses, who had also turned him down. He was averaging about one marriage proposal per month when Williams's engraving, titled "Neptune's Last Resource or the Fortune Hunter Foiled, a Sketch from Heathen

Figure 9. Caricature of the Hottentot Venus and the Duke of Clarence, 1811. © The British Library Board. Reprinted by permission of the British Library (George, Catalogue, X.0981/776, vol. 9, no. 11748).

Mythology" (see fig. 9), appeared depicting him as a long-bearded admiral seeking to seize Sartjee's assets. Pulling on her money bags, he makes his proposition in verse:

> Since golden Long my suit denie,
> Some other fortune now I'll try,
> No Venus Barton I'll come o'eer
> For wealth's the Goddess I adore.
> Dear Venus if report says true,
> Your charms has claim'd the public view,
> Great Neptune kneels in humble state,
> Pray on your rump grant him a seat;
> There shall he ride triumphant still,
> And your bright gold his pocketts fill.

To this appeal, Sartjee, smoking her pipe, responds:

> Ha Massa Neptune vat you Vant?
> Me quite up to all your Cant,

For if Missi Golden Long would have you
You would not come to me to sue
And leave your Wife and Pickaninies
To come and try to take my Guineas.

The portrayal of Sartjee as a financially well-endowed young woman may be indicative of public awareness of her remarkable success in show business. Occasionally one finds in the press of that day waggish suggestions that she might now make an advantageous match for an ambitious suitor: "The damsel, it is said, has picked up some cash, and may become a desirable object in the eyes of some of our minor fortune-hunters."[13]

The notion of the Hottentot Venus as an object of amorous attention was, of course, something that the satirists continued to play upon. In another engraving called "Love and Beauty—Sartjee the Hottentot Venus," which appears to have been done by Williams and published in October 1822, she is presented with a coy expression on her face and a well-armed cupid on her rump who warns, "Take care of your Hearts!!"[14] The image of her is again copied from Lewis's poster, though the pose is reversed.

That poster must have had wide circulation, for it reappears in a number of prints by such master caricaturists as George Cruikshank, Thomas Rowlandson, and William Heath. Cruikshank's tendency was to set the famous profile of the Hottentot Venus somewhere in the background or borders of his work, letting it contribute another dimension of absurdity to the central satirical idea he was developing. Thus, we see her as an aside in arguments aimed at the education of surgeons,[15] the teamwork of musicians,[16] the lavish pomp of the royal family and the self-indulgent voluptuousness of the prince regent,[17] the pretentious grandeur of public military monuments,[18] and the social chaos caused by abolitionists. The latter print, known as "The New Union Club," is full of grotesquely racist humor and includes unflattering images of William Wilberforce and Zachary Macaulay.[19] Rowlandson's "Exhibition at Bullock's Museum of Bonepartes Carriage Taken at Waterloo"[20] and Heath's "All the World's a Stage,"[21] in both of which Sartjee's portrait hangs on the back wall as a comic filler, contain far less savage satire.

Another place where the image of the Hottentot Venus turned up was on the five of clubs in a deck of playing cards (see fig. 10) known as transformation cards because the artist sought to transform the stylized suit numbers into elements of pictorial design.[22] The hats and wigs of the spectators as well as the body of the performer's guitar were shaped as clubs and placed where the five clubs customarily would appear on a playing card. The caption reads "The Hottentot Venus showing her agility," and Sartjee is seen doing her song and

Figure 10. Playing card featuring the Hottentot Venus, 1811. Reprinted by permission of the Guildhall Library, London, and London Metropolitan Archives.

Figure 11. Caricature of a naval officer, the King of Tombuctoo, and his daughters, 1818. © The British Library Board. Reprinted by permission of the British Library (George, Catalogue, X.0981/776, vol. 9, no. 13043).

dance before an attentive male audience that includes a soldier and sailor seated in boxes adjoining the stage. The sailor is ogling her body as he removes her cloak. The fact that the Hottentot Venus was one of fifty-two images selected to convey the flavor of London life in 1811 attests to her high popularity. She had danced her way into the mainstream of popular culture in the metropolis.

Further evidence of Sartjee's influence on the popular imagination may be glimpsed in prints in which she herself does not appear but her anatomy does in depictions of other Africans. An example is Cruikshank's "Puzzled Which to Choose,"[23] a spoof of the possible consequences of far-flung colonial ventures. The "King of Tombuktoo" [*sic*] (see fig. 11) is shown offering his daughters in marriage to a naval officer who seems reluctant to make a selection from such exuberantly healthy specimens. Cruikshank, who also drew "The New Union Club," was one of the most overtly racist of British caricaturists of this period.

It is interesting to contrast these English caricatures of Sartjee with two that were done in France a few years later (see figs. 12 and 13).[24] The French were equally impressed with the endowments of "la Vénus Hottentote," and after the Battle of Waterloo they made adroit use of such fundamental eccentricities to comment satirically on the kilts of Scots guards who were part of the army of occupation in Paris. Sartjee, presented by one artist in the attitude of the

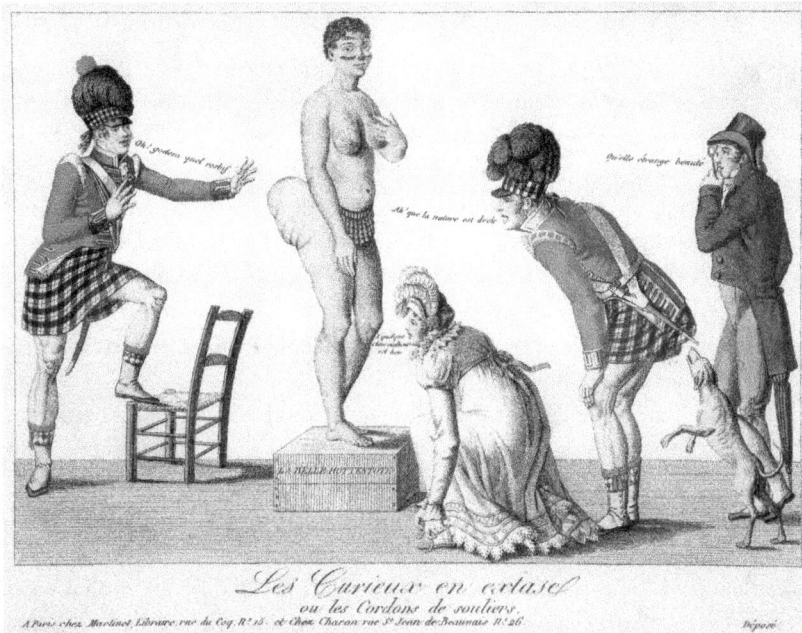

Figure 12. French caricature of the Hottentot Venus and Scots guards, 1815. From author's collection.

Figure 13. French caricature of the Hottentot Venus and spectators, 1815. From author's collection.

Medici Venus, looks more modest and dignified than the spectators surrounding her, not all of whom are British. French women were reportedly excited by the new fashion in kilts, especially on windy days.

French artists also have given us the most accurate portraits of this celebrated exhibitionist. Cuvier commissioned a team of artists to paint her in the nude from several angles, and he subsequently used some of these images to draw invidious distinctions between black and white races (see fig. 4).[25] Even in death, the Hottentot Venus lived on in Europe as a symbol of the backwardness and bestiality of Africans. She became emblematic of the exotic otherness of sub-Saharan Homo sapiens.

In Georgian England, caricature was one method of distancing Africa from Europe. By exaggerating a physical anomaly that by European aesthetic standards already seems ludicrously overdeveloped, artists and their audience could laugh at Africa's claim to human equality. By comparing the buttocks of Sartjee to those of Grenville and other "Broad Bottomites," they could draw ironic, superficial equations that affirmed reflexively the deep differences that were assumed to exist between the so-called civilized and uncivilized races. Georgian caricaturists thus offered visual confirmation of one of the dominant myths of his day: that Africans were so decidedly inferior to Europeans that it was conceivable they were more akin to brutes than to human beings. The Hottentot Venus was displayed as a spectacular example of what could well be a missing link in the great chain of being. Georgian caricature, by making this ordinary woman seem far more bizarre than she really was, helped to dehumanize the image of Africa.

3

Ira Aldridge at Covent Garden

The appearance of Ira Aldridge as Othello on the Covent Garden stage on April 10, 1833, was an unprecedented event in British theatrical history. No other black performer had been seen on the boards of one of London's patent theaters in the early nineteenth century. London already had a significant black population numbering ten thousand or so,[1] most of them from the New World rather than directly from Africa, but they tended to remain placed among the lowest of the working class and poor, never rising to positions of higher visibility in the elite culture of the metropolis. So Aldridge, an African American billed as "a native of Senegal," was a unique phenomenon in his day. Here was a young "African," purportedly a veritable Moor, attempting to enact the major black role in the Shakespearean canon at one of England's national theaters. The announcement of his appearance there immediately stirred controversy.

Aldridge was risking quite a lot, for Covent Garden was known as a theater where a single performance could make or mar an unknown actor's reputation. It was a rigorous testing ground for provincial actors who had attracted attention outside London and had thereby earned an opportunity to display their talent before a large metropolitan audience. Being invited to perform at a patent theater in the capital was a sign of professional recognition, but it was no guarantee of success. The performer would have to please not only the manager who had hired him and the numerous critics whose job it was publicly to evaluate him but also the people from all walks of life who had paid to see what he was able to do on stage. For an actor this was a chance of a lifetime. Those who succeeded stood to gain a substantial boost in their careers, leading possibly to riches or at least to regular employment in London or elsewhere. Those who failed might be quickly forgotten or ignored and might never have another opportunity to prove their competence on the boards of a patent theater. So the stakes were quite high for any actor who took the stage at Covent Garden for the first time. The trial could materially affect his future.

The sports writer Pierce Egan had remarked that "no set of men suffer more from *hopes* and *fears* than actors in their state of probation to acquire the London stamp, and numbers of 'great creatures,' with all their talents and exertions, are doomed to a life of obscurity in the provinces, realizing little more than *empty* houses, *empty* cupboards, and *empty* pockets till the curtain falls on their chequered existence—'full o sound and fury, signifying nothing.'"[2]

Aldridge, of course, was not entirely unknown in London.[3] He had launched his career there by performing for several months at the Royalty Theatre and the Royal Coburg Theatre in 1825 and later for several days at Sadler's Wells, the Royal Pavilion Theatre, and the Royal Olympic Theatre in the winter of 1829–30, but these were minor playhouses that did not attract the amount of media attention that routinely was given to productions at Covent Garden and Drury Lane. Also, he was billed in those early years as Mr. Keene from the African Theatre in New York City; now he had dropped the homonym alluding to Edmund Kean and was presenting himself under his real name, Mr. Aldridge, but with a fictional ethnic identity—"a native of Senegal." Some critics remembered his earlier appearances and quickly branded his Senegalese charade as fraudulent. A few knew of his theatrical activities elsewhere in Britain and were unimpressed with his credentials.

Aldridge had worked hard to improve his acting in the more than seven years he had been on tour in the provinces. He had learned to speak English with the semblance of an acceptable British accent; had performed in more than forty plays, assuming a variety of tragic, melodramatic, and comic roles; had starred in hundreds of productions mounted at theaters large and small in more than fifty cities and towns; and had acted with well over six hundred actors and actresses on these circuits.[4] He had a wealth of experience to draw upon, some of it acquired in very difficult circumstances, and he had managed to survive and eventually thrive while undergoing this grueling regimen of constant itinerant touring. To add to his box office appeal in places where he was unknown, he had cagily and proudly reinvented himself as an African.

However, in London it was the stereotype of an inept "African Tragedian" from New York's African Theatre that was best remembered, for such a bumbling performer had been lampooned by England's leading mimic, Charles Mathews the Elder, in his *Trip to America,* a popular one-man show in which he regaled audiences by representing more than a dozen eccentric characters he claimed to have encountered on a tour of the United States. The black actor whose foibles he imitated was a buffoon who spoke in dialect, mixed and mangled famous lines from *King Richard III* and *Hamlet*, and incorporated a Negro folksong, "Possum up a Gum Tree," into his rendition of Shakespeare. It didn't matter that the performer Mathews had actually seen in New York was someone other than Aldridge. When Covent Garden announced the imminent appearance of an African actor as Othello, some theatergoers assumed that Aldridge was the barbarous thespian who had served as the model for Mathews's hilarious "African Tragedian."[5] The very notion of an uncouth African spouting Shakespeare was still alive as a joke in the metropolitan imagination.

To make matters worse for Aldridge, Gilbert Abbott à Beckett, the maliciously witty editor of London's most successful satirical paper, *Figaro in London*, had seen him perform in Lancaster the previous September and had expressed astonishment that

> a stupid looking, thick lipped, ill formed African calling himself the African Roscius [had posted] placards about Lancaster saying that he appears there previous to his fulfilment of his engagement at Drury Lane Theatre. Now we expect this to be a hoax. . . . this African *Roscius*, as he modestly styles himself, appears to us nothing but an ordinary *Niger* [*sic*] and we predict a fearful failure should he on the strength of his skin be suffered to trifle with the patience of a metropolitan audience. . . . We don't believe he is to appear at Drury Lane, for we do not think that the manager would commit himself so far as to engage a person who has for some years past been traversing the country with idle beasts [*sic*] of his royal lineage and sooty face, and who has occasionally prevailed upon the Coburg management to permit him for six nights to split the ears of the groundlings in that proverbially anti Critical region of the Metropolis. . . . This stage struck chip of an alleged royal block has long been in want of a wholesome reduction, and will we trust profit from the one that we have tardily and very reluctantly administered.[6]

This ill-natured attack may have been enough to scuttle whatever contractual arrangements had been made between Aldridge and Captain Polhill, the lessee of Drury Lane, for Aldridge never appeared there, and it wasn't until several months later that Covent Garden approached him with an offer of employment. Such was the power of the satirical press, and à Beckett was prepared to administer another equally unwholesome reduction of the self-styled

"African Roscius" as soon as he learned that Aldridge was about to set foot on the Covent Garden stage.

Figaro in London, founded in December 1831, was à Beckett's first successful venture in journal publishing.[7] Modeled on the popular *Figaro* of Paris, this four-page penny weekly aimed to provide the same kind of "sparkling, sharp-flavored and high-relished" satirical commentary.[8] The journal had two mottos printed on its masthead, the first a couplet credited to Lady Montague: "Satire should, like a polish'd razor keen / Wound with a touch that's scarcely felt or seen," and the other a statement from Croker's *New Whig Guide*: "Political Pasquinades and Political Caricatures are parts (though humbles ones) of Political history. They supply information as to the personal habits, and often as to the motives and objects of public men, which cannot be found elsewhere." Light but informative satire was to be the hallmark of this new *Figaro*.

Coming at a time when political reform was a leading issue of the day, à Beckett's journal was welcomed as a vehicle for free expression of opinions critical of the government, the king, the clergy, the aristocracy, and individual members of Parliament. Some of this criticism, however, was far from good-humored or light-hearted. Certain razor-sharp attacks, especially the caricatures by Richard Seymour that were carried in every issue, cut so close to the bone that à Beckett was warned by a magistrate that "persons holding high offices in the State should never be made the subject of a joke."[9] Nevertheless, the jokes continued, adding to the popularity of the paper. At the end of its first year à Beckett could boast that *Figaro in London* "sells more than four times the number of its namesake in the French capital."[10] Within three years circulation had shot up to seventy thousand, and à Beckett was reputed to be earning in excess of a thousand pounds per year.[11] Ad hominem satire was paying off handsomely.

The theater critiques were particularly pungent. À Beckett did not spare the feelings of actors and actresses whose performances he deplored, yet he was democratic in his distribution of abuse, condemning with equal fervor established stars and young neophytes who did not measure up to his exacting standards. He commented on several shows every week—not just those at the fashionable houses but also productions put on by some of the humblest of minor theaters. When he saw something he liked, he praised it; however, he was best at attacking what he regarded as deficiencies of talent and violations of good taste. And he took special delight in responding with vigor to complaints about the "undue severity" or "ferocity" of his remarks on particular performers, arguing that "we are in fact doing a service to the object of our severity. . . . we wound to heal."[12]

Figaro in London took pride in its principled refusal to accept free tickets to the shows it reviewed:

> Had we taken the bribe of an admission ticket, our theatricals instead of being the terror of bad actors, brainless authors, and venal managers, would have been a mere register of insipid puffs, without any of those delicious gashes at effrontery and pretension which are issued for the periodical delight of a generous metropolis. The nervous tomahawk of true and acute criticism, would never have been seen flying with rapid but nicely discriminating violence about the heads of theatrical charlatans, and the public would have lost the only critic that dares to put the drama and its professors to the test of honest severity. We are determined to persevere in this course of singular integrity, which gains for us the contumely of the few, with the respect and gratitude of the many.[13]

Pleasing the multitudes by wielding such a nervous tomahawk was also a sure way of selling more copies of *Figaro in London*.

One of à Beckett's pet peeves was the management of Covent Garden Theatre by the Frenchman Pierre Laporte, who in the autumn of 1832 had also become lessee of the Italian Opera House.[14] Before this happened, à Beckett had warned that it was "bad enough to let one national theatre fall into the hands of a grasping foreigner, and it would be an increase of the disgrace the country has already incurred, were he to be allowed to monopolize the two principal theatres in England."[15] After Laporte started importing French singers and dancers and the Italian violinist Niccolò Paganini to perform at these theaters, *Figaro in London* protested that he was throwing British performers out of work, thereby "rendering national talent destitute."[16] This nationalistic argument appeared to have some validity, for when Laporte's productions failed to draw enough spectators, he "endeavoured to persuade his poor performers to accept half salaries, but the insolent proposition was rejected by the company with due scorn, and the moneyless enterpriser has been forced for three nights a week to close the doors of Covent Garden Theatre."[17] To deal with this problem, Laporte resorted to his old ploy of bringing in more foreign players, a tactic that further infuriated à Beckett, prompting him to write: "Laporte's management continues to be marked by indiscretion and avarice. Bad pieces, bad actors, and bad houses have hitherto been the distinguishing features of his career, and he has now thought proper to turn Covent Garden into, what we always prophecied [*sic*] he would make it, a receptacle for foreigners. A French troop has been imported to act in Masaniello, which gang usurps the place of many native performers of ability, who being deprived of their regular engagements at a national theatre are sent to starve in the provinces."[18]

Covent Garden's dire financial situation had begun to improve around the turn of the year when *Nell Gwynne*, a new play by Douglas Jerrold, and *Puss in Boots*, a popular pantomime, were added to the offerings, supplementing the singing and dancing in *Masaniello*. It was in mid-January 1833 that Aldridge returned to London expecting to be put to work by Laporte, who may have viewed him as yet another interesting exotic star capable of attracting attention and drawing larger crowds to Covent Garden. However, Laporte apparently decided against employing him immediately, and Aldridge, instead of lingering longer in the capital, headed for Scotland, accepting engagements at Aberdeen, Glasgow, and Edinburgh while waiting for Laporte to call him back.

In the meantime Laporte had given the stage to another young star with a more resonant name — Edmund Kean's son Charles Kean.[19] One wonders why Laporte did not arrange to stage *Othello* with the junior Kean playing Iago to Aldridge's Othello. This possibility must have occurred to him, but he may have been unable to bring it about because Kean may have refused to share the stage with the black actor who had upstaged him in Belfast three and a half years earlier. According to a Russian woman who met Aldridge decades later, Charles Kean, on "learning that Aldridge was engaged to play in the very theatre where he was, angrily refused to play on the same stage with a despised 'nigger.'"[20] This must have been something that Aldridge had told her, and it appears to relate to the time when both actors were under contract to Laporte, for there is no other occasion on record when they were simultaneously recruited to perform at the same theater in London. Kean never played opposite Aldridge in later years, and when he ran Princess's Theatre in London from 1850 to 1859, he never invited Aldridge to perform there. The memory of what had happened in Belfast may have made Kean resolve to have nothing further to do with this formidable black competitor.

Charles Kean's appearance at Covent Garden turned out to be not as successful as Laporte had hoped, so in February he was used sparingly and only in a couple of his father's favorite roles. In March he was given a part in a new play, James Robinson Planché's "Reputation; or the State Secret," a busy melodrama that was repeated eight times in rapid succession with Kean displaying no signal excellence but executing "with care and propriety all that he was intrusted with."[21] The new recruit apparently was not proving to be a great attraction, but that suddenly changed later in the month when his father, who had been performing very sporadically at Drury Lane due to ill health, was refused a loan of £500 by Captain Polhill. In a huff the elder Kean decided to break his contract with Drury Lane and move over to Covent Garden. Laporte immediately cast him as Shylock in *Merchant of Venice* and arranged for him to play Othello alongside his son Charles as Iago a few nights later, on March 25. According to Charles's biographer, "Laporte thought, with sound managerial tact, that the appearance of father and son in conjunction, would be likely to attract money to his almost empty treasury."[22] This it certainly did, almost doubling the amount taken in when the father had portrayed Shylock.[23]

March 25 turned out to be a historic night for another, more fundamental reason, too, for it brought an abrupt end to an era in British theater that had been dominated by the powerful acting of Edmund Kean. Midway through the third act that evening, just after speaking the famous line "Farewell! Othello's occupation's gone!," he collapsed in his son's arms and had to be carried off the stage. This was to be his last performance. England's greatest tragedian died seven weeks later at age forty-six, the victim of a dissolute life style that had sapped his strength and his finances.

Laporte was now in a difficult situation. His most successful show in March, a Lenten sacred oratorio recounting the story of "The Israelites in Egypt; or the Passage of the Red Sea,"[24] was about to close at the end of the month, and this was to be followed by Easter week when the theater itself would be closed. Which star could he bring in to fill the gap left by the Keans? He chose to try Aldridge, casting him as Othello, the very role that Edmund Kean had attempted to perform two weeks earlier.

It was not a tactful choice. When an announcement appeared stating that "Mr. ALDRIDGE (A NATIVE OF SENEGAL) Known by the appellation of the AFRICAN ROSCIUS" (see fig. 14) would open as Othello on April 10, there was an immediate reaction in the press.[25] *Figaro in London* was among the first to condemn the "act of insolence" that was about to be perpetrated

> by the introduction to the boards of Covent Garden theatre, of that miserable nigger whom we found in the provinces imposing on the public by the name of the *African Roscius*. This wretched upstart is about to defile the stage, by a foul butchery of Shakspeare, and Othello is actually the part chosen for the sacrilege. Is it because nature has supplied the man with a skin that renders soot and butter superfluous, is it on the strength of his blackness that he considers himself competent to enact the part of the Moor of Venice. We have before jammed this man into atoms by the relentless power of our critical battering ram, but unless this notice causes the immediate withdrawal of his name from the bills, we must again inflict on him such a chastisement as must drive him from the stage he has dishonoured, and force him to find in

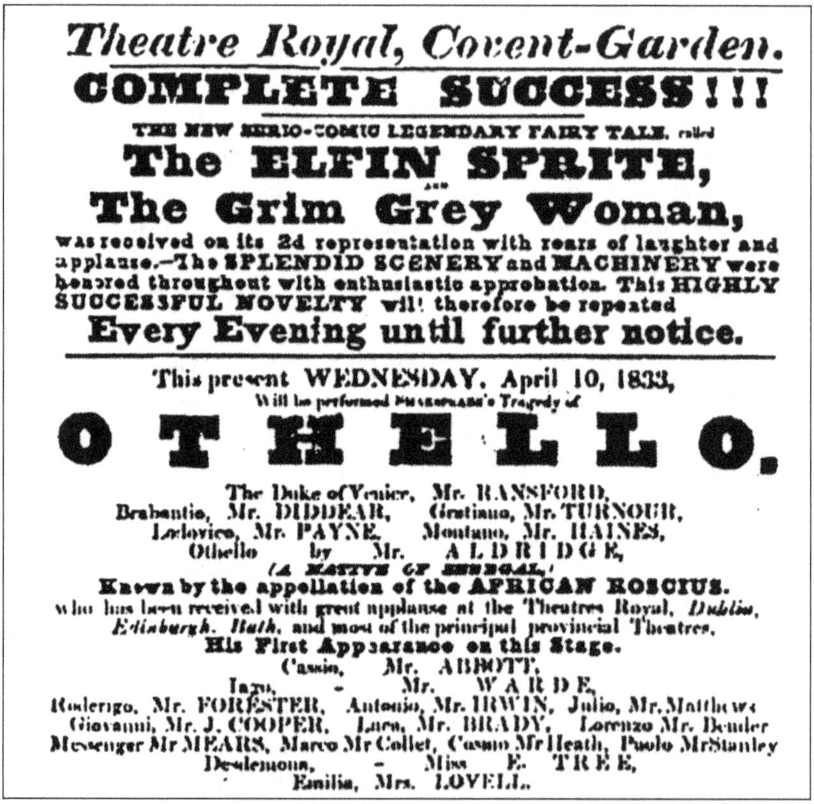

Theatre Royal, Covent-Garden.

COMPLETE SUCCESS!!!

THE NEW SERIO-COMIC LEGENDARY FAIRY TALE, called

The ELFIN SPRITE,

AND

The Grim Grey Woman,

was received on its 2d representation with roars of laughter and applause.—The SPLENDID SCENERY and MACHINERY were honored throughout with enthusiastic approbation. This HIGHLY SUCCESSFUL NOVELTY will therefore be repeated

Every Evening until further notice.

This present WEDNESDAY, April 10, 1833,

Will be performed Shakespeare's Tragedy of

OTHELLO.

The Duke of Venice, Mr. RANSFORD,
Brabantio, Mr. DIDDEAR, Gratiano, Mr. TURNOUR,
Lodovico, Mr. PAYNE, Montano, Mr. HAINES,
Othello by Mr. ALDRIDGE,
(A NATIVE OF SENEGAL,)
Known by the appellation of the AFRICAN ROSCIUS.
who has been received with great applause at the Theatres Royal, *Dublin*, *Edinburgh*, *Bath*, and most of the principal provincial Theatres.
His First Appearance on this Stage.
Cassio, Mr. ABBOTT,
Iago, - Mr. WARDE,
Roderigo, Mr. FORESTER, Antonio, Mr. IRWIN, Julio, Mr. Matthews
Giovanni, Mr. J. COOPER, Luca, Mr. BRADY, Lorenzo Mr. Bender
Messenger Mr MEARS, Marco Mr Collet, Cosmo Mr Heath, Paolo Mr Stanley
Desdemona, - Miss E. TREE,
Emilia, Mrs. LOVELL.

Figure 14. Playbill for Ira Aldridge's first appearance at the Theatre Royal Covent Garden, April 10, 1833. © The British Library Board. Reprinted by permission of the British Library (Playbill 105, Ira Aldridge).

> the capacity of footman or street sweeper, that level for which his colour appears to have rendered him peculiarly qualified.[26]

On the same day that this diatribe appeared, a vigorous response to it was circulated as a handbill by a member of the Garrick Club:

> Base and unmanly attempts are making in certain quarters to prevent Mr. ALDRIDGE, commonly designated the "African Roscius" from making his appearance as OTHELLO, on Wednesday next, pursuant to his engagement at the Theatre Royal Covent Garden, or if he should have the "presumption" to appear, he is threatened with DAMNATION!

His heinous offence is, that he was born in Africa, and though "descended from a line of Kings" his skin is too dark to enable him to personate the "DUSKY MOOR," even though he may possess the genius of a Kean, the classic taste of a Kemble, combined with the dramatic experience of a Garrick!!

To condemn unheard is contrary to the character and known liberality of Englishmen. — Talent let it come from what country it may is deserving of patronage, therefore, fellow countrymen, do not permit a worthy and talented man to be CRUSHED by the slanders and libels of the low and contemptible "catch penny press," the paltry penny critics who have threatened that "he shall be jammed to atoms by the relentless power of their critical (penny rattle? no) BATTERING RAM" if (what think ye is the modest demand?) his name is not immediately withdrawn from the Bills!!!

As a friend to a meritorious though modest and intelligent foreigner, whose able delineations of many of the principal characters of our most eminent Dramatic Writers, has been admitted in the numerous criticisms inserted in the Edinburgh, Dublin, Aberdeen, Bath, Brighton, and other provincial papers (from which the article below is extracted) I beg to ask of a London Audience "fair play" on his behalf when he makes his debut on Wednesday next.

I am the Public's Humble Servant,
'CRITO'

Subjoined was a glowing review from the previous week's *Edinburgh Advertiser* extolling Aldridge's performance of Zanga in *The Revenge*.[27]

The handbill provoked *Figaro in London* to strike back in its next issue, even before seeing Aldridge perform:

> Talking of ruin to a theatrical establishment naturally leads us to the subject of the engagement of the African Roscius, who now styles himself Aldridge, though Keene [*sic*] is the cognomen under which he used to exhibit some seasons ago at the Coburg. When a gentleman indulges in the luxury of an *alias* we must make use of some general term in speaking of him, and he must therefore permit us with all due respect to speak of him neither as Keene nor Aldridge but as the Niger [*sic*]. He seems to be exceedingly irate at our remarks last week, and he or his friends have thought fit to deface the walls of the Metropolis with a slanderous placard attributing to the Editor of Figaro a desire to drive the black gentleman from the stage without a fair trial. We have no

wish to get up a party against him, because it could not be worth our while to take so much trouble, though we have a full right to record our opinions on any public actor we may have seen, and cannot undertake to prevent the public from being most materially influenced by our criticisms. By the time this number gets into the hands of the public the Niger will have appeared, though as we go to press very early in the week in order to supply the whole nation, it is impossible this number of Figaro can contain any notice of the proceedings. We however freely say this, that the African may by possibility succeed; he may by possibility possess extraordinary genius though he certainly did not make it manifest when we saw him in the Theatre at Lancaster. He may have been damped by the wretchedness of the audience, consisting of us (Editorially plural but actually singular) in the Boxes, three loose women in the Pit, and a sprinkling of pickpockets in the gallery. Such a collection might have damped even first rate genius, and if such may have been the case with respect to the African, we shall be the first to acknowledge his talent even in spite of his blackguard posting bills, designed to call in question that critical fairness and philanthropy for which we have established a reputation hitherto unsullied by the venomous breath of calumny.[28]

À Beckett must have made this last remark with his tongue firmly in his cheek, for he certainly would have known that critical fairness and philanthropy were not what the public had come to expect from *Figaro in London* under his editorship. Rather, the journal had established its reputation as a critical battering ram, a nervous tomahawk intent on inflicting delicious gashes on individuals it deemed to be bad actors, brainless authors, and venal managers, many of whom, à Beckett took care to point out, were employed at the Covent Garden Theatre. The editor was a hatchet man viciously swinging a sharp, slanted blade. A rival journal that claimed to offer more objective criticism complained that *Figaro in London* "rests all its pretensions upon the sting of its satire, which is exercised, on all occasions, without, I am afraid, that kind regard to truth and liberality which justice requires."[29] Another periodical, celebrating à Beckett's achievements later in life as a journalist, dramatist, lawyer, and magistrate, began by saying that as a young man he had been "a bitter satirist, the unsparing flagellator of humbug. . . . We well remember the time when nobody cleft his enemy's beaver with a more downright blow than à Beckett."[30] Ira Aldridge certainly must be counted among his many beaver-cloven victims.

Other papers, no doubt primed by à Beckett's slashing attacks, also began to ridicule Aldridge in advance of his appearance at Covent Garden. The *Age* was among the first papers to try to cut him down to size: "Mr. Aldridge, the Nigger, who is underlined to play *Othello* without paint, at Covent Garden in the Easter week, is now, we suppose, a gentleman; but a few years ago he was [the actor] Jemmy Wallack's footman, and, (to use Jemmy's own emphatic words) a very queer one, too. Under these circumstances, we don't pretend to determine what sort of an actor he'll make: one thing is certain—we shan't be there to see!"[31] A week later the critic at the *Age* had changed his mind, saying he was looking forward to witnessing the spectacle: "he had much better have selected Mungo for the opening part, though by the by, we expect to laugh heartily at his personation of the noble Moor."[32] In the same flippant mood, the *Sunday Herald* remarked, "As a Senegal black is advertised at Covent Garden, we should not at all be surprised if the Drury Lane people start a New Zealander 'tattooed at a great expense!'"[33] The *Town Journal*, repeating the gossip that Aldridge had been "formerly a valet to Mr. Wallack," warned that "genius alone will protect him" if such a person dared to set foot on the Covent Garden stage.[34]

After the opening night, however, the reviewer for the *Age*, like so many of those before him in the provinces, felt compelled to admit that the African Roscius had pleasantly surprised him:

> On Wednesday a real black *Othello* in the person of Mr. Aldridge, made his *debut*—for a man of colour it was a very clever piece of acting, void of imitation throughout—occasionally he put forth some beauties, and never out heroded Herod by excessive ranting; his conception of the dusky Moor was generally speaking correct, his enunciation with some few exceptions clear and distinct, and his action graceful; his reception was of the most glittering description, but we much question if the management will profit much by the engagement; some of our contemporaries have blamed the manager for allowing him to appear, we much differ with them in opinion—if Lions, Tigers, Boa Constrictors, and such like animals and reptiles, have been tolerated, we can see no just reason why one of the human race, with only the difference of *complexion*, should be debarred the opportunity of displaying on the London boards, the talent he might possess; therefore we feel no disposition to quarrel with Laporte on that score.[35]

Other papers confirmed that this "Senegalese Lion" was a wonder but disagreed about whether he possessed talent or merely novelty value.[36] Since there were so many commentators remarking on his performance, it may be well to group their reactions into categories that reveal what they most liked and most disliked about his representation of Othello.

First, there were many different opinions expressed about his physical appearance. Unlike some of the unflattering comments made about him earlier at the Royal Coburg, where he was described as knock-kneed, narrow-chested but "considerably humanized" for an African,[37] there was now a general consensus that he was well made, manly, of good height and figure, robust and muscular of frame, with a noble bearing suitable for the role he was playing.[38] He was also said to have an intelligent countenance, a face capable of varied expression, with features "of a negro somewhat refined" that made him look "not unlike the frontispiece portrait of the *Narrative of a Voyage to Senegal.*"[39] There was a good deal of attention given to his color, which was described as light brown or dark olive, and of an "oily and expressive mulatto tint," which "seems to show that he has European blood in his veins";[40] this was thought to be an advantage not only because Othello was a Moor rather than a Negro but also because it allowed audiences to see more clearly the play of emotions on his face.

But there were naysayers too, who found his figure and face unsuitable for the role he was playing. One felt that "in point of physical appearance [Mr. Aldridge] has nothing to recommend him for the part of *Othello* but his complexion."[41] Others complained more specifically about his impassive physiognomy, which was "in every respect unprepossessing," in part because the "conformation of the lower portion of the negro face . . . prevents all Africans from giving effect to, or delineating, at least to an European audience, the changes produced on the countenance by the different transitions of feeling and passion in the mind."[42] Further, Aldridge was accused of having "feet and hands disproportionately large, . . . lips protruding, and chin underhung, his hair woolly, and his eye sullenly dark."[43] In addition, "his foot is ugly, and he walks upon it with the heavy unelastic tread of a dromedary."[44] This catalogue of racial deficiencies reveals a rather deep-seated xenophobia among Aldridge's most outspoken critics.

There was general agreement that he possessed a good voice, which was described as clear, deep, soft, and melodious.[45] One sympathetic reviewer said it "falls on the ear with a melancholy sweetness, which a slight effort of the imagination invests with all the touching interest of the woes that are the inheritance of his countrymen."[46] Another, less enchanted, admitted that the voice was "much better than we anticipated," partly because "it has none of the shrill tuneless croak usually belonging to the West Indian blacks."[47] And a third noted that "like a good instrument in the hands of an unskillful musician, its

Figure 15. Ira Aldridge (commonly known as the African Roscius) of the Theatre Royal Covent Garden in the character of Othello, 1833. © The British Library Board. Reprinted by permission of the British Library (Crach. 1. Tab.4.b.4, Ira Aldridge).

excellence alone, not its management, elicits commendation."[48] In other words, he was endowed with a resonant voice, a remarkable natural gift, but he needed training to make more effective use of it.

Aldridge was also praised for the dignity with which he delivered his lines. He was not a ranter,[49] but in the scene before the Senate he was criticized for being too loud and energetic[50] and in other scenes for being too quiet.[51] One reviewer said, "he also whines occasionally in a manner inconsistent with the lofty nature of the character, and has a disagreeable habit of pumping up his breath."[52] It was this kind of unevenness in his performance that detracted from the good impression he otherwise made as the noble Moor.

Worse, though, were his linguistic faults. In the provinces he had been praised for his excellent diction, which made him sound like a native-born Englishman, but London critics questioned the adequacy of his command of the King's English. They accused him of "peculiar accentuations" that were unpleasantly and vulgarly foreign.[53] One paper surmised that "he was born in Upper Canada, as may be distinctly gathered from his pronunciation of the letter *a*, to which he gives the broad French sound of *ar*."[54] Among other vulgarisms cited were *kep* for *kept*, oppo*site*, ala*b*aster — pronunciations "quite unknown in good society" and attributed to his "humble station" as a former servant.[55] Words themselves were sometimes a problem, for he occasionally added extra syllables, ruining the meter of a line.[56] Moreover, "in passages expressive of excited feelings, he mixes up the sentences awkwardly, not distinguishing the full stops, and altering his words with so much precipitancy that it is difficult, if not impossible, closely to follow him."[57]

But what annoyed critics most were the liberties he took with Shakespeare's text, altering and thereby spoiling it.[58] These changes were of the kind "which neither blank verse will authorise, nor good sense admit the propriety."[59] Examples included the following:

The exclamation to *Desdemona*, "Impudent strumpet!" was colloquialised into "Oh you impudent strumpet you!" The lines,

> That handkerchief, which I so lov'd and gave thee
> Thou gavest to Cassio,

into

> That handkerchief which I so lov'd and gave you
> You must needs give to Cassio.

The line

> You're welcome, sir, to Cyprus—goats and monkeys!

with which Othello *exits* in the fourth act, received this elegant and metrically correct addition,—

> You're welcome, sir, to Cyprus—goats and monkeys
> are *noting* to her!

And in the last act Mr. A. vehemently exclaimed,—

> Had all his hairs been lives, my great revenge
> Had *stummick* for them all!

An emendation of the text by Diddear [playing Brabantio] is also worthy of note:—

> She has deceived her father, and may thee,

was thus given, "e'en though the blank verse halted for't,"—

> She has deceived her father, and may do thee![60]

Aldridge may have been able to modify these lines in the provinces without anyone taking notice or raising an objection, but in London a group of journalists and spectators, some of them experienced actors, knew the play intimately and respected its integrity. They considered any mutilation of the Bard's exact words as an abominable sacrilege. Actors were expected to be letter perfect in their parts. Those guilty of corrupting or misreading a canonical script were thought to be ignorant, undisciplined, and thoroughly unprofessional.

Furthermore, they regarded Aldridge's interpretation of the role of Othello as far too tame and lackluster. "His jealousy did not resolve itself into that sublime madness which we have seen so powerfully represented—that tornado of the breast, which carries with it destruction equally terrible and sudden."[61] "He does not express the individual bursts of feeling, nor the deep and accumulating tide of passion which hurries on the noble and generous Moor to deeds of blood and death."[62] Some felt he was more capable of pathos than passion[63] and was particularly good in scenes with Desdemona, playing them with admirable delicacy of feeling and heartrending effect.[64] Both his weak-nesses and his strengths were traced to a style of acting that was essentially melodramatic.[65] There were the inevitable comparisons to other actors—Kean, Macready, John and Stephen Kemble, Henry Wallack, William Dowton—usually to Aldridge's disadvantage,[66] but a few said he measured up to the best of them[67] and excelled the worst of them.[68] He was called an imitator who displayed no originality,[69] yet at the same time he was credited with having produced new readings and strikingly innovative effects.[70] His death scene, in which he "fell fearlessly with his back to the audience," was thought to be his best, surpassing that of other actors.[71]

Most commentators were of the opinion that Aldridge had not been wholly successful in portraying Othello but that he had given evidence of a sur-prising and very promising talent that could be developed further. They tended to agree with the *Age* that "for a man of colour it was a very clever piece of acting,"[72] and they expressed little surprise that the audience had been very pleased with the performance and had showered Aldridge with applause.

Yet there were still those who believed that the appearance of a black actor in the role of Othello at Covent Garden Theatre was a disgrace to the English stage and an insult to the memory of Shakespeare. Loudest in voicing such criticism were the *Times, Sun, Bell's Weekly Messenger, Weekly Dispatch, Old England*, and the *New Court Journal*,[73] but perhaps the worst assessment appeared in the *Athenaeum*:

Covent Garden

On Wednesday, this establishment (one of the two great national theatres, which are constantly complaining of the decline of the drama, and constantly kicking themselves behind, for fear they should not go down the hill fast enough,) aimed another blow at its respectability, by the production of Mr. Henry Wallack's black servant in the character of *Othello*—*Othello* forsooth!!! *Othello*, almost the master-work of the master-mind—a part, the study of which occupied, perhaps, years of the life of the elegant and classical Kemble; a part, which the fire and genius of Kean have, of late years, made his exclusive property; a part, which it has been considered a sort of theatrical treason for anyone less distinguished than these two variously but highly gifted individuals to attempt; and this is to be personated in an English national theatre, by one whose pretensions rest upon the two grounds of his face being of a natural instead of an acquired tint, and of his having lived as servant to a low-comedy actor. It is truly monstrous . . . [and] sufficient to make

[Shakespeare's] indignant bones kick the lid from his coffin. We have no ridiculous prejudice against any fellow creature, because he chances to be of a different colour from ourselves; and we trust, that we have good taste enough, to take our hats off to genius, wherever we find it; but we are, on the other hand, altogether above the twaddle of helping the drama to bear an indignity of this nature, merely that foreigners may laugh in their sleeves at us, while we quote this silly exhibition as a proof of England's being "the stranger's home." Mr. Aldridge, formerly calling himself, we believe, Mr. Keene, and now distinguished by the appellation of "The African Roscius" is really an extraordinary person; for it is extraordinary, that under all the circumstances, a natural quickness and aptitude for imitation, should enable him to get through such a part as *Othello*, with so little of positive offence, as he does. But there it ends. Looking to his birth, parentage, and education, nothing short of inspiration could possibly make him a fit delineator of Shakspeare's *Othello*; and this is an extent, to which it is not very likely that Providence would choose to go, to produce such a result. That Providence has not done so in this instance, will be amply evident to those who do not permit their judgment to be run away with by that which we have admitted to be extraordinary; who do not let their hands get the start of their heads, nor suffer a false feeling of compassion for the individual, to supply the place of sound and unbiassed [*sic*] opinion. It is impossible that Mr. Aldridge should fully comprehend the meaning and force of even the words he utters, and accordingly, the perpetual recurrence of false emphasis, whenever his memory, as to his original, fails him, shows distinctly that he does not. In the name of common sense, we enter our protest against a repetition of this outrage. In the name of propriety and decency, we protest against an interesting actress and lady-like girl, like Miss Ellen Tree, being subjected by the manager of a theatre to the indignity of being pawed about by Mr. Henry Wallack's black servant; and finally, in the name of consistency, if this exhibition is to be continued, we protest against acting being any longer dignified by the name of art.[74]

This prompted immediate responses from others who protested that Aldridge's performance had not been evaluated properly. *The National Standard* said:

we cannot but consider that the [*Athenaeum*'s] notice of poor Aldridge's enactment of Othello is neither fair, liberal or *genteel*. The writer evidently knows nothing certain of the man of whom he speaks; for he says, "Mr. Aldridge, formerly calling himself, we *believe*, Mr. Keene;" then he is "Mr. Henry Wallack's black servant;"—another, lest Mr. Henry Wallack should fancy for a moment that he is to be allowed to escape scot-free, he is "the servant of a low-comedy actor," (the hyphen connecting "low" and "comedy" being, of course, only inserted as a blind.) But the two grand points of objection urged against Mr. Aldridge are, that he is a "black servant," and that he has neither "birth, parentage, nor education." *He* attempt *Othello*, forsooth!!! indignantly exclaims the editor; *he* venture to undertake a part "the study of which occupied, *perhaps*, years of the life of the elegant and classical Kemble!"—"a part, which the fire and genius of Kean have, of late years, made his exclusive property!" This is rank twaddle. As to Aldridge's being a black servant, we are not satisfied of the fact; but if he were, there are a vast number of very deserving actors and actresses who have emerged from a similar station. Then, as to his "birth, parentage, and education," what were those of the "elegant and classical Kemble?" what were those of the fiery and genius-gifted Kean? What those of half the performers on the stage? If the man has competent talent, (which we are far from vouching for,) there was not any thing preposterous in giving him a chance; another trial having been afforded him, he had a right to fair play and fair criticism, which the *Athenaeum* has not given him.

But the best joke of all is, the protest which is made by the editor, "in the name of propriety and decency," against the interesting Miss E. Tree being subjected to be "*pawed about* by Mr. Henry Wallack's black servant." And this is called criticism . . . [75]

The *Atlas* hammered away at the same points:

The *Athenaeum* objects to the performance of MR. ALDRIDGE, the African Roscius, because he was formerly servant to MR. H. WALLACK. Not being in the secrets of the theatrical world, we were not acquainted with that fact before, but we confess we do not see the logic of the critic's conclusion. . . . Looking . . . to the birth, parentage, and education of *Othello* himself, it might be suggested that nothing short of inspiration could possibly have made him fit to take the head of the Venetian armies. There is nothing more wonderful in MR. ALDRIDGE'S assumption of the character of *Othello*, than there was in *Othello*'s having made such a character.

As for Aldridge's treatment of Miss Ellen Tree, "The critic, if he would be consistent, should also protest against Shakspeare for having made *Othello* paw the gentle *Desdemona*, for, of a verity, the cases are in no way dissimilar; and, of the two, we take it that *Othello* was a lower man than MR. ALDRIDGE, seeing that he was 'sold to slavery,' a degradation to which, we suppose, MR. ALDRIDGE has not yet been subjected."[76] The *Atlas* then returned to the issue of servant and master, giving it a different spin:

> But the critic looks at MR. ALDRIDGE, quoad MISS TREE, as the servant of MR. H. WALLACK, whereas, according to all known canons of criticism, he should look at him as the representative of *Othello*. If the argument be worth any thing, it must lead to the inference that MR. H. WALLACK, having been MR. ALDRIDGE's master, must be a fitter man to play *Othello*. We should like to see MR. H. WALLACK'S *Othello*, or rather, we should not like to see it. The objection is new; it opens a new source of difficulty in critical matters. The mind must cease to be the measure of the actor; he must be judged by an investigation into his private affairs. Now, it is quite clear, we suspect, even to the critic of the *Athenaeum*, that MR. H. WALLACK's servant can play *Othello* in a much superior manner to his master, who, bless the mark, could not play *Othello* at all; but, be his superiority on the stage what it may, his former servitude off the stage damnifies it altogether. Truly the play-bills should be more explicit; they should afford us some more definite clue by which to judge of an actor than his mere intellectual capacity; they should tell us that Mr. Snip has been a tailor, in order that we may know how we are to consider him when he takes upon him to perform *King Lear*.
>
> MR. ALDRIDGE is undoubtedly a much cleverer man than MR. H. WALLACK, and, ignorant of his "low estate," we certainly gave him credit for a talent in his performance which the *Athenaeum* satisfactorily disproves by reference to his situation in the household of MR. H. WALLACK. It is something for the world to know that MR. H. WALLACK had a black servant, which is a sign and token of lordliness: and it is something to know that a black servant can play *Othello* with such apparent ability. Seeing, therefore, that the comparison in this point of view is unfavourable to the master, who is, so far unlike his man, we might pursue the contrast farther into those points of skill on which we may presume MR. H. WALLACK was still more deficient. MR. ALDRIDGE, we take it for granted, could attend table, and

execute all practical offices of a domestic nature, much better than the gentleman in whose service he was employed. We have already demonstrated that he can act better than his master. So far, MR. ALDRIDGE is greatly superior to MR. H. WALLACK. Suppose the master and man were, by some unfortunate accident, dropped upon a desert island, and that they were there obliged to live as they could, and turn such brains as they had to the best account, which of them, we should wish to learn, would be the more likely to acquire the ascendancy? Is it not likely that the man would become the master, and that MR. H. WALLACK would sink from authority into dependence? This is the mastery of nature: and the only difference between us and the *Athenaeum* is, that we recognize the man in his moral development, and the *Athenaeum* takes him in his livery suit.[77]

Here the notion of master and servant was turned completely upside down.

The dispute between *Figaro in London* and the Garrick Club also attracted attention in the press, *Bell's Weekly Messenger* and the *New Court Journal* siding with *Figaro*,[78] the *Sunday Herald* supporting the Garrick Club's argument,[79] the *Morning Post* claiming a neutrality "prejudiced neither in [Aldridge's] favour nor against him, but [witnessing his performance] principally with feelings of curiosity,"[80] and the *Town Journal* dismissing the whole controversy as a publicity stunt employing "every sort of theatrical trick and gag . . . to excite the curiosity or feelings of the public."[81] All of them, biased or not, wound up condemning Aldridge's performance.

When the play ended on his opening night, an enthusiastic audience demanded a curtain call, a relatively new custom that some old theatergoers regarded with disfavor, calling it foolish, injudicious, and in very bad taste.[82] As was his habit in the provinces, Aldridge came forward and expressed his thanks to his auditors for their kindness and encouragement. This sort of speech had worked well when he was on tour, winning him extra applause and commendation, but in London it failed to impress most of those who heard it. They found it too flowery, too carefully rehearsed, and much too lengthy. The *Morning Chronicle* ridiculed it as "a flummery got-by-heart speech about 'gratitude' — 'sunny rays' — 'land of the stranger' — 'pulses of the heart,' &c. &c., which lasted so long that people began to be out of patience, & to show that they were so: during the whole of it, too, Abbott, who had come forward to announce the next night's performances, was obliged to stand by wondering when it would end."[83] The *Morning Herald* and *English Chronicle* called it "an oration as metaphoric as it was eloquent, and which would go far to prove that there is what they call in the Emerald Isle a blarney stone in the vicinity of the Niger."[84] The

Atlas said: "We were sorry that a man who had impressed us with some respect for his good sense, should have committed himself in so silly an exhibition. It is gross impropriety on the part of an actor to return thanks to the audience for supporting him. He might as well turn round, and remonstrate with them if they condemned him."[85] Aldridge evidently learned quickly from his mistakes. When he repeated the character two nights later, it was reported that he did so "with improved effort. He was much applauded. At the conclusion of the last scene, he was loudly called for, but declined coming forward."[86]

Aldridge had originally been scheduled to perform as Zanga and Mungo on his second night,[87] but a playbill announced that "in consequence of the enthusiastic reception of Mr. Aldridge (a Native of Senegal) and by the unanimous desire of the audience, he will have the honor of repeating *Othello* instead."[88] *The Revenge* and *The Padlock* were therefore postponed until Tuesday, April 16, but Covent Garden was forced to close that evening "in consequence of the indisposition of the principal performers there."[89]

Flu had spread throughout London. One paper estimated that "in a population of a million and a half, which is now the number in this overgrown city, at least two-thirds have been attacked by the prevailing Epidemic, or Influenza; some indeed, slightly, but the greater number with severity."[90] A week earlier the same paper had reported, "There is scarcely a house at the West End, perhaps not one, in which some, and perhaps all of the inmates have not been attacked."[91] Theaters were badly affected, losing both patrons and performers. During the three weeks or more that the epidemic persisted, the Italian Opera, Drury Lane, and the Haymarket had to close down for a spell.[92] On Saturday, April 13, the day after Aldridge's second appearance at Covent Garden, manager Laporte received notices of illness from twenty-four members of his company.[93] Under such circumstances, shows could not continue until actors and audiences had sufficiently recovered.

Aldridge's performances did not draw large crowds. Reviews spoke of the theater being thinly attended, and at best only half filled.[94] Covent Garden's financial records reveal that the house drew only £110.12 on April 10, which was less than the amount taken on all but one night in February and all but four bad nights in March. On April 12, however, box office receipts plummeted to only £77.4.6, which set a record for the lowest earnings at the theater in the first quarter of the year.[95] This may have been the primary reason why Aldridge was not allowed to return to perform a third night at Covent Garden, this time as Zanga and Mungo. The devastating flu, plus the negative publicity about his first appearance, may have turned too many people away. It is also conceivable that the flu may have been responsible for Aldridge's subpar performance on his opening night, when he was criticized for the tameness of his representation of Othello. Perhaps he just wasn't feeling well that evening. He had seldom lacked energy when performing this role on his provincial tours.

Some critics thought this actor, "facetiously nick-named 'the African Roscius,'" as the *Times* and *Sun* put it,[96] had failed in his debut at Covent Garden, but one of his staunchest defenders, the *National Omnibus; and General Advertiser*, insisted that this was not so:

> With regard to Mr. Aldridge, we repeat that he is a good actor—as to his asserted failure, we deny it.—The badness of the house was no proof of it.—Mr. Aldridge had the misfortune to appear during the time that the Influenza was raging, and few persons could go to the theatre. It might as well be said that in consequence of Mr. Aldridge's acting, that the Haymarket closed; or that the Opera House, Covent Garden, and Drury Lane, were closed under similar circumstances. There is no doubt that the performers were generally affected with the prevailing disorder, but the public were equally so, therefore, could the actors have appeared, there would have been no one to see them, and it became necessary to close the theatre. We therefore think it most unjust to attribute the thin attendance at the theatre, on the night of Mr. Aldridge's performance, to his want of talent. Besides this dispensation of Providence, Mr. Aldridge has been the victim of an unmanly, vindictive, and unprincipled persecution, got up by a gang of callous, mischievous ruffians, who took the advantage of an unworthy prejudice, which still lingers in the minds of weak persons, in whose ears the sound of "nigger" conveys less idea of a human being than that of villain, burker, or murderer. Because he was black, it was impossible that he could be possessed of intellect, and people did not think it worth while to go and see him. We sincerely hope that, should an opportunity occur, they will remove the stain from the national character, and repair the error into which they have been lead [*sic*] by the *leading* Journal and its worthy "brethren of the press," and support Mr. Aldridge in the performance of the limited number of characters to which the colour of skin alone restricts him.[97]

The "*leading* Journal" referred to here was the *Times*, which had published a damning review of Aldridge's performance saying, "Such an exhibition is well enough at Sadler's Wells, or at Bartholomew Fair, but it certainly is not very creditable to a great national establishment. We could not perceive any fitness which Mr. Aldridge possessed for the assumption of one of the finest parts that was ever imagined by Shakspeare, except, indeed, that he could play it in his own native hue, without the aid of lampblack or pomatum . . . [but his]

Figure 16. Engraving of Ira Aldridge as Mungo in *The Padlock*, 1850. From author's collection.

Othello, with all the advantage of '*hic niger est,*' wanted spirit and feeling."[98] It was this "ill-natured critique of a drunken reporter of a daily Paper" that the *National Omnibus* blamed for persuading Laporte to renege on his commitment to reengage Aldridge to perform "characters in which he would have given more satisfaction"—namely, Zanga and Mungo.[99]

However, à Beckett, wishing to claim full credit for having brought a premature end to Aldridge's appearances at Covent Garden, smugly assumed that the title of "*leading* Journal" belonged to *Figaro in London*:

> One of the greatest triumphs that ever was achieved by the rare union of integrity and severity in the pen of criticism, is the expulsion from the stage of the African Roscius, who, but for the lashing of *Figaro* might still have been suffered to degrade the boards of our national theatre. This man having been announced for Othello, was described by us, who had seen him in the country, as quite destitute of talent;—we were maliciously charged with a wish to injure him, handbills were circulated to excite a feeling against us and a sympathy for the Nigger, when he appears to a house netting £15. 12s. 0d., and confirms by his wretched acting the justice of the castigation we have so liberally dealt out with our relentless tomahawk. The whole press agrees with the opinion we gave before he appeared, and Keene, *alias* Aldridge, *alias* the African Roscius, *anglicè* the Nigger, is unceremoniously kicked off the stage by the naturally indignant newspapers. It is useless for us to say more about him. When he played Othello he doubtless must have had
>
> ———shut up in his brain
> *Some horrible conceit—*
>
> which, might have made him believe himself a genius. We are glad to have saved the national drama a further degradation by thus timely driving away the performer who was most likely to sink it lower than even it is, at this period of quackery.
>
> It is not customary for us to boast, but occasionally events take such a peculiar course, that candour compels us to assume credit to ourselves for some achievement in the cause of right to which we are so ardently devoted. We therefore cannot help expressing, in the most sincere spirit of gratitude, our thanks to our brethren of the whole press, who from the *Times* to the *Omnibus* have acknowledged *Figaro* as the leading Journal in all matters connected with the drama. That

we are so recognised by the press of the country, has been forcibly impressed upon the public mind by the event of last week, for, notwithstanding the applause of the audience at the performance of the Nigger, our *fiat* had gone forth, and the *Times*, &c. with a highly creditable respect for *Figaro*, followed precisely in the spirit of our criticism on the African Roscius. A committee of gentlemen deputed by the lovers of the drama, have applied to us to fix a day for having what they are pleased to term "the HONOUR of presenting *Figaro* with an address on his salvation of the falling drama, by driving the presumptuous black from the metropolitan boards," but as we have only done our duty conscientiously, we respectfully yet firmly decline the proffered distinction. We have no wish for honours however valuable, nor gifts however lucrative, the public good being our sole aim in all those writings the country patronises with so much ardent generosity.[100]

This provoked an angry rejoinder from the *National Omnibus* that heaped scorn on both papers for pretending to be paragons of public morality leading the struggle against degradation of the national drama:

We are obliged, in consequence of a paragraph which has appeared in one of the cheap publications (that is to say, a paper of a low price, for it does not follow, because little money is given for a thing, that it is cheap) to return to the subject of Mr. Aldridge's appearance at Covent Garden Theatre. The paragraph to which we allude, after abusing that gentleman in a most illiberal way, states "We cannot help expressing in the most sincere spirit of gratitude our thanks to our brethren of the press, who, from the *Times* to the *Omnibus* have acknowledged us as the leading journal in all matters connected with the Drama." Now we wish it to be distinctly understood that, as the *National Omnibus* has changed hands and come into our possession, we are not to be held accountable for any "acknowledgement" or concession which has previously been made and that in all theatrical matters, as they are conducted by the press at present, we own no fellowship with "our brethren of the press," most especially that tall towering bully, the *Times*, the *leading* journal as it is called. . . . The other paper which has given rise to the present article calls itself a *leading* journal, (in all matters connected with the Drama), and as far as manly feeling is concerned, the two *leading* journals are worthy [of] each other (*Par nobile fratrum,*) and the rest of their "brethren of the press." For ourselves, we will say if Theatrical criticisms consist in cowardly abuse, vulgarity, and a callous determination to deprive men of bread, as interest or caprice may dictate, "We have no brother, are like no brother." And so much for the two *leading* Journals.

The *National Omnibus* concluded its rebuttal by reaffirming its approval of Aldridge as an accomplished actor, noting with satisfaction that more recently he "has appeared at the Surrey Theatre, and drew very crowded houses on both occasions."[101] Implied in this statement was a suggestion that Aldridge's drawing power increased as the flu season abated. He remained popular with audiences healthy enough to attend the theater. To put it another way, the African Roscius had not failed at Covent Garden. Rather, the virulence of the epidemic and the vicious racism of "*leading* Journals" had conspired to thwart him.

In later weeks Aldridge went on to perform not only at the Surrey but also at the Royal Pavilion and the New City Theatre. The mainstream press tended to ignore most of his performances at these minor venues, but *Figaro in London* continued its relentless campaign against this "unhappy blackamoor"[102] and "quack detected."[103] À Beckett may have desired to prolong the controversy, if only to draw attention to his own role as an influential theater critic.

A long-term consequence of this brouhaha in the press over Aldridge's Othello is that his two nights at Covent Garden are thought to have blighted his early career, making him unemployable at other major London theaters and reducing his opportunities for playing at unfashionable houses outside the West End. He had been condemned as a failure, and theater managers were reluctant to take him on, even though he still had substantial box office appeal as a rarity who could attract large audiences curious to witness a performance by an "African" actor. It is clear that he pleased most of those who came to see him, surprising them with his professionalism and personal dignity. He won admiration and applause not just for his respectable acting but also for having overcome so many obstacles on the path to celebrity on stage. He was a phenomenon who deserved special consideration for what he had been able to achieve against all odds.

Yet there had been organized opposition to the very notion of a black man playing black roles on the British stage. Charles Mathews's memorable burlesque of the antics of an incompetent "African Tragedian" had set the tone of the ridicule that followed, and à Beckett had added acid to the demeaning stereotype, deepening the impression it made on the minds of theatergoers. Aldridge therefore was confronted with a problem of perverted public perceptions right from the start. How could he stand up to such skeptical scrutiny? A last-minute change in nomenclature from Mr. Keene, the African Roscius, to Mr. Aldridge, a native of Senegal, was not sufficient to remove prevailing doubts about a little-known black actor's competence to enact Othello with ethnic authenticity. Aldridge was charged with false pretenses even before he was given a chance to offer proof of his theatrical credentials. He was tried, convicted, and hanged in a kangaroo court of public opinion without having yet been granted the privilege of testifying in his own behalf. The debacle at Covent Garden was a direct result of his prior reification as a racial caricature.

Newspapers of every political persuasion had panned the show. A few liberal papers—notably the *Atlas, Observer, Morning Advertiser,* and *National Omnibus*—defended Aldridge, but others known for progressive and even radical views—*Bell's Life in London, Spectator, Weekly Dispatch, Satirist,* and most famously *Figaro in London*—focused on his shortcomings. Conservative papers such as the *Times, Morning Post,* and *Bell's Weekly Messenger* joined the chorus of condemnation, while the *Age*, notorious for underhanded dealings[104] and fully prepared to laugh at "this bit of ebony"[105] attempting to play Othello, had a sudden change of heart and found it possible to say a few kind words about Aldridge after actually seeing him perform. Others—the *News, Sunday Times, Standard, Morning Herald,* and *Court Journal*—took a middle course, praising this and censuring that, but the general tenor of the London press was negative. Aldridge had indeed failed—at least in the eyes of the professional pundits.

However, the paying customers liked what they saw and applauded his efforts vigorously. To many of them he was a symbol of racial equality—a black man who could think, feel, and express himself as articulately as any other human being. He provided living proof of the educability of Africans, thereby reinforcing arguments against slavery. Undoubtedly a talented man, he deserved to be accepted as a true brother.

Aldridge's performances in London theaters in 1833 happened to coincide with the culmination of a long-fought campaign in Parliament to abolish slavery in British territories. In 1807 the British government had passed a bill that prohibited slave trading by British vessels and the importation of slaves into all British colonies, but slavery itself was not eradicated in these colonies until an "Act for the Abolition of Slavery throughout the British Empire" was finally passed on August 28, 1833.[106] So Aldridge, who had been born in 1807, was on stage in London precisely when the larger issue of colonial slavery was being debated. It is not surprising, then, that his presence there would stir controversy. Many of those who applauded him so enthusiastically would have been supporters of abolition. Some of his opponents may have been of a decidedly different political persuasion.

Historian Lowell Joseph Ragatz has revealed that in the 1820s more than a dozen British newspapers and periodicals had opened their columns to a literary committee of the Society of West India Planters and Merchants "for monetary consideration."[107] The pro-slavery lobby thus funded reportage favorable to their cause. Five of these papers — *Times, Courier, Morning Herald, Morning Chronicle,* and *Globe and Traveller* — had published negative or partly negative reviews of the African Roscius. Four others — *British Press, Representative, John Bull,* and *English Gentleman* — had said nothing at all about him.[108] Whether this negativity was part of a well-financed campaign to discredit Aldridge or was prompted by genuine aesthetic concerns is impossible to determine with certainty, but at this distance it has an unpleasantly political odor. If indeed there were West Indian planters and merchants willing to pay a price to rid London of Aldridge, they must have counted themselves successful, for by July 1833 he was gone, and he did not return to perform on a London stage again until fifteen years later.

4

Clicks and Clucks

Victorian Reactions to San Speech

Homo sapiens have always been fascinated by the diversity and distinctiveness of their own species. People may differ a great deal physically and culturally, but they all recognize one another as related creatures set apart from other animals by a variety of innate characteristics. Indeed, for millennia they have exercised their powers of imagination and reason to explain to themselves the great mystery of their uniqueness in the biological order and to probe with special care the proximity of their kinship to "lower" forms of life. Many religious myths and scientific theories have been concerned primarily with defining man's place in nature.

Yet it is precisely at the margins of the domain delimited as human that the most troubling questions are apt to arise. For instance, although anyone can distinguish quite clearly between an anthropoid ape and a human being, who wouldn't be tempted to imagine some kind of remote genetic connection between them? And if another creature were suddenly to be discovered that seemed to share characteristics of both man and monkey, who could resist placing it in an intermediary position and calling it the "missing link" between the two? Could such a remarkable liminal being possess a soul? Should it be regarded as a man and a brother? Was a half-human brute entitled to full human rights?

These are questions that were debated with some intensity in Europe in the eighteenth and nineteenth centuries, when traffic in the transatlantic slave trade was at its height. However, the questions had started to trouble Europeans much earlier, especially after breakthroughs in navigational technology in the later half of the fifteenth century had put them in direct contact with coastal peoples all over the world. It was only about five hundred years ago, with the first circumnavigations of the globe, that a fairly broad sample of mankind could be surveyed firsthand. These voyages of discovery often brought back human cargo, demonstrating in flesh and blood the diversity of the human species.

Unusual specimens of humanity attracted so much attention in Europe that they gradually became a staple of itinerant popular entertainments, being moved from fairground to fairground, from city to city, and from one country to the next whenever their novelty value as foreign anomalies wore off. But as international trade grew and Europe became more cosmopolitan, these out-landish road shows drew fewer spectators unless they had something really sensational to offer. There was still a good deal of curiosity about strange peoples, and the stranger they were, the better. Crowds would still turn out to view anyone wonderfully freakish, exotic, or bizarre.

For an example of this kind of close encounter with visitors from outer colonial space, let us take a brief look at British responses to a group of "Bos-jesmans" (i.e., San, popularly known in the past as "Bushmen") from South Africa, displayed in various parts of the British Isles between 1846 and 1850.[1] They had been conveyed from Port Elizabeth to Liverpool as "4 servants" of Mr. J. G. R. Bishop, a Liverpool merchant who had lived in the interior of the Cape Colony for a few years.[2] One of the first public notices of their exhibition in November of 1846 stated:

> They consist of two men, supposed to be respectively aged about 35 and 45 years, and two women, aged about 35 and 50, together with an infant of the elder female, about four months old, born during the passage. To these living personages [Bishop] has added a collection of their implements of war, garments, &c., all tending to show how very nearly sentient beings may sink to, or rather have never risen above, the condition of animals unendowed with reason to guide or govern their instinctive propensities. Their appearance has already created considerable surprise among both the learned and the curious; they are of rather diminutive stature, of a dark copper colour, and resemble in some degree the features of the ordinary African. They are supposed to belong to one of the numerous tribes of their benighted country which have not yet emerged from absolute barbarism.[3]

What appears to have made the Bosjesmans particularly fascinating was the fact that they were so different from any people the British had ever encountered

EGYPTIAN HALL,
PICCADILLY.

The most EXTRAORDINARY

EXHIBITION OF ABORIGINES

Ever seen in Europe, landed in Liverpool by the Brig "Fanny," Captain Wheeler, and will be EXHIBITED for the First Time at the EGYPTIAN HALL, Piccadilly,

ON THURSDAY NEXT,
The 20th Instant,

THE BOSJESMANS,

OR BUSH PEOPLE,

Who appeared, for the FIRST TIME in EUROPE, at
EXETER HALL, on Monday last.

They are the most Singular Specimens of that decreasing
RACE OF HUMAN BEINGS,
THE BUSHMEN of South Africa,
VIZ :—

TWO MEN, TWO WOMEN, & A BABY

Of the Bojieman Tribe, from the interior of South Africa, a race that, from their wild habits, could never before be induced to visit a place of civilization. This opportunity of gratifying the man of science and the student in Zoology, has only been obtained by great personal exertion on the part of the gentlemen who have brought them to England at an immense outlay of capital. On the passage to Europe, a baby was born at sea, thus adding to the great interest that must be excited by their appearance. From Moffat the Missionary's Work on Southern Africa, page 53 :—"Poor Bushman! thy hand has been against every one, and every one's hand against thee." For generations past they have been hunted like partridges in the mountains. Deprived of what nature had made their own, they became desperate, wild, fierce, and indomitable in their habits. Hunger compels them to feed upon everything edible. Ixias, Wild Garlic, Mysembry Antharnams, the Core of Aloes, Gum of Acarias, and other Plants and Berries, some of which are extremely unwholesome, constitute their Fruits; whilst almost every kind of living creature is eagerly devoured, Lizards, Locusts, and Grasshoppers not excepted, The poisonous as well as innoxious serpents they roast and eat. They carefully extract their bags or reservoirs of poison, with which they cover the points of their arrows."

From the LIVERPOOL STANDARD.

"BOSJESMANS, OR BUSH PEOPLE, FROM SOUTHERN AFRICA.—Interesting Specimens of a most extraordinary Race of Human Beings have been landed in our Port, they are the Bosjesmans, or Bush People, from the interior of South Africa, of which so much has been written by the Missionaries, and the few who have travelled to that far distant region. They are natives of the country bordering the Great Orange River, 1200 or 1400 miles from Cape Town. They exhibit almost as striking an absence of the Intellectual or Higher Faculties as is observable in the Scull of that Monkey of Humanity, the Baboon, while the preponderance of the animal is almost equally as great. In every respect they are calculated to excite the greatest astonishment, and to confirm with the full those "Tales of Travellers" which we have certainly been inclined to look upon with suspicion. We could scarcely have credited that such a race could be in existence on the earth. That they genuine no one could doubt, in proof of which we give the following extract from a Cape Town Paper of the 24th of December, which we have just received :—
'We understand the Brig, 'FANNY,' Captain Wheeler, which recently left Table Bay for Liverpool, had on board an unusual kind of exportation, viz., two Males and two Females of the genuine Bushman Species, they are in charge of a Mr. J. G. R. Bishop, who has been at considerable trouble and expense in procuring them from the interior. They are authentic specimens of this diminutive and rapidly decreasing tribe of Aborigines, found only in Southern Africa.' "

Hours of Exhibition, from 11 in the Morning until 10 in the Evening.
Admission, 1s. Reserved Seats, 2s. 6d.

Figure 17. Playbill for an exhibition of the Bosjesmans at Egyptian Hall, London, May 1847. From author's collection.

before. The *Birmingham Journal* informed its readers that "the race to which these singular specimens of humanity belong, vegetate in the wilds of South Africa, and are the lowest in the scale of being that have yet been discovered."[4] Aside from their small size and odd features, the Bosjesmans were extraordinary because they owned very few possessions, used only the simplest tools, built no permanent structures, and wore hardly any clothing. All these traits could have been traced to the fact that they were a hunting and gathering people in a warm climate and therefore had no need for possessions or paraphernalia that would impede their mobility, but British spectators interpreted a lack of things as a lack of culture and thought less of the Bosjesmans as a result. Commentators tended to agree with the oft-quoted assessment offered by the learned traveler Dr. Lichtenstein that "there is not perhaps any class of savages upon the earth that lead lives so near those of the brutes as the Bosjesmans;— none perhaps who are sunk so low, who are so unimportant in the scale of existence;—whose wants, whose cares, and whose joys, are so low in their nature:—and who are consequently so little capable of cultivation."[5] In short, the Bosjesmans were presumed to be an utterly hopeless lot.

Yet the very extremity of their "degradation" made them all the more interesting to British audiences, for whenever these visitors deviated even slightly from accepted standards of cultivated behavior, their "foolish" actions were construed not only as further proof of Bosjesman barbarity but also as clear confirmation of British cultural superiority. The more different the Bosjesman appeared, the more comfortable the British felt. It was when the "savage" betrayed some sign of common humanity that the "civilized" expressed surprise and a little concern. John Bull did not fancy seeing himself reflected in this monstrously misshapen mirror. One paper warned that "Britons [may] degenerate if we are overrun any farther by such dirty and ugly monstrosities."[6]

Pictorial representations of the Bosjesmans in the media of the day were not at all flattering, the consensus among observers being that these were exceedingly ugly creatures who differed as much from Europeans in appearance as in intelligence.[7] To heighten the contrast between savage and civilized, some illustrated papers such as the *Pictorial Times* and *Sportsman's Magazine* printed sketches of the Bosjesmans dancing wildly while their fashionably dressed exhibitor stood sedately in the background looking on (see fig. 18).[8] For the show itself a large poster was prepared, illustrated with scenes said to be typical of Bosjesman life: "Quarrels of Bushman," "Fight of Bushman," "Tracing the Footsteps of the Enemy," "Killing the Puff Adder," "Preparing for the Dance," and so on (see fig. 20). Significantly, the borders between the vignettes were lurid with snakes and animal heads.[9] Less sensational images of the women and child in the troupe were used in the fourth edition of a leading ethnological textbook,

Figure 18. Sketch of the Bosjesmans in the *Pictorial Times*, June 12, 1847. From author's collection.

Figure 19. Sketch of the Bosjesmans in the *Illustrated London News*, June 12, 1847. From author's collection.

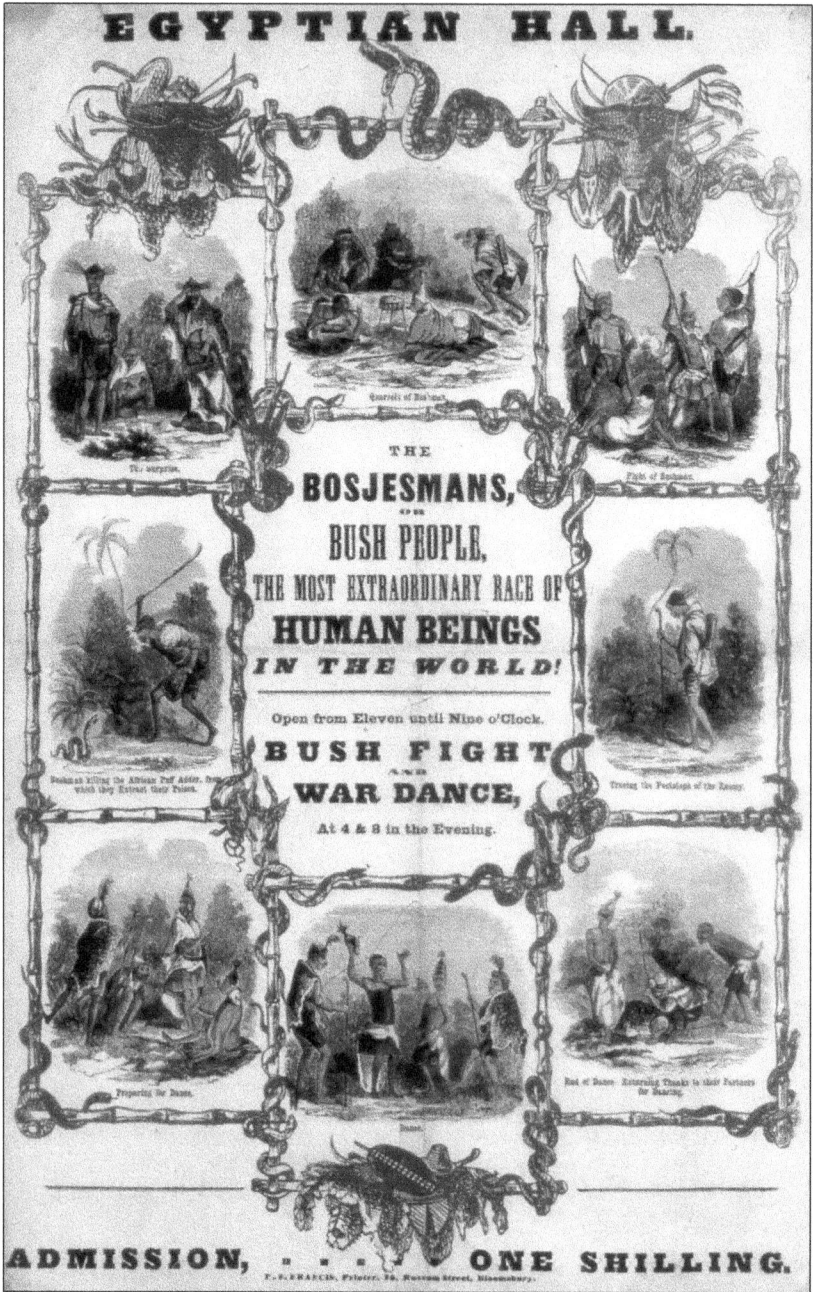

Figure 20. Illustrated poster for an exhibition of the Bosjesmans at Egyptian Hall, London, 1847. Reprinted by permission of the John Johnson Collection, Bodleian Libraries, University of Oxford (Human Freaks).

James Cowles Prichard's *The Natural History of Man* (1855), but even these "scientific" plates did not make them look attractive.[10]

One can find British cultural prejudice displayed quite openly in statements made by newspaper reporters about the Bosjesmans' most undeniably human characteristic—their language. The San phonological system happens to contain a set of implosive consonants, commonly called "clicks," which do not exist in the English phonological system. Since "well over 70 percent of words in Bushman languages begin with a click consonant," this is a very prominent feature in San speech.[11] The number and variety of these click consonants, complicated still further by subtle vowel colorings and significant variations in tone, make San languages, according to a contemporary authority, "from the phonetic point of view . . . *the world's most complex languages.*"[12] All of this complexity was lost on Victorian British auditors, who heard only the unfamiliar clicking and popping noises and drew their own conclusions.

The greatest temptation was to compare these sounds to those made by nonhuman creatures. The *Liverpool Mail* said that "their language—if the singular sounds by which their conversations are conducted can be termed a language—completely puts our alphabet *hors de combat*. It is not unlike the chirps of birds, and is supposed to consist of about twenty words, whose meanings are varied by the pronunciation."[13] The *Liverpool Chronicle* reported, "It is a perfect novelty to hear them talk, their language resembling more the 'click' of turkeys than the speech of human beings."[14] The *Birmingham Advertiser* described the phenomenon as a "singular compound of inharmonious articulations, copiously interspersed with a kind of chirp or click . . . and bearing no remote analogy to the babel of the smaller birds and animals in a menagerie."[15] Other papers drew comparisons to "the clucking of a hen,"[16] "the chucking of fowls or the motion of machinery,"[17] or the sound "used by ostlers to urge their horses."[18]

The *Spectator* offered the fullest and most perceptive linguistic description of the clicks but concluded with an unflattering comparison:

> Three of the consonants, we observed, consisted of these sounds—the noise made by the lips in slightly kissing, as when you kiss your hand; that made by smacking the tip of the tongue against the palate, as you do when tasting a flavour, or as some women do when they express petty vexation; and the clucking noise made with the hinder part of the tongue against the palate to urge a horse or assemble poultry; these three sounds, especially the two former, are consonants of rather frequent occurrence. A vowel sound, often repeated, resembles the French *eu*, but uttered from the chest with the coarse sing-song drawl of a boy driving away birds. The language is as rude and undeveloped, in sound at least, as the physical conformation of the people [who as adults] are

undeveloped children, stricken with senility while their forms are still immature.[19]

There was a similar tendency in other papers to associate unusual phonology with a lack of adequate physical, mental, moral, cultural, or linguistic development. The *Era* described the Bosjesman language as "wholly incomprehensible, for nobody can interpret it. . . . Their words are made up of coughs and clucks—such as a man uses to his nag—anything more uncivilized can scarcely be conceived."[20] According to the *Manchester Guardian*, this language was "singularly barren, exceedingly harsh and unpleasant to the ear . . . its most remarkable feature [being] some inarticulate clicks and clucks."[21] The *Glasgow Examiner* reported that such language consisted of "a series of *clicks* stuck together in some curious philological way, to represent their few and simple ideas."[22] The *Manchester Express* called it "rude and harsh in the extreme,"[23] the Dublin *Warder* said it was "an unintelligible jargon,"[24] and the *Plymouth Times* found it "so imperfect that its sounds can hardly be rendered in writing by any syllables we can frame."[25] The Bosjesmans obviously were not simply a hopeless lot; their ridiculous language betrayed them as a singularly inarticulate hopeless lot.

Some commentators were unwilling to consider them better than dumb brutes. London's *Morning Post* asserted, "They belong . . . to the lowest class of humanity; and the power of speech being excepted, there are many of the inferior animals possessing a greater development of the higher faculties than this savage specimen of the human kind." The only example cited to support this dismissive generalization was the beaver, who "possesses the faculty of constructiveness to a very marked extent." The rest of the article was devoted to illustrating the "marked resemblance" between the Bosjesman and the baboon, orangutan, chimpanzee, and monkey.[26] A reporter for the *Cork Southern Reporter* also felt that in their "brutelike indistinctness of language" as well as in a number of other traits, the Bosjesmans "come so near the Monkey tribe, as to make us almost question their humanity."[27]

Of course, a number of journalists were quite prepared to give the Bosjesmans the benefit of the doubt, principally because these grotesque children of nature were able to speak a language, albeit a simple and somewhat beastly tongue. But no reporters of that day believed that a Bosjesman's rudimentary linguistic competence made him the intellectual equal of a European. That would have been carrying liberal ideas much too far. A correspondent for the *Observer* put it this way: "Their distinguishing characteristic . . . as men is the use of language, but besides that they have little in common—either those now on view, or their brethren in the bush—with that race of beings which boasts of a

Newton and a Napoleon—of a Fenelon, a Milton, and of Dante."[28] No one would dare to attempt to make monkeys out of such distinguished men.

The arrogant ethnocentrism underlying British responses to the Bosjesmans appears to have been typical of European attitudes toward African peoples during the age of imperialism. Certainly Khoisan individuals and groups who had been displayed in the British Isles and elsewhere earlier in the nineteenth century had fared no better in the press. (We have already seen what happened to the notorious "Hottentot Venus" in 1810–15.) Nonetheless, sometimes it is shocking to come across racist remarks made by Victorian gentlemen one might otherwise have assumed to be among the most enlightened observers of the human scene. David Livingstone, for example, speaking specifically of the Bosjesmans, noted that "the specimens brought to Europe have been selected, like costermongers' dogs, on account of their extreme ugliness. That they are, to some extent, like baboons is true, just as these are in some points frightfully human."[29] As we shall see in the next chapter, Charles Dickens, in an essay debunking the romantic myth of the noble savage, concentrated his attention on a troupe of "diabolical" Zulus he had seen perform in London in 1853, but he also made uncomplimentary reference to Catlin's "Ojibbeways" and the Bosjesmans who had appeared on stage earlier:

> Think of the Bushmen. Think of the two men and the two women who have been exhibited about England for some years. Are the majority of persons who remember the horrid little leader of that party in his festering bundle of hides, with his filth and his antipathy to water, and his straddled legs, and his odious eyes shaded by his brutal hand, and his cry of "'Qu-u-u-u-aaa!" (Bosjesman for something desperately insulting I have no doubt)—conscious of an affectionate yearning towards that noble savage, or is it idiosyncratic in me to abhor, detest, abominate, and abjure him? I have no reserve on this subject, and will frankly state that, setting aside that stage of the entertainment when he counterfeited the death of some creature he had shot, by laying his head on his hand and shaking his left leg—at which time I think it would have been justifiable homicide to slay him—I have never seen that group sleeping, smoking, and expectorating round their brazier, but I have sincerely desired that something might happen to the charcoal smouldering therein, which would cause the immediate suffocation of the whole of the noble strangers.[30]

Dickens wasn't alone in desiring that all such people should be "civilised off the face of the earth."[31] Many viewers expressed the same kind of disgust or

Figure 21. Cover of a booklet titled *The Bosjesmans, or Bush People*, 1974 (reprint of 1847 edition). From author's collection.

horror when encountering uncouth specimens from sub-Saharan Africa. Given these unfriendly sentiments in Europe at large and in England in particular; given the state of ethnological science in those days—a science that in the later half of the century was to become increasingly preoccupied with defining racial differences and placing the various ethnic groups of the world on a hierarchical scale of native intelligence measured by such supposedly objective criteria as the shape and size of the skull (measures that were bound to assign small folk like the Bosjesmans and the Pygmies to the bottom rungs of humanity);[32] given, in other words, a propensity among Europeans to deny that other peoples, especially Africans, were their equals in intelligence, industry, and accomplishment, is it any wonder that this century saw Europe move to annex Africa politically, justifying its appropriation of a whole continent's human and material resources as the fulfillment of a divinely ordained "civilizing mission"? Only by dehumanizing the rest of humankind did it become possible for Europeans to shoulder the "white man's burden" in good conscience. At the very heart of European colonial policy, in Africa and elsewhere, was a supercilious belief in the benevolence of cultural genocide. This may have been one reason why the Bosjesmans and other click-speaking peoples of southern Africa who resisted being "civilised off the face of the earth" by Boers and Britons often wound up being slaughtered—like turkeys.

It is interesting to compare the public response to the Bosjesmans with that of a pair of teenagers from South Africa who were put on display in London a few years later. Only three and a half feet tall, fourteen-year-old "Martinus" and sixteen-year-old "Flora," misleadingly identified as "Earthmen from Port Natal" or "Erdmanniges" (a Dutch term), attracted favorable notices, partly because they were much better looking specimens than their predecessors. One lady pronounced them to be "perfectly kissable,"[33] and several papers carried handsome sketches of them (see fig. 22),[34] the *Illustrated London News* noting with approval their "pleasing hue . . . lustrous black eyes . . . perfect docility and mildness of disposition . . . good natural faculties . . . [and] excellent ear for music. . . . Martinus is a fine little savage, beautifully formed, and with well developed muscles. Flora is also a nicely-made child, of more slender and delicate frame, but perfectly healthy."[35] The *Court Journal* reported that they were "most beautifully proportioned. Their faces bear all the physical conformation of the South African races, but are tempered with a very intelligent and even bright expression."[36] The *Morning Post*, agreeing that they were "intelligent in mind and symmetrical in body," said, "in every respect they appear to be of a higher order in the scale of humanity than the savage and filthy Bosjesman."[37]

BOY AND GIRL OF THE EARTHMEN TRIBE, FROM PORT NATAL.

Figure 22. Sketch of the Earthmen in the *Illustrated London News*, November 6, 1852. From author's collection.

A handbill for one of their shows claimed that they were "the only Specimens of this Extraordinary Race ever beheld in Europe,"[38] but this was questioned by a number of informed spectators. They had been dubbed "Earthmen" because they were alleged in South Africa to have slept in hollows in the ground made by burrowing; members of the Ethnological Society of London, noting their resemblance to the Bosjesmans, chose to classify them as "Bushman-Troglodytes, or Troglodyte-Bushmen."[39] However, this designation was challenged by John Conolly, president of the Ethnological Society, who stated:

Figure 23. Sketch of the Earthmen on a British song cover, ca. 1853. From author's collection.

> The name of Earthmen, given to these little Africans, is of very doubt-
> ful propriety, and associated with a more than doubtful account of
> their living in holes burrowed in the earth; for which their delicate feet
> and hands seem unfitted, and for effecting which they are said not to
> have implements or utensils of bone, wood, iron or other material. It is
> very probable that they partly cover themselves with leaves or loose
> earth, not very dissimilar to them in colour, when they wish to elude
> observation. This is said to be the practise of the Bosjesmen.[40]

Like other human curiosities before them, Martinus and Flora danced,
sang, and mimed to entertain their customers, but their "act" differed in one
important respect: they performed entirely in English. They were able to do
this because they had lived for two years with a British family in Croydon before
being exhibited.[41] During that time they had acquired a certain fluency in
English, Flora had learned to play the piano, and together they had built up a
repertoire of songs that included "Buffalo Gals," "I'm Going to Alabama,"
"Annie Laurie," "Poor Uncle Ned," "Britons Never Shall Be Slaves," and a
number of black American tunes.[42] Their musical talents were very much
admired, but audiences were most impressed by their mastery of a "civilized"
tongue. One provincial paper reported that "the most interesting part of the
séance is found to consist in the spritely conversation they carry on with their
visitors,"[43] and another exclaimed that "their knowledge of the English language,
together with their musical proficiency, is very remarkable for the time they
have been in this country, shewing even a greater intelligence than that evinced
generally by the more civilized children of our own country."[44]

To such observers Martinus and Flora were miracles of transformation,
savages transmuted within two years into reasonable facsimiles of pure English
folk. More than anything else, it was their ability to chatter and sing in English
that made them recognizable as fellow human beings; such lively interlocutors
could not possibly be mistaken for baboons, orangutans, chimpanzees, or other
species of monkeys. Soon Martinus and Flora were being hailed as "a direct
Contradiction to the Theory lately set forth, of the Impossibility of Rendering
the Savage a Thinking, Feeling Being."[45] Given this high degree of enthusiastic
public acceptance, it is not surprising that these youngsters were treated more
kindly by graphic artists than the Bosjesmans had been. Their basic humanity
was never in question, so they could be embraced and depicted as bright,
beautiful people. Their fluency in English had won them instant respect and
admiration.

5

Charles Dickens and the Zulus

On December 15, 1852, a steamer, the *Sir Robert Peel*, left Durban carrying passengers and cargo bound for Cape Town. Among those on board were A. T. Caldecott, a prominent merchant from Pietermaritzburg; his son C. H. Caldecott; and, in the steerage compartment, thirteen Zulus whom the Caldecotts were taking to London for the purpose of exhibiting them to the public. The Caldecotts claimed that these were the first "Kafirs from the Zulu country [to be] exhibited in England" and that it had long been A. T. Caldecott's wish

> that the English public should be gratified with a sight of the interesting savages, by whom he was surrounded in the fertile and flourishing colony of Natal. On various occasions he has endeavoured to form a party to accompany him across the ocean to Great Britain, but their own reluctance, their fear of the voyage, the difficulties to be overcome before the colonial government would permit them to embark, and other causes rendered for a while all his efforts nugatory. By dint of continual perseverance; by telling the poor fellows the grand sights which awaited them; by engaging one this month and another the next; and by promising to each a good and just reward for their services, he was at length fortunate enough to secure eleven men, a young woman and a child. But the consent of the people themselves was not all that had to be obtained. It was necessary that the British government should sanction their removal. Mr. Caldecott memorialized the authorities

accordingly. Fortunately the circumstances of having been thirty-three years in Africa, and his being known as a merchant of respectability, and a highly honourable man, influenced the government in his favour.[1]

However, since trafficking in slaves had been outlawed by the British government barely nineteen years earlier, the Colonial Office in Natal granted Caldecott's request only "on condition that he [enter] into a recognizance, binding himself in a sum of £500 and two sureties of £250 each" to guarantee that the natives accompanying him would do so voluntarily, would be well treated on the voyage and in England, would be reported and, if necessary, produced to the secretary of state for the colonies, would be paid for the services they performed, and would be brought back to Durban no later than eighteen months after their arrival in England (4–5). To all these conditions Caldecott readily agreed, and early in January 1853, after exhibiting his troupe in Cape Town for a few days, he sailed with them out of Table Bay on a ship headed for London, arriving there in March after more than two months at sea.

There was good reason to suppose that the English public would be curious about the Zulus. Reports of the military prowess of this tribe had been filtering back to the English since the days of Shaka thirty years before.[2] Dingane's massacre of the Boer leader Piet Retief and some of his followers in 1838 and the devastating retaliation of the Boers at the battle of Blood River later that same year probably were still remembered by British adults who had been following the fortunes of Europeans in South Africa. In 1840 Dingane was overthrown by Boers working in alliance with his brother Mpande (Panda) who, as the new king of Zululand, granted them most of the territory south of the Tugela River, territory that the British annexed in 1843 as the Colony of Natal. From 1848 to 1851, the years just preceding the visit of Caldecott's Zulus to London, more than 2,700 British immigrants had arrived in Natal. The first substantial books about Natal and its peoples had started to appear in London in the 1830s, and during the period of the Great Trek (1835–44) there were frequent reports in the press about frontier skirmishes and full-scale "Caffre" wars. So there must have been considerable curiosity in Britain about the aggressive natives who inhabited this remote corner of the empire and occasionally created problems for white settlers.

But even without such a reputation, the Zulus would have been an interesting novelty in Victorian England. Blacks had been seen in London for centuries and were becoming quite numerous in the city by the middle of the nineteenth century, but most of these early residents and visitors were ex-slaves from North America or the West Indies—blacks, in other words, who had become Westernized to some extent. Africans and other so-called primitive peoples were still a relatively rare sight in even the most cosmopolitan European capitals, and it was not uncommon for exhibitions to be held to display such peoples to audiences that had only heard or read of their remarkable appearance and strange habits. They were the human equivalents of unique specimens in a botanical garden or metropolitan zoo and were treated rather like visitors from outer space. The science of ethnology was just getting established in Britain in the 1840s, and learned professors as well as uneducated laymen would flock to these exhibits to study the latest arrivals from exotic lands overseas. During the months that the Zulus were on stage in London, there were competing exhibitions of such peoples as the "Earthmen" (described in the previous chapter) and the "Aztec Lilliputians" (whose reported "capture" in an "alleged mysterious city lately discovered in Central America" was dismissed by at least one newspaper as a "cock and bull story,"[3] and was later thoroughly discredited by the secretary of the Ethnological Society of London, who regarded these dwarfish creatures as nothing more than profoundly retarded and deformed children hauled up for public display by mercenary hucksters[4]). Yet each of these three unusual groups—Earthmen, Aztec Lilliputians, and Zulus—were honored by being summoned to give a command performance at Buckingham Palace for Queen Victoria and her children. They were sought out by Crown and commoner alike.

The Zulus became one of the most popular shows in London during the summer of 1853. A. T. Caldecott, a canny businessman, had spared no expense in mounting the exhibition. He had rented St. George's Gallery (formerly known as the Chinese Museum) at Hyde Park Corner for the performances and had hired Charles Marshall, one of the most highly regarded painters and set designers of his day, to paint authentic scenery that could be changed mechanically to suit the time, place, and action depicted—a rather recent innovation in stage technology.[5] Two months were spent preparing the troupe for the first performance on the evening of May 16, and daily advertisements were placed in leading papers and journals throughout the exhibition's three-month run in London.

These efforts paid off handsomely. When the show opened, performances were given every evening at eight o'clock and Wednesday and Friday afternoons at three o'clock. By June 1, a third matinee had been added, and three weeks later there were afternoon and evening performances daily. To provide background information on the Zulus and Natal, Caldecott's son wrote a thirty-two page pamphlet titled *Descriptive History of the Zulu Kafirs, Their Customs and Their Country, with Illustrations* (see fig. 24), which was sold for sixpence during performances at the gallery. But even this was not enough to satisfy London's appetite for so unusual an attraction. On July 25, the *Times* carried

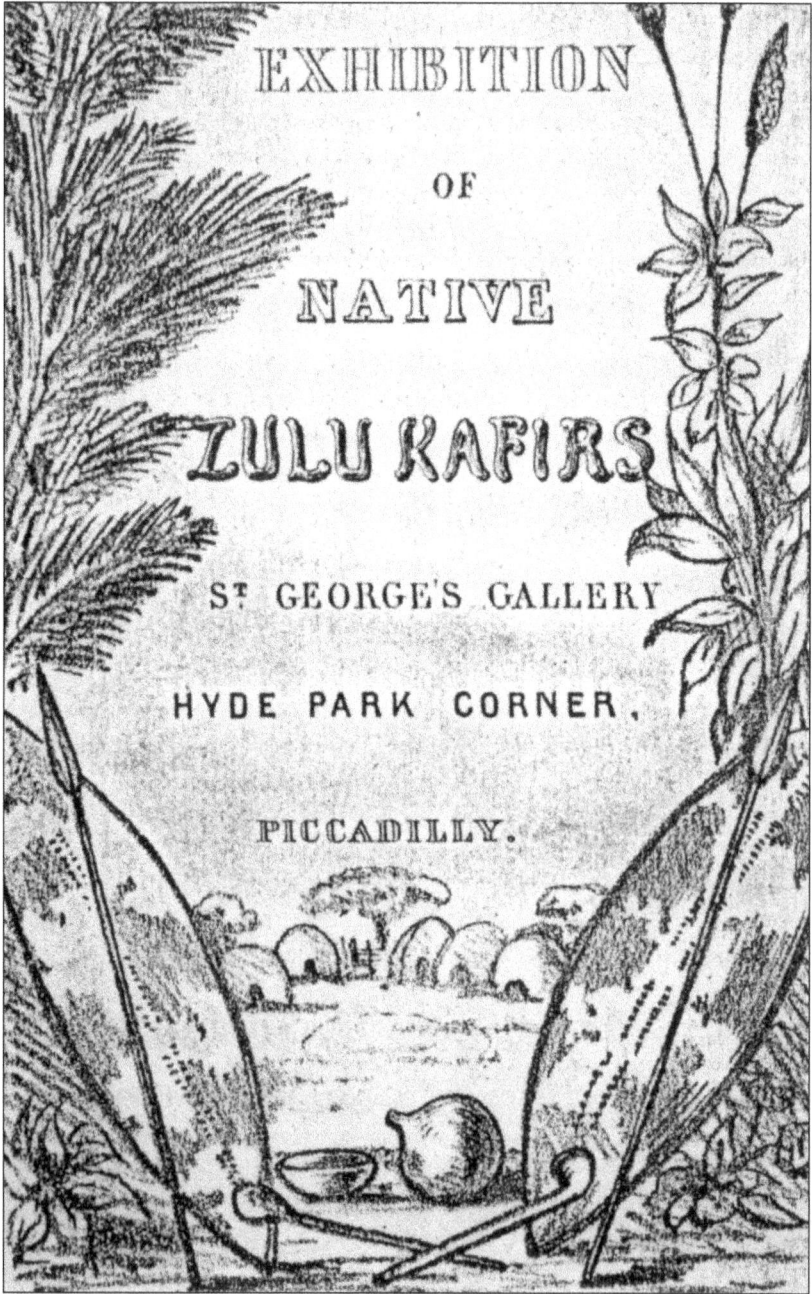

Figure 24. Cover of a booklet by C. H. Caldecott titled *Descriptive History of the Zulu Kafirs, Their Customs and Their Country*, 1853. Reprinted by permission of Yale University Library (Nkd84 1 1853).

an announcement by Caldecott: "In consequence of the increasing interest excited by this extraordinary and pleasing EXHIBITION, arrangements have been made to meet the public wishes, by which visitors will be allowed to see and converse with this interesting tribe daily from 11 to 1 o'clock, during the remaining period of their performance in London."[6]

Before the troupe left in mid-August to tour France, Belgium, Germany, Prussia, and possibly some of the English provinces, a second pamphlet on them had been published that reprinted several enthusiastic reviews of their performances and provided more information on the sanguinary history of the Zulus under "warlike and ambitious" Essenzingercona (Senzangakhona), "terrible" and "despotic" Chaka (Shaka), "cruel and treacherous" Dingarn (Dingane), and "their present king, Panda [Mpande], [who] is to a consider-able extent imbued with civilization, [having] got the good sense to prefer trading to fighting."[7]

What helped to make the Zulu exhibition more popular than other ethno-logical displays was the fact that it was an extremely dramatic performance, not a static sideshow. The performers acted out incidents said to be typical of Zulu life and did so with great fervor. The advertisement placed in the *Times* on the day the show opened stated that the exhibition would illustrate "in an extensive and unexampled manner, that wild and interesting tribe of savages in their domestic habits, their nuptial ceremonies, the charm song, finding the witch, hunting tramp, preparation for war, and territorial conflicts."[8] To explain some of the scenes, Caldecott's son served as interpreter and master of ceremonies, lecturing briefly on Zulu customs and traditions before they were enacted on the stage.

The earliest review of the "Caffres at Hyde-Park-Corner" (as they came to be called) appeared in the *Times* two days after the premiere. It is worth quoting in full because it is typical of the response of British theater critics to this novel entertainment:

> Although there have been several attempts to render Caffre life familiar to the English public through the medium of exhibitions, nothing in this way has been done so completely or on so large a scale as the new exhibition opened on Monday evening in the rooms formerly occupied by the Chinese museum. Eleven Zulu men, with a woman and a child, are assembled into a company, and instead of performing one or two commonplace feats, may be said to go through the whole drama of Caffre life, while a series of scenes, painted by Mr Charles Marshall, gives an air of reality to the living pictures. Now the Caffres are at their meal, feeding themselves with enormous spoons, and expressing their

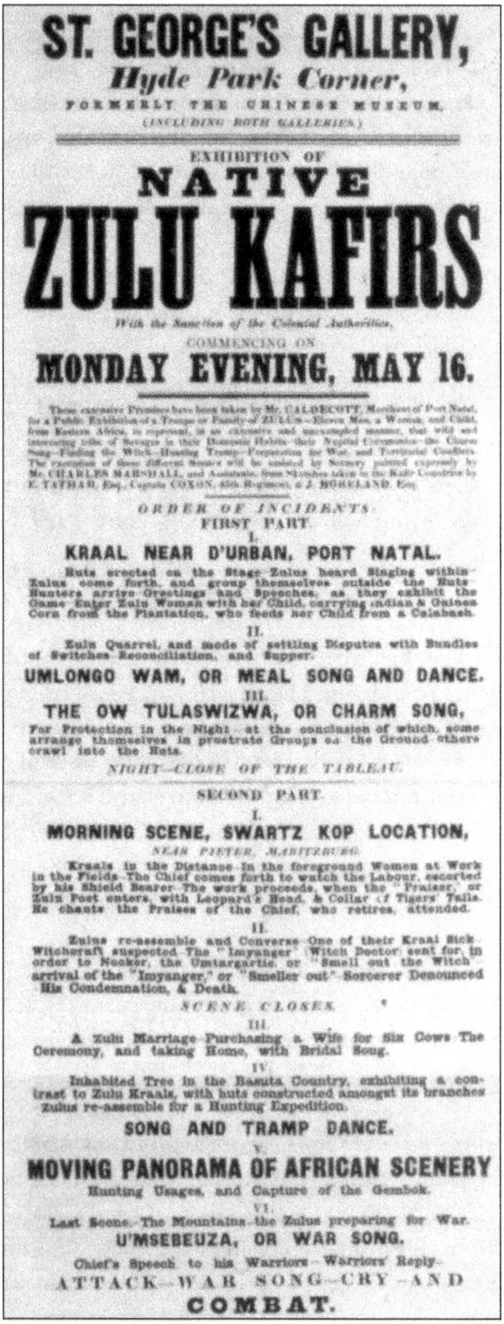

Figure 25. Playbill for the Zulu Kaffirs at St. George's Gallery, Hyde Park Corner, London, May 16, 1853. Reprinted by permission of the John Johnson Collection, Bodleian Libraries, University of Oxford (Human Freaks 4 [84]).

satisfaction by a wild chant, under the inspiration of which they bump themselves along without rising in a sort of circular dance. Now the witchfinder commences his operations to discover the culprit whose magic has brought sickness into the tribe, and becomes perfectly rabid through the effect of his own incantations. Now there is a wedding ceremony, now a hunt, now a military expedition, all with characteristic dances: and the whole ends with a general conflict between rival tribes. The songs and dances are, as may be expected, monotonous in the extreme, and without the bill it would be difficult to distinguish the expression of love from the gesture of martial defiance. Nevertheless, as a picture of manners, nothing can be more complete; and not the least remarkable part of the exhibition is the perfect training of the wild artists. They seem utterly to lose all sense of their present position, and, inspired by the situations in which they are placed, appear to take Mr Marshall's scenes for their actual abode in the vicinity of Port Natal. If 11 English actors could be found so completely to lose themselves in the characters they assumed, histrionic art would be in a state truly magnificent.[9]

Other reviewers singled out many of the same features of the exhibition for comment—the excellent scenery, the impressive physical appearance of the Zulus, the spirited and uninhibited acting. A columnist in the *Athenaeum*, after noting how the physiognomy of the Zulus differed from that of West African Negroes, went on to say: "Most of the men have a fine muscular developement [*sic*], and they exhibit considerable strength in some of their exhibitions on the stage. One thing is very striking in those performances,—that is, the almost perfect dramatic effect with which these wild men play their parts."[10] The reviewer for the *Spectator* was equally impressed with the "considerable dramatic propriety" of the performances but found several of the scenes highly amusing:

The Zulus—fine well-formed men, of fleshy frames but attenuated legs—get up the quarrel, and discuss the chances of war, with a great appearance of being in earnest about it all. In this point, and in its life-like character, to which the accessories contribute, the exhibition transcends all others we have witnessed of the kind. The charm-song and the proceedings of the witchfinder or "smeller out" were especially expressive and forcible in their pantomime. As for the noises—the howls, yells, hoots, and whoops, the snuffling, wheezing, bubbling, grovelling, and stamping—they form a concert to whose savagery we cannot attempt to do justice.[11]

Figure 26. Sketch of the Zulu Kaffirs in the *Illustrated London News*, May 28, 1853. From author's collection.

The *Illustrated London News* initially described the exhibition as a "picturesque drama [consisting of] a series of scenes which charm by their spirit and *vrai-semblance*" and often excite laughter by depicting incidents "more amusing than anything in a farce,"[12] but in its next issue printed a sketch of one of the scenes in the show (see fig. 26), gave brief biographical details of several of the performers, and elaborated on what it had found particularly entertaining:

> After a supper of meal, of which the Kaffirs partake with their large wooden spoons, an extraordinary song and dance are performed, in which each performer moves about on his haunches, grunting and snorting the while like a pair of asthmatic bellows . . . but no description can give an idea of the cries and shouts—now comic, now terrible—by which the Kaffirs express their emotions. The scene illustrative of the preliminaries of marriage and the bridal festivities might leave one in doubt which was the bridegroom, did not that interesting savage announce his enviable situation by screams of ecstasy which convulse the audience.
>
> The Zulus must be naturally good actors: for a performance more natural and less like acting is seldom if ever seen upon any stage.[13]

The "Zulu Kafir Exhibition" was obviously good theater and deserved to become a smash hit.

On May 26, after the show had been on for a week and a half and the first rave reviews had appeared, Charles Dickens went to see it, inviting his friend John Leech to accompany him.[14] Dickens may have been in need of relaxation for he was terribly overworked at the time. Not only was he writing the final chapters of *Bleak House* in monthly installments and the middle chapters of *A Child's History of England*, but in addition he was quite busy editing *Household Words*, a popular weekly journal he had launched in 1850. As might be expected in such circumstances, the Zulus turned out to be more than mere transitory entertainment for him; they became grist for his prolific mill. Shortly after witnessing their performance, he wrote a humorous essay titled "The Noble Savage" that appeared in a subsequent issue of *Household Words*. Though he made reference to such peoples as the "Ojibbeway" (American Indians) and the Bushmen who had been on display in London earlier, he focused his attention primarily on Caldecott's Zulus, using them as hilarious examples of the ignobility of uncivilized man. The essay has been called "one of the most effective philippics of our language,"[15] and there can be no doubt that Dickens, with his incomparable flair for comic exaggeration, achieved his aim of debunking the Romantic myth of the "noble savage," but today this piece of Dickens's writing is seldom commented on by scholars or teachers of Victorian literature, possibly because the views expressed in it are embarrassing and offensive to a contemporary sensibility.[16]

Here is how the onslaught begins:

> To come to the point at once, I beg to say that I have not the least belief in the Noble Savage. I consider him a prodigious nuisance, and an enormous superstition. His calling rum fire-water, and me a pale face, wholly fail to reconcile me to him. I don't care what he calls me. I call him a savage, and I call a savage a something highly desirable to be civilised off the face of the earth. I think a mere gent (which I take to be the lowest form of civilisation) better than a howling, whistling, clucking, stamping, jumping, tearing savage. It is all one to me, whether he sticks a fishbone through his visage, or bits of trees through the lobes of his ears, or birds' feathers in his head; whether he flattens his hair between two boards, or spreads his nose over the breadth of his face, or drags his lower lip down by great weights, or blackens his teeth, or knocks them out, or paints one cheek red and another blue, or tattoos himself, or oils himself, or rubs his body with fat, or crimps it with knives.

> Yielding to whichsoever of these agreeable eccentricities, he is a
> savage—cruel, false, thievish, murderous; addicted more or less to
> grease, entrails, and beastly customs; a wild animal with the question-
> able gift of boasting; a conceited, tiresome, bloodthirsty, monotonous
> humbug.[17]

From here Dickens goes on to grumble about the way some people whimper
over the savage "with maudlin admiration" and pretend that "the tenor of his
swinish life" is preferable to "the blemishes of civilization." He cites the "miserable jigs" of the "Ojibbeways" and the "horrid" pantomimes of the Bushmen
as evidence of the degenerate nature of such peoples, and then reinforces his
argument by taking a long look at the Zulus.

> There is at present a party of Zulu Kaffirs exhibiting at the St. George's
> Gallery, Hyde Park Corner, London. These noble savages are repre-
> sented in a most agreeable manner; they are seen in an elegant theatre,
> fitted with appropriate scenery of great beauty, and they are described
> in a very sensible and unpretending lecture, delivered with a modesty
> which is quite a pattern to all similar exponents. Though extremely
> ugly, they are much better shaped than such of their predecessors as I
> have referred to; and they are rather picturesque to the eye, though far
> from odoriferous to the nose. What a visitor left to his own interpret-
> ings and imaginings might suppose these noblemen to be about, when
> they give vent to that pantomimic expression which is quite settled to
> be the natural gift of the noble savage, I cannot possibly conceive; for it
> is so much too luminous for my personal civilisation that it conveys no
> idea to my mind beyond a general stamping, ramping, and raving, re-
> markable (as everything in savage life is) for its dire uniformity. But let
> us—with the interpreter's assistance, of which I for one stand so much
> in need—see what the noble savage does in Zulu Kaffirland. (339)

It is apparent that Dickens relied heavily on the ethnographic information
supplied in young Caldecott's lecture, but he supplemented what he heard with
his own observations of the Zulus in action. It is interesting to compare the
descriptions of Zulu life and customs in Caldecott's later pamphlet (which
presumably grew out of his lecture) with Dickens's version of how these wild
creatures conducted their affairs. The accounts were often quite similar, though
Dickens had a tendency to stress graphic details and toss in amusing asides to
his readers.

For instance, young Caldecott, after describing the land, racial background, and material culture of the Zulus, devoted one entire chapter of his booklet to Zulu "Laws and Government" and another to "Zulu Characteristics." Since he based his remarks on Nathaniel Isaacs's *Travels and Adventures in Eastern Africa, Descriptive of the Zoolus, Their Manners, Customs, with a Sketch of Natal* (1836), it is perhaps best to begin with Isaacs's account and to observe how this was transmuted via Caldecott into vintage Dickens. Isaacs regarded the Zulus as "the most extraordinary people in existence" and "zoolacratical government" as

> the most incomprehensible government with which any known nation
> on the face of the earth is conversant. . . . Its outline, however, may be
> said to be perfectly simple—namely, despotic. . . . It is monarchical, it
> is true; but apparently neither hereditary nor elective, the succession
> depending on the murder of the existing monarch, which usually takes
> place when he begins to exhibit either of those two signs of age—
> wrinkles or grey hairs. In this case, the criminal who performs the
> bloody deed, or directs its execution, is perhaps a son or some other
> member of the royal family. When the throne has become vacant by
> the sacrifice of the monarch, it usually happens that civil disputes settle
> the succession. . . . When the monarch is firmly seated on his throne—
> which is seldom or never accomplished without, as it were, wading
> through blood to it—he becomes an absolute king, or "inquose." His
> name then becomes sacred, and adoration is paid to it. . . . The power
> of the monarch is indeed not only despotic, but even atrocious: for he
> can command indiscriminate massacres by his nod. . . . [His warriors]
> are a morose, sullen, savage set of monsters, fit only for deeds of darkness
> and for the devastations of war; and these are their sole occupations.[18]

As for religion, Isaacs says simply, "[The Zulus] have none" and "are unquestionably the most superstitious creatures on the face of the earth."[19]

That young Caldecott followed Isaacs very closely, at times even slavishly, can be seen quite plainly in his description of Zulu government as most nearly resembling "a perfect despotism":

> The king is absolute; there is no liberty of the subject; a nod from the
> monarch consigns anyone to death, no matter whether guilty or inno-
> cent. At the command of his ruler a father must murder his own un-
> offending child, brother must slay brother, or a husband destroy his

wife. Appeal is death to the appealer. It is a monarchical government, but apparently neither hereditary nor elective. The succession depends on the murder of the existing sovereign, which usually takes place when he begins to exhibit the signs of age. The criminal who performs the deed, or directs it, is usually the son, or some other member of the royal family. When the throne has become vacant by the sacrifice of the monarch, a dispute and some additional murders settle the succession. . . . When the king becomes firmly seated on the throne, he is called an "Inkosa." His name then becomes sacred, and adoration is paid to it. (19)

In his chapter on "Zulu Characteristics" young Caldecott also asserted: "In his present savage state [the Zulu] has very little idea of morality and none whatever of religion. Behind his agreeable outward bearing, he conceals the most vindictive feelings, and a capacity for perpetrating the most atrocious cruelty. Impulsive, emotional, and excitable even to frenzy, he makes no effort to control his impulses, nor at any time reasons upon the abstract justice of his deeds (21–25)."

Dickens compressed all this information into a brief paragraph that conveyed the essence of what he had learned from Caldecott about Zulu law, government, and character:

> The noble savage sets a king to reign over him, to whom he submits his life and limbs without a murmur or question, and whose whole life is passed chin deep in a lake of blood; but who, after killing incessantly, is in his turn killed by his relations and friends, the moment a gray hair appears on his head. All the noble savage's wars with his fellow-savages (and he takes no pleasure in anything else) are wars of extermination— which is the best thing I know of him, and the most comfortable to my mind when I look at him. He has no moral feelings of any kind, sort, or description; and his "mission" may be summed up as simply diabolical. (336)

Dickens then went on to poke fun at the way in which Zulu marriages were contracted. Here his description seems to be based as much on the performance he saw as on the lecture he heard. Young Caldecott's written account also appears to owe a great deal to personal observation, though portions of it were taken directly from his two primary sources, Isaacs's *Travels* and Captain Allen Francis Gardiner's *Narrative of a Journey to the Zoolu Country in South Africa* (1836). Here is how Caldecott introduces the subject of marriage:

A Zulu marriage festival is a very noisy and animated affair. Preliminary matters having been gone through, the bridegroom, in company with his friends, seats himself, and waits the arrival of the bride, who comes escorted by the people of her tribe. She is tastefully attired; her hair being decorated with feathers, in imitation of a coronet, and her skin well oiled and polished for the occasion. Rows of beads in varied colours are suspended round her neck, and she brings many strings of beads with her. The overture is as often made by the women as the men. The bride's father usually sends a cow with her as a present. When she arrives in the presence of her future husband, she and her attendants perform a dance, accompanied with as large an amount of noise as they can conveniently get up for the occasion. It is the aim of the lady, on this occasion, to appear as agile as possible in the presence of the bridegroom's friends, and that which she may lack in grace she compensates for in expertness. The ballet being finished, and all present being satisfied with the lady's performance, her friends proceed to settle the important business of how much she is worth. They value her at six cows. Her lover offers three: the offer is rejected. Very much clattering and haranguing takes place, but at length the bargain is struck at the price originally demanded; and the bridegroom is made a happy man by the gain of a wife and the loss of his six cows. (25)

Dickens turns this "very noisy and animated affair" into a raucous unmusical comedy in which the bridal barter and "ballet" are pictured as uninhibited haggling punctuated by ear-splitting ejaculations and frenzied foot-stomping.

If he wants a wife he appears before the kennel of the gentleman whom he has selected for his father-in-law, attended by a party of male friends of a very strong flavour, who screech and whistle and stamp an offer of so many cows for the young lady's hand. The chosen father-in-law—also supported by a high-flavoured party of male friends—screeches, whistles, and yells (being seated on the ground, he can't stamp) that there never was such a daughter in the market as his daughter, and that he must have six more cows. The son-in-law and his select circle of backers, screech, whistle, stamp, and yell in reply, that they will give three more cows. The father-in-law (an old deluder, overpaid at the beginning) accepts four, and rises to bind the bargain. The whole party, the young lady included, then falling into epileptic convulsions, and screeching, whistling, stamping, and yelling together—and nobody taking any notice of the young lady (whose charms are not to

be thought of without a shudder)—the noble savage is considered
married, and his friends make demoniacal leaps at him by way of
congratulation. (336)

Dickens gets even more dramatic when describing Zulu witchcraft, a
subject calculated to amuse a Victorian public skeptical of the efficacy of any
form of non-European divination. Young Caldecott, who shared this prejudice with his London audience, may have helped to shape Dickens's negative
attitude toward Zulu sorcery, but it is apparent that the spirited enactment of a
witch hunt by Caldecott's troupe made a very powerful impression on him, one
that he tried to replicate for others in onomatopoeic prose. Before looking at
Dickens's account, however, let us see how young Caldecott presented this
custom, which he frankly regarded as "singularly absurd":

> The Zulus believe illness to be always the result of witchcraft. When
> any of their tribe are taken ill, the services of the *Inyanger* or witch-
> finder are called into requisition, to nooker or smell out the *Umtugartie*
> or witch, who has caused the illness of the invalid. They abhor the
> tiger-cat, or *Imparker*, as they call it, and believe it to be as necessary a
> companion to the witch of the Zulu, as a black cat is thought by some
> people, to be indispensable to the witches of more civilized nations. The
> witch-finder, or *Inyanger*, makes his appearance, attired very demonia-
> cally in shaggy strips of fur; all the people seat themselves before him.
> He dances in their presence, flinging himself about in the wildest manner
> imaginable; then smells the ground, and eventually pouncing upon one
> of the party present, declares him to be the person who has bewitched
> the sick man. The *Inyanger*'s assertion is unhesitatingly believed, and the
> denounced individual is at once hustled away by his neighbours, and
> beaten to death with their knob-kerrees. It is almost needless to add
> that these Inyangers are the vilest imposters. (27–28)

Dickens substitutes a grizzly bear for the leopard (or "tiger-cat" as it was called
in South Africa then) and spells phonetically all the Zulu words introduced by
young Caldecott, but otherwise his account is fairly faithful to the substance
and tone of his source. It differs mainly in its dramatic immediacy and hilarious
sound effects.

> When the noble savage finds himself a little unwell, and mentions the
> circumstance to his friends, it is immediately perceived that he is under
> the influence of witchcraft. A learned personage, called an Imyanger

or Witch Doctor, is immediately sent for to Nooker the Umtargartie, or smell out the witch. The male inhabitants of the kraal being seated on the ground, the learned doctor, got up like a grizzly bear, appears, and administers a dance of a most terrific nature, during the exhibition of which remedy he incessantly gnashes his teeth, and howls: "I am the original physician to Nooker the Umtargartie. Yow yow yow! No connexion with any other establishment. Till till till! All other Umtargarties are feigned Umtargarties, Boroo Boroo! but I perceive here a genuine and real Umtargartie. Hoosh Hoosh Hoosh! in whose blood I, the original Imyanger and Nookerer, Blizzerum Boo! will wash these bear's claws of mine. O yow yow yow!" All this time the learned physician is looking out among the attentive faces for some unfortunate man who owes him a cow, or who has given him any small offence, or against whom, without offence, he has conceived a spite. Him he never fails to Nooker as the Umtargartie, and he is instantly killed. In the absence of such an individual, the usual practice is to Nooker the quietest and most gentlemanly person in company. But the nookering is invariably followed on the spot by the butchering. (336)

Dickens's next subject was the Zulu "Praiser" whom young Caldecott described as a "Poet-laureate" and a

most uncouth-looking individual, dressed in the skin of a leopard, or a tiger-cat, the head of the animal forming his own head for the nonce, and his occupation being to utter, through the leopard's mouth, and in very deep-toned words, the attributes and excellencies of his superexcellent monarch. The more he disregards the laws of punctuation in performing his duty, the better he acquits himself. We subjoin a portion of his eulogy, printing the epithets as they are spoken, without any intervening pauses — "Thou who are as high as the mountains thou noble elephant thou black one thou who art as high as the heavens thou who art the bird who eats other birds thou who art the great cow and the peace maker!" &c. &c. &c. (27)

Dickens anglicizes the praise song and throws in a few more animals unknown in the African subcontinent but again captures the vigor and spectacle of the Zulu performance at Hyde Park Corner.

There suddenly rushes in a poet, retained for the purpose, called a Praiser. This literary gentleman wears a leopard's head over his own,

and a dress of tigers' tails; he has the appearance of having come
express on his hind legs from the Zoological Gardens; and he inconti-
nently strikes up the chief's praises, plunging and tearing all the while.
There is a frantic wickedness in this brute's manner of worrying the air,
and gnashing out "Oh what a delightful chief he is! O what a delicious
quantity of blood he sheds! O how majestically he laps it up! O how
charmingly cruel he is! O how he tears the flesh of his enemies and
crunches the bones! O how like the tiger and the leopard and the wolf
and the bear he is! O, row row row row, how fond I am of him!"—
which might tempt the Society of Friends to charge at a hand-gallop
into the Swartz-Kop location and exterminate the whole kraal. (337)

The last example Dickens gives of the culture of this uncultured people is
their colorful preparation for battle. A war song had been performed as part of
the show at St. George's Gallery, and Dickens, as usual, based his description
of the custom on both what he had seen and what he had heard from young
Caldecott, whose booklet put it this way:

> War is the principal business of a Zulu Kafir. Before going to battle the
> king calls a council of his chief men. He appears among them arrayed
> in a mantle of tigers' tails, and with an attendant behind him holding a
> shield above his head. The particulars of the projected campaign are
> detailed, and one warrior after another steps forward to give his advice.
> Though in the presence of his monarch, he does not speak coolly, nor
> conduct himself with modesty, but utters his opinions with a howl,
> emphasizes them with a jump, and bangs his shield with his assegai to
> enforce their justness, and the strength of his own convictions. When,
> at length, the place of action is determined upon, the warriors rush off
> at once to where the conflict is to take place, singing with savage glee
> their war song on the way. (28–29)

Now here is Dickens expanding on the subject:

> When war is afoot among the noble savages—which is always—the
> chief holds a council to ascertain whether it is the opinion of his brothers
> and friends in general that the enemy shall be exterminated. On this
> occasion, after the performance of an Umsebeuza, or war song—which
> is exactly like all the other songs—the chief makes a speech to his
> brothers and friends, arranged in single file. No particular order is

Figure 27. Poster of the Zulu Kaffirs, the Aztec Lilliputians, and the Earthmen at Cremorne Gardens, London, September 15, 1853. Reprinted by permission of the John Johnson Collection, Bodleian Libraries, University of Oxford (Human Freaks).

observed during the delivery of this address, but every gentleman who finds himself excited by the subject, instead of crying "Hear, Hear!" as is the custom with us, darts from the rank and tramples out the life, or crushes the skull, or mashes the face, or scoops out the eyes, or breaks the limbs, or performs a whirlwind of atrocities on the body, of an imaginary enemy. Several gentlemen becoming thus excited at once, and pounding away without the least regard to the orator, that illustrious person is rather in the position of an orator in an Irish House of Commons. But, several of these scenes of savage life bear a strong generic resemblance to an Irish election, and I think would be extremely well received and understood at Cork. (337)

Dickens followed this up with a paragraph playfully suggesting other parallels between the ceremonies of the noble savage and the practices of civilized man in Europe, but he returned to his main theme in his concluding statement: "My position is, that if we have anything to learn from the Noble Savage, it is what to avoid. His virtues are a fable; his happiness is a delusion; his nobility, nonsense . . . and the world will be all the better when his place knows him no more" (339).

Although it sometimes appears so in this essay, Dickens was not really recommending genocide. He was very much the Victorian pragmatist striving to puncture an inflated Romantic conception of the dignity of "primitive" peoples. The Zulus were simply a convenient case in point, a group so far removed from Europe in custom and culture that they could easily be held up as examples of an underdeveloped race obviously in need of moral improvement and mental refinement. Dickens did not suggest that such peoples be exterminated; rather, he wanted them "civilised off the face of the earth." He believed in cultural, not literal, genocide.

Yet it is interesting to note with what contempt Zulu customs, traditions, and institutions were viewed by the London audiences who saw this troupe perform. The performers obviously overstepped the boundaries of Victorian decorum when they sang and danced, but their antics presumably would not have provoked so much hilarity among spectators with cultural traditions more closely akin to those of the performers themselves. Underlying the reaction of Dickens and other English viewers was a broad streak of undisguised racism, a belief that the Zulus were morally and mentally inferior to Europeans. The numerous comments on their smell, their bizarre modes of dress (and undress), their noises, their monotonous songs, rabid incantations, and wild demoniacal dances, betray an arrogant assumption that the Zulus were overgrown children of nature who had not yet developed the inhibitions, self-discipline, and manners that distinguish more civilized folk. They were savages pure and simple, primitives in the raw.

Of course, one cannot really blame the Victorians for being so ethnocentric. Nineteenth-century Europe, with its numerous civil and international wars, was not exactly a showcase of ethnic tolerance, and inadequate opportunities for meaningful face-to-face cultural contact with representatives of the non-Western world hindered Europeans from learning much about the human beings who inhabited the rest of the globe. In an illuminating study titled *Stereotyping: The Politics of Representation*, Michael Pickering demonstrates how in the Victorian era

> Africa became known about almost entirely through Western cultural myths and stereotypes. Although new data was steadily forthcoming, this was continually filtered through European preconceptions, or simply ignored if it did not conform with existing images of what became known as the "Dark Continent." . . . Fitting Africa and Africans into what [Victorians] already knew, and how they already thought, made their image of Africa a largely European construct created to suit European needs. Europeans imagined the African in their own regard, as a non-self standing over against themselves. In this respect, Africa was an absence filled up by the presence of European discourse about it.[20]

And this discourse was further skewed by meretricious physical evidence presented on stage to Victorian spectators. There were no documentary films or television specials then to bring more accurate images of foreign peoples to the drawing rooms of London. The Zulus were therefore merely a spectacle, a carnival act consciously designed to play up their "abnormalities"—that is, their radical deviation from European norms of dress and behavior. It would be ethnocentric of us to expect audiences who saw them more than a century and a half ago to react with a more modern sensibility and to come away from such a performance with a richer understanding and appreciation of Zulu culture.

Indeed, one wonders if this would be possible in Europe or America even today. There is strong evidence to suggest that it would not. If we examine the reviews of more recent black South African performances in London and New York, we find remarkable echoes of those antiquated Victorian attitudes. More than a century was to elapse before a second black South African musical managed to reach the London stage. This was *King Kong*, a jazz opera set in Johannesburg's shantytowns, which ran for more than eight months at Princes Theatre in 1961. Though the script was written and produced by white South

Figure 28. Sketch of a later troupe of Zulus in the *Illustrated London News*, January 14, 1865. From author's collection.

Africans, though the setting was urban rather than rural, though the hero was an Othello-like boxer who strangled the woman he loved and then committed suicide, drama critics yielded to the temptation to fasten on what seemed to be the crudest aspects of an animated performance. In London the *Times* called it "a piece of naive but vital indigenous art" and went on to say:

> The naivety, the rhythm and the vitality have a characteristic colour and manner of their own. They seem to be conditioned by the particular locality to which the characters belong; and it is perfectly easy to take what appear to us as stage clumsinesses in our stride and to yield ourselves up to the rhythm and the vitality.
>
> Mostly the dances are frankly erotic, with the dancers using their hips and legs, or they are war dances with the gangsters seeking to strike terror with their foot movements. The songs are always strongly, if seldom melodiously, sung. . . . There is also a wildly uninhibited gangster dance culminating in a murder and an enchanting wedding hymn warmly lit and beautifully dressed which also culminates in a murder.[21]

Except for the gangsters, this almost sounds like a revival of the "Caffres at Hyde-Park-Corner."

King Kong was a harbinger of things to come. In following years no fewer than four Zulu musicals were brought to London, and all received similar reviews. In 1972 *Umabatha*, an attempt to tell the story of Shaka as a super-sanguinary Macbeth, met with this startled response:

> Before the murder, Mabatha (Macbeth) takes snuff and sneezes; an approved method of achieving second sight, which brings him the vision of an assegai. His letter to his wife is communicated as a drum message. And the three witches are transformed into *sangomas* (witch-doctors) who upset all Western notions of the sinister by conducting jolly dances round the cauldron shaking with seemingly innocent laughter. The most surprising thing about the whole show is its apparent good humor. . . .
>
> The dances are built on a uniform beat to a short melodic fragment, and when one of these ostinatos starts building up the stage really catches fire. The shields go down to the ground while a leader whirls demonically in the foreground, executing high-kicks up to his chin, and bringing in the group with a pounding one-footed beat.
>
> The effect is as stunning visually as it is to listen to: a mass of moving skins and weapons transforming separate members into a single in-domitable animal, bent on celebration, joy, or killing, but unstoppable no matter what its objective.[22]

Singing, dancing, and drumming were also singled out as the most impressive features of *Kwa Zulu*, a musical that opened in London in July 1975.[23] But an even more enthusiastic response greeted the musical gyrations in *Ipi-Tombi*, which premiered a few months later and ran for years in London. The *Times* called it "all ululating leaps, steatopygous flourishes, and tableaux of warriors framed in russet skybroth silhouette," which added up to "an evening of exotic escape."[24] The *Sunday Times* went further, hailing it as a "thrilling production, presented with a verve, an *éclat*, a technical brilliance, a richness of voice in the singing, an excitement and a precision in the dancing which I do not believe that even the best American musical could rival. It is a riot of colour and movement, yet it is as controlled as the changing of the Guard. Every member of the huge cast is superb."[25]

Ipi-Tombi did not win such unrestrained applause when it traveled to New York in January 1977. The fact that the show was picketed by antiapartheid groups may have made some critics think twice about the political significance of the atmosphere of joy, happiness, and innocence being conveyed by the black performers, but it did not stop a few reviewers from indulging in the usual clichés about African atavism. The dances, *Time* magazine exclaimed, "illustrate how close to nature some Africans apparently still are. The gestures, the rhythms and the sounds indicate an unbroken totemic relationship with animals. The members of the troupe slither like snakes, stalk like the great cat family of the jungle, stamp and trumpet like elephants. This is all done with an agility, grace and energy that is breathtaking. The lead drummer (Junior Tshabalala) plays with galvanic fervor and propels the best number in the show, a warrior dance, into a Dionysian frenzy."[26]

Dickens would have loved it. Such a performance would have proved to him that savages are no nobler now than they were 150 years ago, thereby reinforcing his belief that "between the civilized European and the barbarous African there is a great gulf set."[27]

If Zulus were more recognizably human on stage, we might be challenged to accept them, at least in imagination, as our brothers and sisters. But when they sing, dance, and drum as demonically as they do, then obviously they come from a different world and must be kept in their proper place, always a good distance from Europe and America. Such performers, no matter how diverting, serve to increase the great gulf of misunderstanding between Westerners and Africans and thus perpetuate the pathology of racism. Dickens clearly is not dead yet.[28]

6

A Zulu View of Victorian London

When one reads what Dickens and other Victorian commentators said about the Zulus they saw onstage in London, one naturally wonders what these South African performers may have thought of the peoples and places they encountered on their travels. How would the British have looked to them? Given their own cultural orientation, their own aesthetic preferences and ethnocentric attitudes, how would Zulu visitors have responded to what they found in a city like London? What would have impressed them? Which sights would they have regarded as odd, puzzling, or disconcerting? How would they have interpreted some of the strange things they saw? Fortunately, an unusual document that has long been out of circulation provides a basis for answering some of these intriguing questions. Reprinted here is the text of a dialogue between one of the Zulu performers Dickens saw and a group of Zulu elders in Natal to whom he was reporting what he had seen abroad. The conversation was taken down by someone fluent in Zulu (presumably a missionary working in the area), and was published in English translation in one of the last numbers of the *Natal Journal*, a missionary quarterly from Pietermaritzburg that survived for only two years before expiring for lack of adequate financial support.[1] The entire document is reproduced here, including the editor's prefatory remarks and parenthetical interpolations.

A South African Native's Picture of England

[A few years ago certain natives of the colony of Natal were conveyed to England for purposes of exhibition. They remained in the British Islands, and in

European countries, for about a year, travelling from place to place, and seeing a great deal. It so chanced that, subsequently to their return, one of the party, who had made good use of his eyes, was induced to tell of what he had seen, in the presence of several older men of his own race. The following sketch of the scene, and report of the experiences of the traveller, is made by an eye and ear witness, who was present at the time, and who was eminently qualified, by a thorough acquaintance with the native language and peculiarity of character, to preserve an accurate record of what passed. Every expression that is attributed to the narrator was actually used by the young native in communicating his experiences to his companions. The account of the conversation may accordingly be pursued by the readers of the *Natal Journal* with exceeding interest, as furnishing a trustworthy and vivid picture of the aspect civilized matters assume in semi-barbarous eyes.—Ed. *Natal Journal*.]

Upon a certain occasion not many moons ago, an intelligent young Zulu, of about twenty-two years of age, sat on the floor of a large room in the city of Maritzburg, surrounded by twenty older men of the same race—most of them persons of rank and influence in their tribes, and some of them old enough to be the young man's grandfather. The countenance of the young man was open and clear; but the faces of the elders were clouded with doubt, or fixed in the impassable mould of incredulity, which barbarians of experience and dignity so well know how to assume. The occasion of the gathering was that the young Othello had undertaken to speak of "the dangers he had passed," and to re-count his adventures in strange lands. In place of "antres vast and deserts idle," he, however, had to tell of the wonders of civilization, things more incredible to the rude dwellers of the kraal, than if the narration had been of "men whose heads do grow beneath their shoulders." He had crossed the wide ocean, and visited the white-chiefs in their island home beyond, and he had now to bear his testimony to their surprising cleverness and power. For some time the entire party sat in uninterrupted silence, the old men unwilling to admit curiosity, and eyeing their travelled entertainer. At last one of the seniors put an end to the probationary silence by saying—

"Well, young man, it is said you are older than we are; you have travelled further, and seen more; you have crossed the sea. Now tell us of your wanderings, and what you have seen; but do not pour lies upon us."

"Yes, father," replied the youth deferentially (for the reader must know that great respect is always shown by these people to age as well as rank), "I have crossed the sea; I have seen London, the great place of the English; I have also crossed another sea, and seen the 'great places' of other white nations; and there is another great sea, which I did not cross; and beyond that live still other white nations. I will tell you no lies; but what my own eyes have seen can I relate to you."

The old councillor said, "Go on, my son, begin with the sea."

The young traveller proceeded to say, "I must first tell you that when we left this country to go to England, we had heard from Englishmen much about the greatness of the English—how numerous they were; what an old people, and how rich they were; and what wonderful things they possessed. We shall now see the truth of all this—every man magnifies his own country to strangers. When they told us, they did not think we should go there to see for ourselves. We did see, and that which we saw far exceeded what we thought was exaggeration. I cannot tell you all I saw. I should not expect you to believe me if I did, because I saw before I could believe. When we left this country, the tax (native hut-tax) had only just been established; and when we asked why we had to pay? we were told that in every country people paid taxes. We did not believe this either; we thought that when another's property is wanted, a hole can always be found in the fence. We determined to investigate for ourselves, and bring back the truth. We did so; we enquired all over England, in France, in Germany, in Prussia; wherever we went all said they paid taxes, and that everyone they knew paid taxes; so we concluded that where the world ends, there ends taxation! These are the two things we agreed together to enquire into and find out, and we found as I have told you."

"Going on the sea was hard to us; but we said, we will try; others have gone, and gone safely; should we be selected for a different fate because we are black? At first the ship went well enough; soon it began to lean from side to side, and it felt so loose in the water, we said it will fall over; we saw no reason why it should remain upright; presently we became very sick, and could eat nothing, and we thought we should die; our hearts turned behind us, and we lamented for our friends; at length, however, we found ourselves recovering, and the ship still keeping its right position, and we said all may yet go well with us. We reached Cape Town. Until we had seen England, we thought Cape Town was a great place, but then we saw otherwise. After leaving the Cape, we lost sight of the land, and we thought, how can the ship find its way without a path—before, behind, and on every side, is nothing but sea? we bewailed our condition, and said we shall all die in this waste together; but the white men laughed at us, and told us that they saw their way in the sky—that the stars were their guides, and the sun their path, and that they had not lost the way; we hoped this might be true, but we could not see such a path, and we could not believe; we said, however, surely these people do not die joking, for if we die, they must also. After some time the captain said we should see land the next day, and this would prove that he knew where he was; we said, we shall see; the next day truly we did see land; then our fears ceased, and our bodies melted into comfort; this land, however, was not England, but some island in the sea which we were to pass by. In the third month of being in the ship we saw England; then we were told that we were in the mouth of a river, and soon after, that London was before us; those who knew London saw it; our eyes, however saw nothing but a cloud of smoke, then houses, and presently poles standing out of the water, like reeds in a marsh, and these were the masts of the London ships; we went in among them, and our ship stood still—and we found ourselves in London, the great place of the English!"

One of the listeners enquired how large this great place was? the young man replied, "We never saw the end of it; we tried hard to find it, but could not; we ascended a very high building like a pole (the monument), to see where it ended; but our sight was filled with houses, and streets, and people; we heard that many people, born and grown old there, had never seen the end of it, and we said, if such is the case, why should we, who are strangers, look for it? we gave it up.

"The people are so numerous that they tread on another; all day and all night the streets are crowded; we thought some great thing had happened, and said, let us wait till the people have passed on, but they never did pass; if anyone falls down he is trodden upon and dies, there is no rising again for him, unless his own strength helps him; the surface of the earth is too small for the people, and some live under the earth, even under the water" (an allusion to the shops in the Thames tunnel).

"That must be a lie, young man," exclaimed one of his listeners.

"I hate a liar," said another.

"Perhaps it may be true," suggested a third, "let him explain."

"No, chiefs! it is no lie," replied the young man, "for I saw it with my own eyes; the London river is as broad as one part of the Bay of Natal; over it they have built a bridge which people and wagons can cross upon; there are also boats by which you can get over on the water: and under the river is a passage cut, through which wagons and people can go to the other side, without knowing that they have passed a river at all, for the water is above them; and it was here that I saw the people living."

One of the chiefs enquired, "If wagons and people can pass on a bridge over the water, and they can cross with boats on the water, why should they make another passage under the water?"

The young man said, "I asked as you ask, and was told they made it so because they wished to have it so."

Chief, "But where is their light—it must be dark where they live?"

Young man, "Fire gives light."

Chief, "Did you go among the crowd in London?"

Young man, "Only while holding the arm of a white man, for people lose themselves in London, and are sometimes never heard of; we were told that two brothers got separated in the streets, and it took a letter from one, two months to find the other, and he was in London all the while; you know how fast letters always travel."

Chief, "Young man, if you speak the truth you are old, for you have seen much; we are but children."

Young man, "Besides the crowds in the streets on land, the water is covered with large and small ships, all full of people, going up and down it, who never go into the large sea, and I was told they live on the water because there is no room for them on the land: when I saw all these people, I thanked for you that England was not joined on to this place, for if it were they would trample you into the earth with their boots."

Chief, "Did you see any black people in England?"

Young man, "I saw a few, but although they had black faces they had long hair, and I heard that they came over another sea."

Chief, "Are the houses of London large?"

Young man, "They are so tall that they shade the streets from the sun till midday; the spirits of the place live in the highest parts of some of the buildings, where men never go, and day and night utter a wailing sound, which I heard" (this is probably an allusion to the chimes in the churches).

Chief, "What kind of country is England? what grass grows there?"

Young man, "I never saw any country, and there is no room for the grass to grow—except it is fenced in like a field of corn it would all be trodden down; I went from London to other parts of England, but I only saw houses and fences; I never saw open country, and believe there is none any where more open than this Umgungundhlovi (the town of Pietermaritzburg); a man is never alone in England, he could not be so where I was, but I travelled so fast my eyes were puzzled."

Chief, "How?"

Young man, "I travelled in a wagon drawn by another wagon, but I never could understand; what I know is, that it went so fast, that if you were to start from this place at daylight in the summer time, to go to Durban (fifty miles off) you could go there and be back again by gun-fire the same morning" (this would be from half-past four to nine a.m.)

"No! no!" exclaimed his hearers, "that is faster than a horse can go!"

Young man, "A horse! when you want to go quickly in this country you ride on a horse, but there you take the horse with you into the wagon, and he feeds as he travels."

Chief, "That is too much for us; you are laughing at us. What is it you say?"

Young man, "One wagon draws a great many others; it goes so fast that a horse cannot keep up, therefore you take your horse with you; when you have arrived at the place you are going to, you mount him, and ride about to finish your business quickly, in time for the return of the wagon; having done this, you put him back again into the wagon to be taken home with you."

Chief, "And what is this wagon that draws the other wagons along?"

Young man, "I do not understand it myself; I could only make out what is a large kettle on wheels, full of water, with a fire under it to make it boil; but before it boils other loaded wagons are tied behind it, for the moment it does boil it runs away on its own road; and if it were to boil without the wagons being fastened to it, I do not know where it would go to."

Chief, "But does going so fast not break the wagons?"

Young man, "It has its own roads, upon which nothing else travels; they are straight and level; valleys are built up, and hills bored through for it, and strips of iron are put into the ground to keep it right."

Chief, "Did you ever see a hill bored through?"

Young man, "I passed through many; a stranger thinks his road goes over the hill, but all at once he finds himself going through it, in darkness, and sparks, and a fearful noise."

Chief, "If there are so many people in England as you say, do not these wagons kill the people?"

Young man, "These roads are guarded, and the people take care of themselves, few prefer death."

Chief, "Are there any cattle in England?"

Young man, "There are none here; I never saw a cow give milk, or a fat ox, till I went to England."

Chief, "But you say there is no open country; where do they graze?"

Young man, "They are kept in stables like horses, and their food is cultivated."

Chief, "Is there any beef in London?"

Young man, "It was in London that I saw beef."

Chief, "Where did it come from?"

Young man, "I enquired about that very point, for I could see but few oxen, and still there was plenty of beef; and I found that they were brought from a distance in wagons, feeding all the time; for instance the oxen to be slaughtered here tomorrow—supposing this to be London—are just now leaving Delagoa Bay, in those wagons drawn by the hot-water wagon; in England oxen do not draw wagons, but ride in them, and I saw a herd of them coming into London on the tops of the houses; there was no room for the road on the earth, so they built it over the houses."

Chief, "When you began, young man, we asked you not to pour lies upon us; we are no longer children, we are full grown men; how can a road be built over houses such as these we see?"

Young man, "I tell you what I saw, I add nothing of my own; I saw oxen come over the houses of London, and they are not like these; I see no houses here; in England the horses live in better houses than the gentlemen do here."

Chief, "You said the cows give plenty of milk in England."

Young man, "One there gives as much as a kraal full would here; the milker tires before the milk is finished."

Chief, "What kind are they?"

Young man, "The kind we call *Amafalalani*; they have large bodies and short legs; they stay in houses; when I looked at them I was sorry for them, for although they gave so much milk they never felt the sun."

Chief, "How much is the money that buys them?"

Young man, "Many pounds are paid for one cow; but London is the place where money is made, they don't look at it there."

Chief, "Are the people of London all rich?"

Young man, "Many are rich and many are poor; in such a great place there is all that is beautiful, and all that is bad."

Chief, "How is a rich man known in England?"

Young man, "He is not rich who has not been obliged to build a house to keep his money in; I saw many large houses in London, built for nothing but to keep money in."

Chief, "Did the English notice you black people much?"

Young man, "They noticed us because we are black, for I saw they never noticed each other."

Chief, "Did you hear any news of the country while you were there?"

Young man, "Yes, the English were at war with the AmaRusi (Russians); we saw the soldiers going into the ships to fight them."

Chief, "Where was the fighting carried on?"

Young man, "It was over the sea; I heard that the English never allow any fighting in their own land; whenever they fight they go and meet the enemy in his country."

Chief, "They understand fighting who do that; but did they show any alarm as to who would be beaten?"

Young man, "None at all—they know they will beat; I saw some of the ships of the AmaRusi brought in which had been captured by the English; it is only the soldiers who go to fight, war makes no difference to the people."

Chief, "Did you see the Queen?"

Young man, "Yes, we were taken to her house—it is very large, looks to have been built long ago; is surrounded by high walls, and guarded by soldiers; we were taken into a large room, in which it was said the Queen saw people who came from other countries; many persons, all belonging to the inside, came to look at us, and we stood wondering at what we saw; presently we perceived from all the gazers leaving us, that the Queen was coming—we thought these were many of them great men, but they knew themselves to be too small to stand in her presence—all left us but our conductors, and we feared to stay where our superiors had considered themselves unworthy to remain; the Queen however approached, and we saluted her with our '*Bayete*' (native royal salute); one of our conductors was then called to explain to her all about us; I was also called to answer questions about this country—Chaka, Panda, the Zulus, and Faku—I was asked about old Zulus, who had died long ago, and whose names I only recollected after my return to this country, for I had heard my father talk of them. When we found ourselves so near the Queen, we felt that we were not far from the edge of a precipice; but when she spoke our fears ceased, for we saw she only wanted to look at us; but who can tell all that we saw there—they showed us the Queen's carriage, fastened and covered with gold, the dresses of the men who sit in front and behind it the same, as also the dresses of the horses who draw it.

An acquisitive old listener remarked, "It might be profitable to walk behind it; it is said that riches are often found in the paths of the great."

The young man resumed, "We were shown the stables where the horses were kept; those belonging to the Queen's guard are all black, very beautiful; then we looked at the buildings themselves, but came away without knowing where the Queen herself staid [*sic*], the place is so large no one can know unless he is told.

Chief, "What kind of person is the Queen?"

Young man, "Not tall, but good looking; she is like any other English lady in her own house; it is only when she goes out that you see she is the mistress of the land; she rides in this shining carriage, surrounded by great gentlemen on horseback, and the soldier guards, with metal covers to their heads, riding their black horses; when there is no path for anyone else, a way is always found for her; when she passes all hats are taken off, even the great of the land do not omit to uncover their heads, for she is passing who owns them all; it is then that even a stranger, who knows not, would say, this must be the Queen of the land."

Chief, "Did the Queen give you anything?"

Young man, "No, we were told that we must go again before we left, but we never did."

Chief, "You said you went over another sea, and saw other white nations."

Young man, "Yes, we crossed the sea, and saw the AmaFulansi (French) and the AmaBelgi, the Amagermani and the AmaPulusi (Prussians); we saw all their 'great places.'"

Chief, "Are they like London?"

Young man, "Their houses are; but in size they are all children to London; we could walk from the middle of either of them to the outside in any direction, and return the same day; but London we never saw where it ended, or where it began, although we were bent upon doing so."

Chief, "Which are the largest of these great places?"

Young man, "Paris is large, and so is Berlin; I said Paris was the largest, but if a man contradicted me I should think he has seen as well as I, and might be right; but London is the mother, and could hold one in each arm."

Chief, "Are the people there as rich as those in London?"

Young man, "They themselves confessed to us that the greatest riches were in England."

Chief, "Did you recross the sea, and go back again to England?"

Young man, "Yes, but one of our party died in Berlin."

Chief, "What more did you see in England?"

Young man, "I saw more than I can tell you, and yet I saw nothing; some of our party staid behind because they said they wished to see more; I saw men ascend into the skies, and go higher than the eagle; I saw dogs carry letters, and monkeys firing off guns; I saw a horse dance to a drum, and when he had finished make a bow to the people who were looking at him; I saw elephants, seacows, tigers, and crocodiles, living in houses; I saw snakes handled by human hands; I saw a boa coil himself round an Englishman, put his head into the man's mouth, and then uncoil himself when he told him; I saw men standing on their heads and walking on their hands for money, and paid my own money to see him do it."

Exclamations of "Hau! hau!" followed the narration of this string of wonders. "By Chaka!" said one of his hearers, "the young man is inventing now; where did the men get wings who went into the skies?"

Young man, "I saw all that I tell you; the men did not go up with wings, but in a basket (a subdued "Au!" from several showed that they thought the young man was becoming incorrigible)—the basket was tied to a large round bag filled with smoke; it looked like a large calabash, with the mouth downwards, and the basket hung beneath; in this two people sat, and when the bag was let go it went up with them. I looked at it till my eyes were tired, and it became smaller than a bird; they took up sand with them, and poured it on the people beneath, some of it fell on me."

Chief, "Did you see them come down again?"

Young man, "No, I did not; but people said the coming down was danger-
ous, because the thing mostly went where it liked, not where the people in it
wanted; sometimes they found themselves on the top of a tree, or a house, or in
the water."

Chief, "What did they go up for?"

Young man, "I don't know; they told me there was some work they went up
to do, but what it was I did not hear."

Chief, "It is hard to believe this, but if it is true the white people have large
livers" (much daring).

Young man, "If you were to go where I have been you would say so."

Chief, "Do you speak the firm truth in what you say about the wild animals
and snakes?"

Young man, "Yes, I saw all I tell you; I saw animals from this country, and
others which I had never seen before."

Chief, "May we believe you?"

Young man, "You may, for it is all true; why should I tell you lies in praise
of others? did you not hear me say, that when we went to England we thought
all we had heard from the English was exaggerated, and when we saw for ourselves we said we had heard nothing?"

Chief, "We have heard, and if you have any more to tell us that is true, go
on."

Young man, "I saw many things that were good to me, and many that I did
not like. When a man dies in the streets (and many do, because the streets are
always full), if he has no brother or friend he is taken to a house, and his things
hung up, and he is cut open and salted, and papers put out to ask who he is;
and if no one claims him he is taken to the doctoring houses, and cut up and
dried; and if one dies, and they do not know his disease, they cut him open and
look at him. We were taken to one of these doctoring houses, and when we
were at the door we saw dead men standing up as if they were alive, so we
feared to go in."

Chief, "Why is all this done?"

Young man, "Because they say the doctors learn to cure the sick, and because they don't want to bury more than they can help, for the ground is but
small; in England people make ready places for burying themselves in, as we
here make kraals for our cattle, and in these one generation is buried by the
side of another."

Chief, "No wonder they come to Natal, if their own country has grown so
small for them; but this cutting up dead people looks as if they knew how to
'takata' (use witchcraft)."

Young man, "They may know that also, for they know everything; but I heard that the doctors were the people who liked dead men, and that if the graves were not taken care of their people stole the bodies for them; we were also told that the man of our party who died at Berlin was only buried because we were there, and that he was afterwards taken out and cut up, to see if he was made inside like the white people."

Chief, "Where there are so many people there should be much food; but if land is so small, food must be scarce."

Young man, "The people are like the grass, but food is more abundant; at first we thought, where shall we get food when there are so many people of the country to eat it themselves—we did not see it growing, or where it could grow, but we learnt afterwards that money brought the food of other countries there; for a sixpence a man can fill himself there much better than here, and have more than he can eat."

Chief, "Is there umbila (Indian corn) in England?"

Young man, "Plenty, but we never looked at it; we eat [*sic*] bread and drank beer; we only liked umbila after we came back to this country."

Chief, "Have you any more things to tell of?"

Young man, "I have many more, but I cannot recollect them now; I did not see what I wished to see, the houses where clothes and iron things were made; we were always promised to see them, but did not; some of our party refused to come back, because they wished to see these and other wonders; I saw, however, where they are made, and the people that make them, and found that our belief was not true, that a race of people with only one eye were the only makers of them. We went to the house where the money is made, but the soldier would not let us go in—he said that not even an Englishman was allowed inside—but we heard them making money very fast from where we were; there is English money distinct, and French money distinct; all countries have their own money; and when an Englishman goes to France he buys French money from the money houses, where I saw heaps for sale, to use in France, and the same when a Frenchman comes to England."

"But although I have told you so much I have told you nothing, for I was only beginning myself to see when I left; I saw but one thing—the number and power of the English, and all the white people; when I went from this country, I thought that the blacks were beyond the whites in number, but when I saw for myself I concluded there were no black people at all; men say many things, and that the whites are but few—it is only because they have not yet come; if they were all here they would dig down the mountains and build up the valleys, and we should be like dogs on a flat, howling for their homes; we know no work— they can work for themselves—there is nothing they cannot do; and we! what can we do? I often thought of you in England, and that you knew not the truth on this point; that you believed you were strong, while you were nothing; and that it would put an end to many false thoughts if every chief in Natal could be taken to see England."

Chief, "Young man, we thank you for your news; you have made us older than we were, but you are older still, for you have seen with your eyes what we only hear with our ears; as you say, eyes are more to be relied on than ears, and it would be well to see as well as hear; but what old man would cross the sea?"

7

Dr. Kahn and the Niam-Niams

One of the most interesting European efforts to merge show business and ethnographic science took place at Dr. Kahn's Celebrated Anatomical Museum near Piccadilly Circus in London in December of 1854. Joseph Kahn, allegedly a German doctor of medicine, had made a profitable business of exhibiting wax models of anatomical wonders at various centers of learning on the Continent before moving to London to cater to Victorian curiosity about the human body. His museum contained hundreds of natural and artificial preparations illustrating such physiological phenomena as the formation of the human embryo (seen as through a microscope), the development of the fetus, the process of deglutition, the anatomy of the skeleton, muscles, arteries, veins, and nerves, the development of the face and genital parts, the deformation of various bodily parts (including a special display on the "dreadful effects of tight lacing"), and the occurrence of monstrosities and other extraordinary aberrations. For "medical gentlemen" (i.e., anyone interested in exploring these mysteries further) there was also an obstetrical room, where closer attention was given to sexual organs and childbirth, and a pathological room, where venereal disease was illustrated in all its ulcerous varieties. Among the more memorable sights here were preparations showing "gangrene and mortification of the scrotum," "elephantiasis of the female sexual parts . . . the result of onanism," and the "figure of a man who had his penis torn off by a horse, rendering the constant wearing of a small silver tube necessary for the passage of urine."[1] Needless to say, this was sex education of a very engaging kind—lurid but illuminating, serious but slightly kinky. Separate hours had to be established for ladies who wanted to see these marvels. To top it all off, Dr. Kahn made himself available in an adjoining office to anyone who needed professional advice or treatment for venereal disease. And as a sideline, he sold replicas of his most popular wax models.

Dr. Kahn's contribution to ethnological science took the form of a "Gallery of all Nations [consisting] of a series of figures representing the different varieties of the human race, and arranged with due regard to geographical position and mental development. . . . Explanations are given every hour, pointing out the peculiarities of each race, and embellished with anecdotes of their manners and customs."[2] The 1853 *Catalogue* of the museum stated: "Here will be found in one view the graceful Circassian, the angular Copt, the erect European, and the ungainly and ill-poised Ethiopian; the agile Arab contrasted with the languid and effeminate Hindoo; the gigantic Patagonian in juxtaposition with the squat and stolid Laplander; and the keen and warlike native of North America side by side with the immovable and pacific Chinese."[3] The accompanying lectures were given by a "Dr. George Sexton, F.R.G.S. and F.E.S.," who at other times had been employed by Dr. Kahn to speak authoritatively on such topics as food, air, tobacco, lactic acid, eyesight, brain disease, and the mutiny in India.[4] Ethnological expertise must have come easy to so versatile an expert.

On December 27, 1854, an astonishing new anatomical attraction was advertised in London's *Morning Herald*: "NIAM-NIAMS, or the Tailed Family (Man, Woman and Child) from Central Africa, are NOW EXHIBITED, for the first time in Europe, at Dr. KAHN'S MUSEUM." The ad may have led some readers to expect that these curious creatures could be seen in the flesh, but anyone entering the museum would have discovered that the Niam-Niams were only three more waxen figures in the Gallery of Nations. However, nobody could deny that these Africans were fundamentally different from all the other folks on display, for each of the three—mama, papa, and baby Niam-Niam— sported what Dr. Sexton sententiously described as "a caudal appendage, called in common or vulgar language, a tail."[5]

The belief in people with tails has had a rather long history, stretching back at least as far as Ptolemy (second century A.D.), who maintained that in his time they lived on certain islands. Marco Polo (twelfth century) claimed that there were such people inhabiting the kingdom of Lambry (in the vicinity of Sumatra), and later travelers reported finding them in Egypt, Tripoli, Borneo, Formosa, and the Philippine Islands.[6] Linnaeus, in fact, had placed some credence in the seventeenth-century account by a Swedish sailor telling of a race of cannibals "with tails like those of cats" living on one of the Nicobar Islands in the gulf of Bengal. In most of these stories the people endowed with caudal appendages were said to be black, but there was at least one example cited of a teacher of mathematics in eighteenth-century Scotland whose tail, "about half a foot long, which he carefully concealed during his life . . . was discovered after his death." An enthusiastic advocate of the theoretical possibility of "an elongation of the rump-bone" was James Burnett, better known as Lord Monboddo, who wrote of tailed people in his six-volume study *On the Origin and Progress of Language* (1773–92),[7] but his views had been immediately dismissed as eccentric, irrational, and sacrilegious; James Boswell had alluded to him as a "grotesque philosopher."[8]

What revived the debate about caudal appendages in the middle of the nineteenth century were contemporary reports by French travelers who claimed to have seen tailed anthropophagi called Niam-Niams and to have heard corroborating accounts of them from many other African peoples as well as from slave dealers. These travelers were no ordinary tourists but explorers sent out on official expeditions by the French government. Their reports were taken seriously by the Academy of Sciences in Paris, and other explorers who had collected anecdotal evidence of the existence of tailed people in the same general vicinity delivered supporting papers on the subject at meetings of the Oriental Society and Geographical Society in Paris. Within a few years Niam-Niams supposedly had been sighted not only in their native land (usually said to be located somewhere in "Central Africa" between the gulf of Benin and Abyssinia— a vast expanse of uncharted territory) but also in the slave quarters of Mecca and Constantinople.

By 1854 a book and a pamphlet on Niam-Niams had appeared, and the topic was getting a lot of play in French academic journals.[9] The book, du Couret's *Voyage au pays des Niam-Niams*, was reviewed in the London *Literary Gazette, and Journal of Science and Art* on October 28, 1854. Just a week earlier a reputable French medical magazine had carried a circumstantial summary of new findings on the question of tailed men, prompting the British medical journal *Lancet* to give some attention to this interesting tale in its November issue. While Dr. Kahn may have been aware of the earlier controversy in France, he seems to have been inspired to take action only after the story had appeared in the British medical media. But then he moved very swiftly: within a month he had his three Niam-Niams molded and mounted and had published a pamphlet titled *Men with Tails*.

This pamphlet, which was sold for sixpence at the exhibition, contained an introduction by Dr. Kahn, "Essay on the Anatomical View of the Question" by Dr. Sexton, reprints of the articles that had appeared in the *Lancet* and the *Literary Gazette*, and an "engraving of a Group of these Extraordinary Beings." In his introduction Dr. Kahn said that in addition to the testimony offered in the sources quoted, he himself had

received a few weeks since, a communication from a valued friend of
mine who has spent many years in Africa, and who is now in Constantinople, wherein he informs me that he has on two or three occasions
come in contact with the Niam-Niams, and had one with him which he
intended to bring to this country, until a few days before he posted the
letter to me, when, to his great regret, the tailed man died. The skeleton,
however—which will probably be almost as interesting to the scientific
as the living man—my friend still has with him. Having, therefore,
received this intelligence, together with drawings of a group of these
curious species of humanity, I have taken the earliest opportunity of
adding models of them to my collection, trusting they may both interest
and instruct those who derive pleasure from the study of the various
branches of science relating to man.[10]

Sexton then weighed in with his "anatomical view," which consisted of a preface
applauding the continual progress of science, a long series of rhetorical questions
concerning caudal appendages, and a corresponding string of pat answers
bolstered by glib hypotheses about the proliferation of lower vertebral bones.

Yet what, after all, is there remarkable in men with tails? What law of
nature does it violate? What axiom in natural science is it in opposition to? What established principles of anatomy does it overthrow?
We answer, none. . . . A tail is simply an elongation of the vertebral
column. . . . What is the difference in these parts, between those animals
with tails, and those destitute of that appendage? Simply this: that the
coccygeal vertebrae are more numerous. And what is therefore to
prevent the existence of an additional vertebrae or two in some of the
races of man? Nothing.[11]

The evidence Sexton supplied to support these assertions was entirely specula-
tive but included mathematical theorems and an impressive chart, taken from
Agassiz, Gould, and Wright's *Outlines of Comparative Physiology* (1851), that gave
vertebral bone counts for various mammals, birds, reptiles, and fishes.

The articles reprinted from the *Lancet* and the *Literary Gazette* were much
more cautious about coming to a firm conclusion, but they reviewed the French
explorers' accounts at some length, retailing all the pertinent anatomical details that had been published in Paris up to that time. The *Lancet* opened its
column by asking a few rhetorical questions of its own: "Are we truly promoted
monkeys? . . . What if Lord Monboddo, the much ridiculed, should have the
laugh on his side?" But no attempt was made to answer such questions. Instead,

the *Lancet* suggested that more hard evidence was needed to prove "our affinity with the monkey tribe": "Whether the Niam-Niams will be a creation of Oriental fancy, like the Yahoos of Captain Gulliver, or a race actually existing, it is at any rate an object of interest to extend our ethnological inquiries in Central Africa. Should any enthusiastic traveler determine to solve the question, we counsel him to bring home the finest-tailed specimen that can be found."[12]

The *Literary Gazette* devoted more space to the matter, quoting copiously from passages in du Couret's narrative that emphasized the animalistic appearance and cannibalistic nature of the Niam-Niams. Here are some of the descriptive details singled out for translation:

> The Niam-Niams, or Ghilanes (their name signifies cannibals), form a race of men who have a great similitude to the monkey. Shorter than other negroes, they are rarely more than five feet high. They are generally ill-proportioned; their bodies are thin and appear weak; their arms long and lank; their feet and hands larger and flatter than those of other races of man; their lower jaws are very strong and very long; their cheek-bones are high; their forehead is narrow and falls backwards; their ears are long and deformed; their eyes small, brilliant, and remarkably restless; their nose large and flat, the mouth large, the lips thick, the teeth big and sharp, and remarkably white (they sharpen their teeth). Their hair is curly but not very woolly, short and not thick. What, however, peculiarly distinguishes this people, is the external prolongation of the vertebral column, which in every individual, male or female, forms a tail of from two to three inches long. . . . They live in numerous bands, in a completely savage state, without any clothing, and feed on what they get by the chase or fishing, on roots, and on plants and fruits, which without the least labour a bountiful Paradise puts within their reach, and causes to grow spontaneously. They are armed with small lances, bows and arrows, and they poison the latter skilfully; with clubs of very hard wood; with shields made from the skins of the elephant, rhinoceros, hippopotamus, and crocodile; they often seek quarrels with neighbouring negro tribes with the sole object of carrying off their women, to whom they are very partial, their children, and other victims, whom they devour without pity. They are idolatrous. Formerly the Arabs bought great numbers of them from the slave-dealers (Djelabs), but at present they will not take any of them, because the children belonging to this race who were sold to them became, on growing up, dominated by the ferocious instincts natural to their species, and devoured the children of their masters.[13]

An example was then given of a middle-aged Niam-Niam slave who had been captured as a young boy and carried off to Mecca, where he had been converted to the Islamic faith. Even though he was a devout Moslem and had lived so long abroad that he had forgotten his mother tongue, he still retained a "frightful appetite" for human flesh that his master sought to allay by tossing him large pieces of raw mutton from time to time. The slave himself was said to be self-conscious and genuinely worried about this strange dietary preference but claimed that it was an instinctual penchant that he could not control, no matter how hard he tried. In other words, once a Niam-Niam, always a Niam-Niam. Eating people just came naturally to anyone with a caudal appendage. It was a genetically acquired characteristic, custom-tailored to fit a backward African tribe at the very bottom of all humanity.

Dr. Kahn made the most he could out of such details. The figures he constructed to represent the Niam-Niams in his Gallery of all Nations were not only fitted with tails but also framed as cannibals. The description he wrote to accompany the engraving of these "marvellous beings" was based entirely on du Couret and stressed the unsavory symbolic significance of the alertness in the male Niam-Niam's eye, ear, and nose:

> The man, in his rude and savage state—diminutive stature, black skin, large flat negro foot, long arms, repulsive figure, large jaws, enormous mouth, high cheek bones, narrow and receding forehead, long ears, thick lips, large white and sharp teeth, curly hair, vertebral column prolonged, so as to form a tail about three inches in length, and, in a word, a frame approximating toward the lower animals—is seen leaning upon one of his implements of warfare; his eye keenly piercing the distant view, and watching for prey (human, or otherwise); his ear intently listening to catch the first faint sound of approaching footsteps; his large broad flat nose, with the nostrils expanded, sniffing the air—even this sense appropriated to the uses of discovering prey, and detecting danger.[14]

One could almost hear this Niam-Niam murmuring, "Yum-yum!"

The number of spectators Dr. Kahn conned with this extraordinary exhibition is not known, but the British scientific community at large—with the possible exception of Dr. Sexton—appears to have been skeptical of the whole enterprise from the outset. The *Literary Gazette* refused to take sides on the issue

> for if, on the one hand, it be hard to believe that M. du Couret, M. de Castelnau, and other distinguished scientific men, are foolish victims of credulity, or dupes of impostors, on the other hand it is not a little

Figure 29. Cover of a booklet titled *The Niam-Niams or the Tailed Family of Central Africa*, 1855. Reprinted by permission of the Wellcome Library, London.

singular that the precise whereabouts of the Niam-Niam country is not described, and more singular still, that none of the tailed race should have yet been sent to Europe, though, as we are told in the book before us, they are by no means rare at Mecca, in the towns on the coasts of the Red Sea, and in the Arab slave markets.[15]

John Conolly, president of the English Ethnological Society, was not at all impressed with the French explorers' accounts because so many of them were based on hearsay rather than on actual observation: "These particular descriptions seem scarcely reconcilable with entire error, or defective observation, or downright falsehood; but are still very far from being satisfactory, or even credible. The evidence of tails remains, indeed, still as defective as that adduced long ago by Lord Monboddo. We never arrive at the actual person who has visited the tailed nations."[16]

In Conolly's view, Dr. Kahn's exhibition, based on such flimsy evidence, was "at least rather premature." It was probably no more than a tall tale in wax.[17]

But most of the spectators drawn to Dr. Kahn's Celebrated Anatomical Museum may not have been so incredulous. Indeed, they may have been predisposed to believe in any fabulous foreign tale put before them, especially if it came out of Africa. In the public mind the humanity of Africans was still in question, and Dr. Kahn, by capitalizing on the curiosity aroused by reports of tailed cannibals in Central Africa, was only pursuing this question to its logical end. Niam-Niams may have been merely a half-baked figment of the European racial imagination, but in 1854–55 the British public ate them up.

8

The United African Twins on Tour

A Captivity Narrative

On July 11, 1851, near the small town of Whiteville in Columbus County, North Carolina, Jacob and Monemia, slaves of Alexander McKoy, had another child, but this one turned out to be quite different from the seven who had been born to them earlier. For a starter, the newcomer weighed in at seventeen pounds, a big child even for a stout woman like Monemia, who at that time already may have weighed considerably in excess of two hundred pounds herself. But it wasn't merely the impressive size and weight at birth that made this child extraordinary. Rather, it was the wonder that she had been born at all, for Millie-Christine (or Christine-Millie, as she was alternately known) was a genuine *lusus naturae* of the kind known to science as a living "pygopagus symmetros" and to show business as "a perfect protoplastic bifaceous beauty." In other words, she was a pair of conjoined twins, a freak of nature possessing two complete bodies that, in her case, through some mysterious accident of anatomical formation *in utero*, had been joined indissolubly at the lower spine.

When she grew up, she turned this singularity to her own advantage and earned a good living in the exhibition trade in the United States and Europe. Since part of her act consisted of singing duets with herself, she became known professionally and popularly as the "Two-Headed Nightingale." But during her childhood, when she was owned, exhibited, and kidnapped by one unscrupulous manager after another, she was usually billed as the "United African Twins" or simply the "African Twins." In the United States in those days the ethnic marker "African" meant only that she was black—that is, recognizable

131

by her color as someone clearly of African ancestry, albeit born in North America. But the term was deliberately given additional exotic resonance when, at the age of four, she was first exhibited in the United Kingdom. Her exhibitors evidently felt that in some British cities and towns something could be gained not only by showing that she was conjoined but also by claiming that she had been born in Africa and transported to the New World with her enslaved parents. Thus, to anatomical novelty they attempted to add abolitionist appeal. Millie-Christine's early professional career as a freak with a fabricated African past merits further scrutiny, for it sheds some light on black show business strategy in the British Isles in the decade preceding the American Civil War.

For the basic facts of Millie-Christine's first few years in the United States we can turn to a pamphlet biography sold between 1881 and 1889, a decade when she was in her thirties and starring in the John B. Doris Great Inter-Ocean Largest and Best Show on Earth as well as at a number of American fairs, expositions, and dime museums.[1] Though some of the details reported do not correspond exactly with those in an earlier pamphlet published in her late teenage years and purportedly "told in 'her own peculiar way' by 'one of them,'"[2] the Doris biography offers the fullest account of the tawdry events that led to her first tour abroad. One can learn from such a narrative the perils of being a living symmetrical pygopagus in ante-bellum America.

> During her first eighteen months of her life nothing of importance occurred to Millie Christine worthy of note. She grew as other girls grow, learned to walk at twelve months old, was of a lively and agreeable disposition, and at fifteen months began to talk with both her mouths. She was cheerful and active as any girl of her age, with every appearance of robust health. Her vivacity and goodness, together, no doubt, with her peculiar formation, rendered her the almost idolized child of the mother and a general favorite of both old and young, and every attention and kindness was bestowed upon her.
>
> At this time Mr. McCoy [*sic*], being a man in very moderate circumstances, a plain farmer, thinking the girl would become a burden to him, and annoyed with the frequent visits of strangers to see her, determined to dispose of her. He was not long in finding for her a purchaser, a person by the name of Brower, who offered $10,000 for her, seeing the possibilities of the child in the way of an exhibition. But inasmuch as this Brower was not possessed of the requisite cash to back his faith, and only offered to give a note of hand for the purchase money, Mr. McCoy naturally desired some responsible person to whom to look for the money in case of the non-payment of the note when due. This

person was ultimately found by Brower in Mr. Joseph P. Smith of Wadesboro, North Carolina, and Mr. McCoy finally parted with Millie Christine, in consideration of Brower's note for $10,000, endorsed by Mr. Smith.

The happy Brower, in full possession of his prize, at once departed for New Orleans, in obedience to a request from the medical faculty of that city, asking that she be brought there for a scientific examination.

Rooms were taken and every preparation made for the contemplated examination, after which she was to be placed on public exhibition. It had been arranged, prior to their leaving home, that their presence in the city should be kept as quiet as possible, as the desire to see her would undoubtedly be very great and might interfere with the examination. This precaution was not strictly regarded, and soon the rooms and the passages leading thereto were literally besieged with anxious crowds of people eager to get a sight of her.

The examination, however, at length took place and proved most satisfactory, every physician in attendance concurring in pronouncing her Nature's greatest wonder. Being endorsed by the medical faculty, she was now put on public exhibition, but from want of proper management she succeeded but indifferently.

Mr. Brower being quite ignorant of the business he had undertaken despaired of success after a few more efforts. About this time he became acquainted with a certain adventurer who hailed from Texas and boasted of his immense tracts of land in that State. This swindler proposed to purchase the girl by giving for her lands, at a fair market valuation, to the amount of forty-five thousand dollars, and Brower, having full confidence in the would-be millionaire, concluded the bargain by giving possession of the girl, and was on the following day to receive the deeds in due form. The day arrived, but neither the Texan nor the deeds were forthcoming, and then for the first time the unpleasant fact broke upon him that he had been completely duped. To gain some knowledge of her whereabouts was now his first effort, but so adroitly was everything pertaining to her abduction managed that no clue to her, or even the direction she had been carried, could be gained, and every effort for a time to learn anything of her proved futile.

Mr. Brower, after weeks of useless search, becoming convinced that, for the present, further efforts to regain her would only prove useless, determined to return to North Carolina and impart to Mr. Smith his loss, and to the mother the sad intelligence of the abduction of her daughter. Words are inadequate to describe the anguish of the parent on learning the fate of her child. For a time she was perfectly frantic, during six days refusing food, and for the same number of nights her eyes did not close in sleep. Her excellent character, uniform kindness and amiable disposition had made her a general favorite, so that everything that could be was cheerfully done to comfort and soothe her mind. She was promised that no amount of money should be spared, no effort left untried to procure her much-cherished child. How truly this promise was kept the sequel will prove. Brower and partner were bankrupt and Mr. Smith expected no assistance from them. But before anything could be done to recover the child it was necessary that the original owner should be compensated for his loss in the transaction. Christine Millie had been spirited away to parts unknown, and all that Mr. McCoy had to show for her was Brower's note for $10,000; and as Brower could not pay this money his endorser, Mr. Smith became the responsible party and accepted the responsibility. He at once paid the purchase money in full to Mr. McCoy, and took from him a deed which made him the exclusive owner, under then existing laws, of the person of Millie Christine. The proviso, "wherever he could find her," was of course understood, and in order to quiet the mind of her mother and convince her that, whenever found, the child would be restored to her care, Mr. Smith purchased the father, mother and seven children, a transaction of course involving a large sum of money, all of which was dependent for its recovery on the recovery of Millie Christine herself.

The question then arose, where was she, and if found how was she to be recovered, if at all?

Mr. Smith found in the person of Mr. T. A. Vestal, of Selma, Alabama, one of the shrewdest detectives in the country, and Vestal at [once] commenced operations with the assistance of two other detectives, and ultimately gained intelligence of her in the city of Philadelphia, though not before the lapse of some fifteen or eighteen months.

Vestal heard from a negro barber, whose confidence he had obtained, that about a year ago a child answering her description had been in the city, and for a time had been secreted in a cellar on Pine street. The cellar was found, and through the influence of bribes, it was ascertained from an old woman still living in a portion of the house to which the cellar belonged that the child had been carried to New York. The next day Mr. Vestal started for that city to prosecute his search, and remained there five weeks. Every effort was made, but no further intelligence of her could be learned. If anyone knew of or had seen her there, their mouths were sealed to the influence of money or persuasion.

Mr. Vestal began almost to despair, yet determined not to yield his cherished object. He had every reason to believe she was alive, for when taken from New Orleans she was in excellent health. The papers had been watched closely by him, and no account of the death of anyone answering her description had been noticed, which certainly would have been the case had she died. From New York he proceeded to Boston; from thence to Philadelphia, and ultimately to Newark, New Jersey. There, for the first time, he got definite information of her. He learned from a man then keeping a drinking house that at one time, when engaged as a cabman in the City of New York, he had been hired to convey a girl answering her description to a sailing vessel, the name of which he did not remember, bound for and ready to sail for Liverpool; that he had seen the vessel depart, and knew the child was aboard of her when she sailed. Acting on this valuable information, Mr. Vestal immediately returned to North Carolina and urged on Mr. Smith the necessity of following her. Mr. Smith determined to make the attempt, and accordingly prepared for the journey. Accompanied by the mother of Christine Millie, he reached New York, took the steamship Atlantic, and after a pleasant voyage reached Liverpool. There they learned that the child had been on exhibition in that city, also in London, Leeds and other places. (2–5)

Millie-Christine's itinerary between New Orleans, where she had been abducted by the unnamed Texan "swindler," and Liverpool, where she had been conveyed by two other showmen, still needs to be fully reconstructed. The Doris biography offers little information on these years except to state that "the Texan, although shrewd enough to dupe Brower, was in turn made a dupe himself. Arriving in Philadelphia, on their way from New Orleans, he fell in with two showmen, Thompson and Miller [*sic*], who soon succeeded in getting possession of the girl, and it was they who carried her to, and in whose possession she was found in England" (7). The identification of Thompson and Millar as Millie-Christine's tour managers in Great Britain was correct, but the details of the transaction in Philadelphia that put her into their hands were far more complicated than the Doris biography suggests. Philadelphia, after all, was in a northern state that did not countenance slavery. How could two northern showmen "get possession" of a black child who had been bought and sold and kidnapped in the south as a slave? The British press offers some insight into this puzzle, so let us turn our attention to the other side of the Atlantic and follow Millie-Christine's peregrinations in a part of the world where indigenous slavery had been more or less abolished for three-quarters of a century.

Figure 30. Sketch of the African Twins, 1855. Reprinted by permission of the John Johnson Collection, Bodleian Libraries, University of Oxford (Human Freaks 2 [88]).

The Liverpool papers report that the "United African Twins" and their "guardians," "Professor" William Millar and Mr. William Thompson, arrived in Liverpool at 2:30 p.m. on July 24, 1855, aboard the ship *Arab*, which had sailed from Quebec, not New York City. The next day the twins were displayed before "leading members of the medical profession," who issued the following statement:

> We have examined carefully to-day the African twins. They are completely united below the body, posteriorly, by a bony union, and the band of communication is in all about nine or ten inches in circumference. With the exception of these parts the bodies of both are perfect. They are interesting, lively, and intelligent little people, and have nothing of monstrosity in their appearance. It is impossible to see them without being pleased with their manners and lively chattering.
>
> John O'Donnell, M.D.
Thomas Inman, M.D.
Thos. Lewis, M.B.
Thomas Blackburn
P. Macintyre, M.D.
W. Wright Manifold, M.D. and Surgeon
B. Bickersteth[3]

Newspapermen were also invited to inspect the girls and to publicize their peculiarities, not the least of which was a colorful life history that Millar and Thompson had concocted for the occasion. The *Liverpool Mercury* carried the whole bogus biography:

> The united twins were born in Africa, and when a year old were taken, together with their parents and three brothers and sisters, and sold into slavery at Cuba. They are named Christianna and Melley, and are the youngest of the family to which they belong. They are five years old. As regards their history, it may be stated that early in the year 1853 Dr. Maginley, of North Carolina, while on a visit to a fellow-collegian, Don Pedro Estevano, at Cuba, heard of these extraordinary children, and, on learning their history, expressed a desire to purchase them. He accordingly entered into arrangements for that object, and took them with him on his return to the United States. Shortly afterwards Dr. Maginley died, when the children were sold with the remainder of the goods and "effects" of his estate, and they were thrown upon the world.

> The purchaser, who had paid $400 for them, with the intention of
> exhibiting them, brought them for that purpose to Philadelphia; and
> Pennsylvania being a free state, and the little slaves "not being run-
> away negroes," the Government, by a judgment of the court, declared
> them free, and appointed Professor Millar and Mr. Thompson their
> guardians; and they annually, for five years, pay a certain sum to the
> state for the purpose of purchasing the freedom of their parents and
> brothers and sisters, to whom they will be united when manumitted. . . .
> under these circumstances they are entitled to the sympathies of the
> benevolent as well as the attentive examination of the scientific.[4]

The family manumission fable was a clever ploy, for spectators could now
go to the show in good conscience, feeling they were contributing to a worthy
cause, not just gawking at a rare freak. The Caribbean connection added some
interest too, though Millar and Thompson may have arbitrarily selected Cuba
as the twins' first North American home merely because they had hired a "lady,
long resident in Cuba and the slave states of America," to accompany the girls
and provide "information relative to the conditions of the slaves in those
places."[5]

The twins got a very good press during their two-week stay in Liverpool.
The *Liverpool Chronicle* called them "a natural wonder, a study alike for the pa-
thologist and the physiologist, which far exceeds in interest and curiosity the
celebrated Siamese twins, and throws the Aztec abortions completely in the
background."[6] The *Liverpool Mail* agreed, noting that "their countenances are
pleasing and expressive, and their general appearance such as to create a most
favourable impression upon the mind of the visitor. . . . In the presence of
strangers the twins are exceedingly lively, and exhibit the usual aptitude for
chattering peculiar to children of their years. There is everything in their appearance to interest, and nothing repulsive to the most fastidious."[7] As for their
mental abilities, the *Liverpool Courier* testified that "these children are exceedingly intelligent for Africans. They speak English, (Yankee version,) and are
very amusing in their manners."[8] By the end of the second week it was being
reported that "these little phenomenas [were] . . . natives of some country up
the river Congo" who had "features perfectly Ethiopean."[9] Encouraged by
such reports, hundreds of people turned out to see them, and the exhibition
had to be moved from Queen's Hall, Bold Street, to the Theatre Royal, where
they came on after the nightly Shakespearean production.

No sooner had this Liverpool run ended than Thompson and Millar
hustled the twins off to London, apparently intending to display them before
even larger audiences in the capital. But Millar appears to have had some

Figure 31. Playbill for the African Twins at the Theatre Royal Liverpool. © The British Library Board. Reprinted by permission of the British Library (Theatre Royal Liverpool Playbill, August 10, 1855, 243).

entrepreneurial ideas of his own, for the London *Sun* of August 20 carried a brief notice that

> William Miller [*sic*], a person in the employment of Mr. William Thompson, the proprietor of the African twins, absconded on Tuesday night, and carried off those interesting specimens of Nature's freaks, from the Bedford Hotel, Covent-garden, where Mr. Thompson and his charge were staying. Information has been given to the police, and the offender fully described as being about 43 years old, 5 feet 10 inches high, dark moustache and whiskers. The twins are five years old, joined at the back. A reward has been offered for the apprehension of Miller [*sic*] and recovery of the twins.

If we count the snatching from New Orleans by the Texan swindler as their first abduction, and their removal from New York or Quebec to Liverpool by Millar and Thompson as the second, this unexpected disappearance from London engineered by Millar must count as their third kidnapping within a period of about thirty months. Thompson, of course, issued a hue and cry and a week later left London without pausing to settle his hotel bills, for the twins, according to press reports, were about to be shown by Millar in Dundee, Scotland.

Millar, after absconding with them and their Cuban companion to this northern outpost, had gone about the business of preparing them for exhibition in the same manner he and Thompson had employed in Liverpool. "Eleven of the principal medical men in town" were invited to a private examination of Millie-Christine, and their testimonial on "the most interesting and extraordinary instance, not even excepting the 'Siamese Twins,' of living departure from the ordinary human structure," appeared in a Dundee paper the next day.[10] Millar may have been naive to assume that this notice and an advertisement he had placed in various local papers would escape Thompson's attention, for the press in southern England quickly picked up the story and commented on it. Even though Millar intended to stay in Dundee only a short time, he did not move quickly enough to elude his former partner. Within a few days the Dundee papers reported:

Kidnapping Extraordinary

> On Wednesday afternoon about three o'clock considerable excitement prevailed in the neighbourhood of Union Street, in consequence of the abstraction of the African twin children, then exhibiting in the Thistle Hall. It appears that the children are claimed by more than one party,

but nothing could justify the desperate and lawless manner in which they have been wrested from Mr. Miller [*sic*], who has lately had them in his possession, as they were taken from the arms of the nurse in the most brutal manner, and the nurse herself received bruises and injuries, the children, too, suffering from the rough usage of the contending parties. While the scene was transacting, a meeting of clergymen for a religious purpose was assembled in an adjoining room, and one of the gentlemen were in conversation with the keeper of the twins at the door of their apartment, when two men dashed past them into the room, seized the infants, and, by the aid of some accomplices, in spite of all the opposition that could be offered by the parties present, carried them down stairs, rushed into a cab which they had in waiting, and in a few minutes disappeared. While the struggle was going on, cries of "murder" and "robbery" were heard, and the police were called, but the officers declined to interfere. This was the cause of some surprise, until an immediate representation was made at the police office of what had occurred, and to their still greater surprise were informed by the acting official that he believed the officers on duty had been instructed not to interfere between the claimants of the children. The law of England will not allow of children being held as property, but some means ought to be adopted by the authorities to prevent a recurrence of this disgraceful affair, as the lives of the children are in imminent danger, and we certainly believe that the whole party ought to have been brought before the authorities, and the matter definitely cleared up. Who was or is proprietor of the infants is not the question, but the justice of permitting two or three men to enter a public building, and from a private room carry off by sheer force two infants in the most helpless conceivable condition, eminently endangering their lives, ought not to be tolerated.[11]

Another paper, comparing the abduction to an incident from *Uncle Tom's Cabin*, expressed amazement that the police had not interfered: "Of course they could not be expected to decide to whom the children belonged, but they were bound to preserve the public peace which was unquestionably outraged on the occasion. . . . The men who carried away the children were at least guilty of a breach of the peace, and ought to have been arrested."[12]

The fullest newspaper report, appearing a week later in the *Dundee Courier*, offered some new information and editorialized at length on what it called

a very violent and unseemly proceeding, which, besides being of a highly questionable nature suggests considerations deeply affecting the rights of humanity. . . . The assailing party succeeded in carrying off the booty; and the person at its head exhibited, we are told, a paper purporting to be a deed by the State of Pennsylvania, constituting him guardian of the children. The document not having been shown to any Magistrate, there was no one present either qualified or entitled to decide as to its authenticity—still less as to its effects in a question of disputed ownership occurring in this country. . . .

The first reflection which naturally suggests itself on a consideration of the case is that the party claiming the children, if legally entitled to them, ought, before attempting to vindicate his rights, to have shown his credentials to some Magistrate, instead of proceeding at his own hand to reclaim his alleged property *brevi manu*. If he felt conscious of possessing a valid title—and only that could justify his act—there was no reason why he should not have gone about the business in a legal and formal manner. But the next and far more cogent consideration is—what right of property could any party have in these unfortunate children? If they are, as we understand, the offspring of Slaves brought from Cuba, and if it was on such ground that the alleged deed of the State of Pennsylvania proceeded, then we apprehend that within the limits of the British Empire such a document is utterly void and valueless. The law of this country does not recognise the power of Pennsylvania, or of all the States in the Union, to confer a right of property in human beings; and the circumstance of the curious formation of these Twins can never abridge their claims to the protection of our merciful laws, or deprive them of that liberty which is the inalienable possession of every one who sets foot on British soil. We enter not into the question betwixt the competing claimants; but, if we are correct in our views, there will be some difficulty in either of them establishing a valid title to the subject of dispute before any Court in this kingdom. On a point of this kind it is scarcely necessary to refer to authority; but the celebrated case of Somersett, decided in 1772, as it bears directly on the present, may be cited. In that case it was decided that a negro, when brought to England, owes no service to an American or any other master. James Somersett had been made a slave in Africa, and was sold there; from thence he was carried to Virginia, where he was bought, and brought by his master to England. Here he ran away from his master, who seized him and carried him on board of ship, where he was confined in order to be sent to Jamaica and sold as a slave. While he was thus detained, some one interfered in his behalf, and Lord Mansfield granted a *habeas corpus* ordering the captain to bring up the body of James Somersett, with the reason of his detention. The whole circumstances having been fully stated, and discussed in the Court of the King's Bench, the Court were unanimously of opinion that the return was insufficient, and that Somersett *ought to be discharged*. It has been well observed—"Liberty, by the English Law, depends not upon the complexion; and what was said even in the time of Queen Elizabeth, is now substantially true, that the air of England is too pure for a slave to breathe in." In these circumstances, it is somewhat difficult to conceive how any right of property in the African Twins can be maintained in this country; and as for the Pennsylvania document, it is only so much waste paper in such a question.[13]

The key issue, in other words, was not one of kidnapping or of disturbance of the peace but rather one of slavery. Could anyone in the British Isles—Millar, Thompson, or anybody else—claim a proprietary right to profit from the exhibition of small black children who had been acquired as property? The fourth abduction of Millie-Christine had raised an important humanitarian issue.

On fleeing Dundee, Thompson rushed directly to London where, accompanied by Mr. E. T. Smith, the lessee of Drury Lane Theatre, he produced the United African Twins at the Bow Street Police Court so the presiding magistrate there could see that they had been recovered from Scotland. Before Thompson had gone up to Dundee, he and Smith had taken the precaution of seeking advice from this magistrate as to how to proceed against Millar and had been counseled to take whatever steps they thought proper. Those steps having now led to the desired result, Mr. Smith duly reported that "the owner of the children had followed them to Scotland, and had taken 'forcible possession' of them," but the legal and moral implications of this mode of rescue may have been lost on the magistrate, who appears to have been distracted by the novelty of seeing such children in his court.

> When the magistrate inquired, good humouredly, if they could speak, Mr. Smith requested their attendant to "set them on," upon which they began singing the nigger melody "o, Susannah" with a gusto that induced his worship to require their speedy removal to a more fitting arena for the exercise of their vocal powers. The little things, who seemed to enjoy the joke amazingly, were not to be stopped until they had finished one verse of the song, upon which they were removed from the court, exclaiming "Good morning gentlemen," as they left.[14]

Smith then wrapped the children up in a large carpet to conceal them from the crowd waiting outside, and he and Thompson carried them off. Humanitarianism may well have been smothered and forgotten amid the "good humor" displayed on this occasion by the magistrate, the twins, and their profit-conscious carpetbaggers.

The following week Smith arranged for the leading medical men in London "and those otherwise interested"[15] to examine Millie-Christine in the saloon of his Drury Lane Theatre. The next step was to put her on public display at Egyptian Hall, Piccadilly, where the same old abolitionist pitch was used to encourage attendance. However, this time there was more information given about Thompson's managerial role, and Millar's Scottish caper was mentioned as an added come-on.

> They were born in Slavery; and their Guardian, appointed by the Orphan Court of Philadelphia, United States, legally apprenticed them to Mr. Thompson, of that City, who instantly freed them from their degrading bondage, and determined to appropriate the receipts arising from their Public Exhibition to the purpose of emancipating the parents of the children, who are at this moment Slaves on a North American Plantation. The better feelings of humanity, as well as the strongest impulses of curiosity, are therefore to be jointly gratified by their inspection. As already stated in the public prints, they were feloniously abducted from the Bedford Hotel, Covent-garden, by the man who had charge of them, and recovered in Dundee, Scotland; the Scottish authorities, as well as the metropolitan magistracy, having taken the warmest interest in their situation.[16]

Natives of Philadelphia might have been curious to know how Thompson managed to emancipate Millie-Christine in Pennsylvania, a northern state that did not recognize slavery, but to the average Londoner, such niceties of American political geography must have mattered little. One could go to this exhibition and see singing black infant conjoined twins who had recently been kidnapped and whose parents still were slaves. At only two shillings and sixpence (one shilling for children) this was getting very good value for one's money.

The advertisement in the London papers encouraged patrons to see the show immediately, for the twins would soon be leaving England "as they are now *en route* to the French Capital, where they have received a special invitation, and will thence return to Philadelphia, to complete their filial mission."[17] However, a cursory glance at scattered reports in the British provincial press makes it clear that Thompson was in no hurry to convey Millie-Christine back

Figure 32. Sketch of the African Twins at Egyptian Hall, Piccadilly, September 1855. From author's collection.

to Philadelphia. In February of the following year they were performing in Stamford, in May in Sheffield, and in December in Birmingham. No doubt they had played in many other cities, towns, and villages as well during the eighteen months they had been on tour in the British Isles. But it was in Birmingham that Thompson's luck finally ran out, for here Mr. Joseph P. Smith, his wife, his attorney Luke Blackmar, Detective J. Vestal, and the twins' mother Monemia suddenly arrived on the scene. To reconstruct this part of the story we can return to the point in the Doris biography where this pursuing posse of friends, relatives, hired hands, and slave masters had finally reached Liverpool:

> Seated in a promiscuous crowd of traders and traveling clerks one eve-
> ning, in front of his hotel, her name was introduced, and [Smith] learned
> that a short time before she had been on exhibition in Glasgow, Scot-
> land. Immediately they started for that city, but on arrival found that a
> short time before she had been taken back to England, and was then in
> Birmingham. So to that city they posted, and on their arrival, to their
> joy, found she was then on exhibition. It now became necessary that
> extreme caution should be used, lest their long-cherished object would
> be frustrated on the very eve of consummation. The impatience of the
> mother knew no bounds; scarcely could she be restrained from rushing
> to the exhibition-room and defiantly claiming her child, supposing the
> sordid wretch who then had possession of it would recognize her
> claims. She was, however, at length convinced of the imprudence of
> such a course, and submitted to wait until the case had been placed in
> the hands of the proper officers. Accordingly the Chief of Police and a
> select body of his assistants were called and a true statement of affairs
> given. The American Consul was also waited upon and consulted. He
> immediately took a lively interest in the matter, and advised that the
> arrival of the Americans be kept unknown to the exhibitor until they,
> in company with a protective force of police, should enter the hall that
> evening; and, should the child recognize the mother among the audi-
> ence, it would be *prima facie* evidence of the facts attempted to be estab-
> lished by them, and used as such in case of litigation. Accordingly, the
> impatience of the mother was restrained until the hour of the gathering
> of visitors, when a portion of the police (selected for the purpose and
> disguised), Mr. Smith and the mother, procured tickets of admission
> and entered the hall, as casual visitors, impelled only by the general
> curiosity. No sooner, however, had the keen eye of the mother caught a
> glimpse of her long-lost child, than she uttered a scream of such heart-
> rendering pathos that the audience simultaneously rose to their feet,

wondering and astonished. The mother, overpowered, fell fainting to the floor. When resuscitated, she wildly threw her arms about, crying in most piteous tones, "My own child! O! give her to me! Do not take her away again; she needs my care! Where is she? Where is she?" While this scene of excitement was going on, the exhibitor attempted to secrete the girl in an adjoining room; but an honest Scotchman, divining his intentions, placed his back against the door, and, bringing himself into a position that would have delighted a pugilist, cried out: "Yell nae tak' the bairn ayant the door, maun ye wallop me first, an' I'm nae thinkin' ye'll soon do that."

Such a scene of excitement as this denouement created has seldom been witnessed. The women fainted, and the men, learning the true state of affairs from the Chief of Police, who mounted the stage for the purpose, threatened with immediate and summary punishment the sordid villain who had stolen, for the purpose of gain, a helpless child. He managed, however, to escape by jumping from the second story window, which hazardous feat alone, for the time, saved him from certain and well-merited punishment.

The mother, recovering, took the child, and they were conveyed to the hotel, where, for the first time in three years, she slept with it in her arms, forgetting, in the possession of the fondly-loved and long-lost one, the days and nights of anguish she had spent during its absence, and dreamed of naught save happiness and pleasure to come. But her troubles were not to end here. The prize was too rich to be thus easily given up by interested ones. So, on the following morning, a writ of *habeas corpus* was served upon them, requiring the appearance of mother and child before the Court of Admiralty, to show cause why she was taken from the custody of the exhibitor. Here the Consul again proved a friend and true American, by demanding the child as an American citizen, and requiring it, as a minor, to be placed in charge of the mother, and that protection be given her to maintain her maternal rights.

Voluminous proofs, giving an accurate description of mother and child, together with all necessary facts bearing upon the case, had been carefully procured and carried there, in case of necessity. Upon these the Consul spoke a short time, when the judge, arising, declared it useless to occupy more time, for, from the opening of the court, the case had been decided by the Bench. "The child should be given into the custody of its lawful mother. If it was not the child of the defendant, then mother never bore a child. Every lineament, every feature, every look betokened it; every spectator in his inmost heart felt, yes, knew it to be her child, almost as certainly as though they had see it every hour since its birth." A long and hearty shout of approbation at this decision ascended to the dome of the stately old building.

As soon as order was restored, the plaintiff determined to make one more effort; so, calling the attention of the Court to the fact of their knowledge of his ability to perform as he promised, he said he was ready then and there to settle upon the mother the sum of ten thousand pounds sterling, and deed to her an elegant house, in which she could spend the rest of her days in luxury and comfort, if she would remain in England and give him possession of the child until she was eighteen, to all of which flattering offers she only turned a deaf ear, preferring, as she said, "to return and live, as she had done, in the land of her birth, with those she had known from infancy, and among her kindred and her friends." . . .

Mr. Smith, the mother and the subject of our sketch, being now free to depart, made their preparations openly to return. The *Atlantic* had made a return trip, and was then at the Liverpool docks. The now happy party again took passage upon her and, after a prosperous voyage, reached New York. There they took the cars and were soon landed safely in the good old State of North Carolina. (5–7)

This is accurate enough for a show business biography, but the Birmingham press can be called upon to supplement the factual base of the story. Thompson, who lately had been advertising the twins as having been born in "Tamboo, Africa,"[18] and who had never had any dealings with Joseph P. Smith or Monemia, must have been stunned by the ambush laid by the American vice-consul, and it is not surprising that he took the matter to court. After all, he had been forcibly dispossessed of a very valuable show business property, and he did have official papers from Philadelphia to support his claim to be their guardian. Here were their old slave master and a black woman whom Thompson refused to believe to be their mother trying to steal the twins away to North Carolina, where they would presumably return to a slave's life on Smith's plantation. Thompson could thus present himself as a champion of Negro emancipation and human rights.

But the American vice-consul, Mr. Underhill, was solidly on the side of Smith and Monemia, and the striking resemblance between the twins and their mother could be adduced as persuasive circumstantial evidence of their consanguinity. The tack taken in court, however, took another interesting turn when the solicitor representing Underhill, Smith, and Monemia argued that "the instant that coloured female touched the soil of England she became a free woman, and was entitled to protection and to all the advantages of the English laws. She now came into the court, to demand that her children be restored to her," and the solicitor "could not see upon what pretence they could be detained from her."[19] This neatly undercut Thompson's stance as Millie-Christine's designated protector. On what grounds could a free five-year-old child be protected from her natural mother, who now was also a free person?

The solicitor went further and asserted that Thompson was indictable for the offence of "enticing a child away from its parents," a felony punishable in England by transportation for fourteen years. Moreover, the solicitor was prepared to show that Thompson had obtained possession of the children by fraud; this he would do, if necessary, by calling as a witness in court the man "who was a co-thief with Mr. Thompson in their abduction"[20] — in other words, his previous partner "Professor" Millar!

All this was too much for Thompson, who had to be reprimanded for bursting in and interrupting the solicitor at this point. Though Thompson's attorney tried to raise a series of legal objections and offered "to show from documents, in his possession, that the children were apprenticed . . . to Thompson, for the purpose of learning to exhibit themselves,"[21] the case was finally settled in favor of Smith and Monemia, the children being placed under the protection of the American vice-consul Mr. Underhill, who immediately turned them over to their mother.

Thompson, however, was not about to give up so easily: "After some further remarks, the parties left the court. Mr. Thompson was very much excited, and, when outside the court, harangued a small crowd of persons hanging about the entrances, and endeavoured to persuade them to assist him in taking the children away forcibly, offering them rewards for their assistance. They declined aiding him, but listened to him as long as he liked to talk."[22] Thompson then went to the press to present his side of the story. The *Birmingham Mercury* reported: "He states, and produces official documents to sustain his version of the affair, that, after several wanderings, the children reached Philadelphia, and were there publicly exhibited by a man, whose drunken habits incapacitated him from taking the necessary care of the children. The Orphan Court interfered, and appointed Mr. Freeman Scott as their legal guardian. This person eventually apprenticed them for five years to Mr. Thompson, and this document, officially signed, Mr. Thompson has with him."[23]

Thompson evidently felt terribly cheated and may have believed that Millar was at the bottom of the plot to take Millie-Christine away from him, for the "Professor" had earlier threatened to send to America in order to get the twins back into his own possession. But if the Doris biography can be trusted on such matters, Thompson and Millar must have quickly resolved their differences, for they soon turned up in America together as reunited business partners in hot pursuit:

> Astonishing as it may appear, scarcely had the party reached home when those who had caused so many sleepless nights and days of anguish and trouble made their appearance in Charlotte, distant from the girl's home fifty-five miles, evidently intent upon another attempt to regain the rich prize they so fraudulently had possession of for a time, but now wrested from their avaricious grasp. The citizens of Charlotte, learning of their presence and intentions, concluded to give them an admirably fitting suit, composed of good *tar* and excellent *feathers*, and the freedom of the streets for promenading, with the company of a lusty negro to keep time to a *quickstep*, on the end of a large tin kettle.
>
> Thompson and Miller [*sic*], by accident, learning the intentions of the Charlottins, concluded "discretion was the better part of valor" and decamped by night, and since then nothing has been heard of either in North Carolina, and the only thing to remind you of their visit to that section is the chorus of a negro song heard at the corn shuckings.
>
> > Massa Tomsin run a race;
> > Oh! Ho! O-O-O yah!
> > He beat de fastest hoss in de place;
> > Yah, oh yah! O ha! (7–8)

A Charlotte newspaper editorial describing the same event refers only to Thompson and tells a somewhat different story of how and why he was "drummed out of town":

> On Sunday morning last a man calling himself Thompson, from Philadelphia, arrived in Charlotte and put up at the Mansion House. During the day it was found that he was tampering with the slaves of the place, he having approached a trusty negro man named Elias, belonging to Mr. Sam'l Taylor, on the subject of freedom, asking him if he did not desire freedom, that it was wrong for a negro to work for a white man, that the negroes ought to be free, &c. Elias told him that he had a good master and desired none of the kind of freedom offered by abolitionists. These circumstances becoming known to the citizens, a committee was appointed to wait on the gentleman (?) and examine his credentials.

His baggage was searched but nothing found in the way of incendiary documents. However, his conduct was better proof against him than anything that could be found on his person. When questioned as to his business in this part of the country, he stated that he was in pursuit of the twin negroes which were recently brought from Europe to this country—that he was entitled to them and had come out for the purpose of prosecuting his claims. (These negroes are owned by a gentleman in Anson county, who recently recovered them.) Thompson's story in this regard was evidently manufactured for the occasion, as he certainly was smart enough to know that he stood no chance of getting the etheopian [*sic*] twins. He could not possibly have anything like a plausible claim to them.

Taking everything into consideration, our citizens became convinced that Thompson was an abolitionist, and that his journey South had better be postponed for the present. Accordingly about day-light Monday morning the fellow was aroused from his slumbers by that appropriate old tune, "three little pigs and a short-legged sow," (sometimes known as the "rogues march,") and escorted down to the N.C. Railroad depot where he was invited to take a ticket for Weldon and directed not to show his ugly physiognomy in these parts again.

From our bedroom window we saw that the b'hoys did the thing genteely and maintained order. Monsieur Thompson has reason to congratulate himself that he escaped without a coat of tar and feathers, but as the articles are rather high in market it was not thought prudent to waste them upon him.[24]

From this account it appears that Thompson, a northerner, may have had a genuine desire to liberate Millie-Christine from recapture by her southern slave master Mr. Smith, but considering his earlier behavior in England, he clearly had a very strong financial interest in her as well. He was an aggressive entrepreneur, not merely an aggravating Yankee abolitionist, and only Charlotte's brand of southern hospitality prevented him from making another legal or illegal takeover bid to regain exclusive possession of her.

But now that Millie-Christine was safe and sound back home in North Carolina, how were she and her mother regarded by others? Were they accepted as free blacks or were they still viewed as slaves? Did Joseph P. Smith resume ownership of them or did he honor their British emancipation? A local newspaper, commenting on their return to the United States, could not resist offering some words of southern self-congratulation on the subject:

Recently Mr. Smith heard they were on exhibition in England. Knowing that he could not reclaim them as slaves, he purchased their mother
and took her to England to reclaim her children. . . . the mother's claim
was respected, even in Abolition England, where the rights of the
master are unknown or disregarded.

No effort was spared to induce the mother of these children to
desert her master and remain in England. She said she had seen white
slavery, and it was far worse in civilized England, than African slavery
in the United States. Indeed, so strongly was she impressed with the
misery of white slavery, that she clung to her master and returned with
him home, to endure the misery of negro slavery in North Carolina, as
not only a choice of evils, but as the happiest condition of the African
race.[25]

If this story is true, at least in its logistical revelations, then Smith's purchase of
Monemia had not been a benevolent humanitarian act but rather an effort to
protect his investment in Millie-Christine. And the rescue and repatriation of
such a property had had nothing at all to do with any kind of emancipation.
Smith had merely wanted to restore his twins to "the happiest condition of the
African race" and had been clever enough to make adroit use of the American
vice-consul and the British courts to achieve his objective. As a kidnapper, ole
massa had finessed Thompson.

But this wasn't the last of the abductions. Not long thereafter, on another
ill-fated visit to New Orleans at the end of a four-state exhibition tour, the twins
were stolen away again, and "for two years [were] hurried over the country,
from place to place, and deprived of the fostering care of her natural guardians"
(8). But we should allow the Doris biography to tell the rest of the story of our
heroine and her guardians:

Ultimately, however, Mr. Smith's anxiety and determination were
rewarded, and the child was restored to the arms and heart of Mrs.
Smith, whom it soon came to regard and denominate its "white
mama." Under her care the girl was reared to regard with reverence
and love the Supreme Father of all mankind and speedily grew up into
an intelligent Christian child. She not only became proficient in ele-
mentary education, but, showing a high appreciation and taste for
music, soon became an object of great interest to all visitors at Mr.
Smith's home by the rapid progress she made in that accomplishment.

The year 1860, the dreadful year which brought so much pain and
suffering to the United States of America, brought its own individual

Figure 33. Poster of the African Twins and their mother, 1855. Reprinted by permission of the State Archives of North Carolina (Private Collection 266, Millie-Christine Collection, 1855–1874).

sorrow to the home of Millie Christine. Mr. Smith, after a few weeks of suffering, passed quietly away to a better world, mourned by all who knew him, and by none more than those who called him master. Indeed, it is only due to Mr. Smith and his wife to state, and Christine Millie desires particularly that it be inserted in this sketch of her life, that she experienced at his death rather the affection of one who had lost a beloved father rather than a master. Not only this but other families on [the] estate of the Smiths, while calling the owner and his wife master and mistress, always regarded them in the light of protecting parents.

But the war came on, and with it came those heavy losses which prostrated the fortunes of the Smith family, making of the once prosperous plantation an untilled waste, over which the restless hand of the armed spoiler worked its will. It was then that the kindness of the past found its fruit in the devotion displayed by Millie Christine towards her only living protector, Mrs. Smith, whom she regards with filial affection, and from whom she was fully determined never to separate herself. To retrieve the fallen fortunes of the family she, now free, consented to place herself on exhibition and afford the world the opportunity of seeing the most marvelous physical development which has ever existed in the human family. It may be mentioned here as an interesting fact, showing the strange mutability of human fortunes, that Jacob, the father of this wonderful being, once the slave of the planter McCoy, now owns with his wife Monemia, the very plantation on which he was once a bondman, and on which Millie Christine first saw the light of day, the same having been purchased by her with the proceeds of her exhibitions as a present to her father and mother. (8–9)

So the story seems to have a happy ending. Millie-Christine, after a childhood spent in bondage to many different masters and an adolescence upset by the ravages of civil war, returned to the exhibition stage as a free adult and earned a fortune for herself, her parents, and her "white mama." By making a spectacle of herself, she presumably lived as contentedly as anyone can who has been transformed into a liberated new being yet who remains steadfastly linked to the crippling legacy of her past.

During her early years she had been shamelessly exploited by a series of abductors who did not hesitate to tell lies about her in order to reap fatter profits from her peculiarities. In England, as we have seen, her vaunted manumission was as much a show business gimmick as her alleged Africanness. A southern slave-owner who had purchased her as an infant legally regained possession of her in a Birmingham court by pretending to agree that she and her mother,

BIOGRAPHICAL SKETCH
OF
MILLIE CHRISTINE,
THE TWO-HEADED NIGHTINGALE.

"None like me since the days of Eve—
None such perhaps will ever live."

Figure 34. Cover of a biographical sketch of Millie-Christine, ca. 1871. Reprinted by permission of the John Johnson Collection, Bodleian Libraries, University of Oxford (Human Freaks 2 [181]).

Figure 35. Song cover of the Two-Headed Nightingale, ca. 1871. From author's collection.

having set foot on British soil, were no longer slaves. For much of her childhood she existed as nothing more than a highly moveable property, being hustled from city to city, country to country, continent to continent, sometimes being released abruptly from one form of portable captivity only to be subjected to another somewhere else in the world. Yet so long did she remain attached to those who owned her that the symbiotic relationship between her and her "white mama" did not dissolve after the Civil War. Back in North Carolina her life became intimately linked to another's, and that bond, generated by tradition, habit, and circumstance, grew much too close to sever. So following the Emancipation Proclamation, Millie-Christine, formerly the United African Twins, assumed an even stranger shape: forfeiting her independent binary identity, she voluntarily joined herself to the widow Mrs. Smith and for years they toured together as the strangest triplets in American show business history.

9

Circus Africans

There are many recorded instances of Africans being displayed in Europe and the United States as freaks, curiosities, or biological sports—creatures whose humanity was in question. Sometimes their bodies were exhibited posthumously. A plaster cast of the corpse of the Hottentot Venus, for example, could be seen at the Musée de l'Homme in Paris until 1982, having been displayed naked and unadorned for well over a hundred years. Debrunner tells of four Africans in the late eighteenth century being skinned, stuffed, and enclosed in glass cupboards alongside stuffed exotic animals at the Museum of Natural History in Vienna.[1] In September 1906 at the Bronx Zoo a live Batwa Pygmy named Ota Benga was placed in a cage in the Monkey House with a pet orangutan and a parrot;[2] protests from the black community in New York City eventually led to his release from the zoo and placement in the custody of the Colored Orphan Asylum, but after ten more miserable years in the United States, he committed suicide.

Living Africans of unusual appearance have been in demand in the West both at scientific and educational institutions (museums, universities, labs) and at places of entertainment (theaters, parks, fairs). One reads not only of "Bosjesmans," "Earthmen," and Zulus[3] being exhibited in Britain in the 1850s but also of albinos from Madagascar being shown at the American Museum in New York in the 1860s,[4] of Amazons from Dahomey appearing in exhibitions in Paris and Chicago in the 1890s,[5] and of genuine Pygmies appearing early in the twentieth century in both Britain and the United States.[6] By then the term

"Pygmy" was already in general use as a descriptor of any African less than five feet tall. Indeed, the words "Pygmy" and "Bushman" frequently were used interchangeably or in combination—that is, Pygmy-Bushman.

But the place where many of these peculiar peoples wound up was in the circus sideshow. One of the most famous was Clicko (see fig. 36), a "Bushman" who spent nearly twenty years (1921–38) with the Ringling Bros. and Barnum & Bailey's Greatest Show on Earth. A two-page "Life History of Clicko, the Dancing Bushman of Africa" sold at the circus asserted: "He is as near like the ape as he is like the human. He has a good understanding of things, but with a mind that would correspond favorably with that of a two-year-old child, and we cannot help but wonder if Captain Du Barry [his captor] has not brought Darwin's missing link to civilization."[7] This claim was being made more than a century after Cuvier's pronouncements on the Hottentot Venus.

Perhaps the most celebrated circus Africans in the twentieth century were the Ubangis, the "Dish-lipped Savages from the Belgian Congo" who appeared with Ringling Bros. and Barnum & Bailey in 1930 and 1932 and also with the Al G. Barnes circus in 1932 (see figs. 38 and 39). The Ubangis were actually from the Lake Chad area of French Equatorial Africa, and anthropologists of the day offered at least two explanations to account for their custom of distending the lips of marriageable women with large bamboo plates. One was that this unfortunate people, "often pillaged by their islamised neighbours before the French Occupation, disfigured their women in this way so as to prevent them being taken away by their enemies."[8] The other was that the piercing of a young girl's lips and her wearing of such plates indicated that she was engaged to be married; in other words, the custom was part of a nuptial rite.[9] However, when Ubangi women were exhibited in circus sideshows, the mutilation of their lips was explained by the spieler as a primitive effort to enhance appearance, for "among Ubangi women, the larger the lower lip, the more beautiful the woman is considered to be."[10] The showman's patter about Congolese cosmetic practices was intended to amuse the audiences that were drawn to the sideshow. Humorous postcards of these women smoking pipes or posing with attractive white showgirls were sold at every performance.

Of course, not all the Africans who were exhibited in the "kid show" or "Nig show" (as the sideshow was termed in the circus trade) were physiologically abnormal. Some of them, in fact, looked quite ordinary, a few others even handsome, but these usually were peoples who were presented as being culturally exotic—cannibals, bloodthirsty warriors, stone-age savages. The ethnological tag that came to be attached to most of them was the euphonious word "Zulu."[11]

In the early decades of the nineteenth century, under the leadership of powerful warrior chiefs, the Zulu people had earned a local reputation for

Figure 36. Postcard of Clicko, the Wild Dancing South African Bushman, 1828. From author's collection.

CLICO Wild Dancing

SOUTH AFRICAN BUSHMAN
RINGLING BROS. & BARNUM & BAILEY CIRCUS

CONGRESS OF FREAKS WITH RINGLING BROTHERS AND BARNUM & BAILEY CIRCUS

Figure 37. Photo of Congress of Freaks with the Ringling Bros. and Barnum & Bailey Circus, 1929. From author's collection.

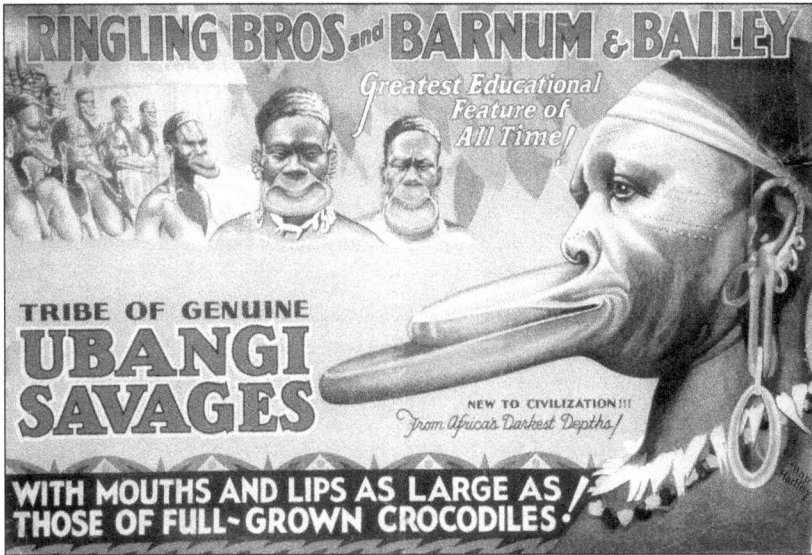

Figure 38. Poster of the Ubangi Savages, 1930. From author's collection.

Figure 39. Photo of Ubangi women with circus showgirls, 1930. Reprinted by permission of the Circus World Museum, Baraboo, Wisconsin.

military prowess. This reputation grew later in the century when they twice massacred British troops in military engagements. The British responded in 1879 by conquering the Zulus and capturing and deposing their chief, Cetshwayo, but the prolonged conflict had made the tribe known internationally as fierce, courageous, and very skillful in battle. Naturally there was a good deal of curiosity about them in Europe and the United States.

Circus entrepreneurs tried to take advantage of this curiosity by recruiting Zulus for their shows. P. T. Barnum even went so far as to offer Queen Victoria's government $100,000 for permission to exhibit Cetshwayo for five years, a petition that did not amuse the Queen.[12] A rival showman outdid Barnum by putting on display three of Cetshwayo's nieces (whom he billed as the chief's daughters, true "Zulu princesses"),[13] a baby, another Zulu chief, and twenty-three warriors who had surrendered to British authorities in South Africa; it has been reported that "their arrival in London was greeted by over one hundred thousand people on the docks and as far up the street as the eye could reach."[14] Other showmen couldn't ignore such palpable signs of popularity, and soon spears, shields, feathers, and war paint could be found in abundance in every sideshow and even in circus "specs" or opening pageants.

Needless to say, many of these Zulu performers were frauds. More than one circus veteran has commented on this in his memoirs: "I recollect at the time of the Zulu war how one showman conceived the idea of exhibiting a number of Zulu warriors. There was only one drawback—not a single Zulu was at that moment in the country. But drawbacks do not exist for the born showman and a party of ordinary niggers were easily made up into Cetewayo's [Cetshwayo's] savage soldiery."[15] Another showman recalled:

> In the side show we had a big negro whom we had fitted up with rings in his nose, a leopard skin, some assegais and a large shield made out of cow's skin. While he was sitting on the stage in the side show, along came two negro women and remarked, "See that nigger over there? He ain't no Zulu, that's Bill Jackson. He worked over here at Camden on the dock. I seen that nigger often." Poor old Bill Jackson was as uneasy as if he was sitting on needles, holding the shield between him and the two negro women. Fortunately for him, about this time the audience was called to another portion of the tent.[16]

However, in the years following the colonial wars against Zulus in South Africa, authentic specimens became more plentiful in both Britain and the United States, and fewer Bill Jacksons had to be employed. The program for Barnum's show at Madison Square Garden in April 1888 advertised "Two

Figure 40. German postcard showing pseudo-Africans, 1800. From author's collection.

Figure 41. American circus troupe with pseudo-Zulus, 1826. From author's collection.

Real African Zulus,"[17] and a naturalist writing in 1885 on ethnological exhibitions at Dime Museums declared quite emphatically:

> The idea that the Dime Museum Zulus were manufactured to order is false. There have been Zulus. These are not, as some of the journalists have wickedly insinuated, Irish immigrants, cunningly painted and made up like savages. They are genuine Zulus; and though we need not believe the lecturer's statement that they fought under Cetewayo [Cetshwayo] at Isandhwalo [sic], and displayed prodigies of valor in order to free their country from British rule. . . . there is no doubt that they would prove terrible enemies in battle. Looking at their leaps and bounds, and listening to their yells and whistles and the rattling of their assegais against their shields, no one can wonder that English cavalry horses were at first afraid to face them.[18]

Some showmen were afraid to face them too and found it more convenient to continue to employ pseudo-Zulus who could be more easily controlled and disciplined. When James Lloyd engaged a dozen bona fide tribesmen for a show that toured Ireland, he found that "their wildness [in performing dances] was disturbingly genuine; this being one of the disadvantages encountered by showmen who, with more honesty than aesthetic perception, prefer Nature to Art. Nature, it has been said, is pulling up on Art; but she has still a long way to go before she produces savages who are equal to the other for show purposes."[19]

That most circus showmen preferred Art to Nature is evident in their use of the term "Zulu," which in American circus jargon gradually expanded its field of reference to include any Negro who participated in the "spec."[20] A black laborer or musician employed by the circus could earn a "Zulu ticket" (a credit slip for more pay) by donning a costume and parading around the hippodrome track in the grand opening pageant. "Zulu" thus became synonymous with artifice and disguise.[21]

Another traditional "African" role filled by black circus employees was that of the "wild man." Not all circus wild men, of course, were represented as coming from Africa; some were said to have been captured in Borneo, Fiji, Yucatan, or some other remote corner of the world. But when they have been black or brown or tan, usually they have been recruited from among negro circus workers, some of whom have been singled out for sideshow stardom because of a physical quirk that made them look a bit odd. Here is Al G. Barnes talking about "Alabam," one of his featured performers: "Unlike most negroes, he could grow a long beard, and I ordered that he keep it long, as it made him conspicuous. He dressed up in fancy trappings and he made a spectacular appearance in the parade. He was also used as a 'wild man' in the side show,

Figure 42. Poster of Amazulu Princess and companions, 1881. From author's collection.

where he would rattle his chains with a display of ferocity that was very impressive."[22] Another American circus manager told of acquiring a "Beast of Borneo" at a very reasonable price: "We had a deformed darkey, in that he was bow-legged, answering to the name of Bow-Knuckle. He was engaged as a canvas-man, but earned fifty cents extra money each day by playing the part of the captive brute. With an excellent make up, including false tusks, a long haired wig, handcuffed, chained and shackled, he only needed growls to thrill the visitors, who were many."[23]

"Uncle" Bob Sherwood, who worked as a clown for Barnum for many years, stated categorically that in every circus the wild man was

> bunk, pure and simple. We called the wild man a "Kie" show. . . . The "Kie" himself is nothing but a negro following an employment which suits him because it does not involve excessive labor. His principal talent is uttering ear-splitting yells. Seldom is he called by his surname. He is either Black Tom, Black Billy, or Black something or other. . . . The Dahomey Giant was a bit of bunk. Merely a seven-foot negro. The Missing Link was only a hairy child. And even the first Wild Man was a fake, just as every wild man, from Borneo, Siam, Yonkers or the Bronx since then, has been a fake.[24]

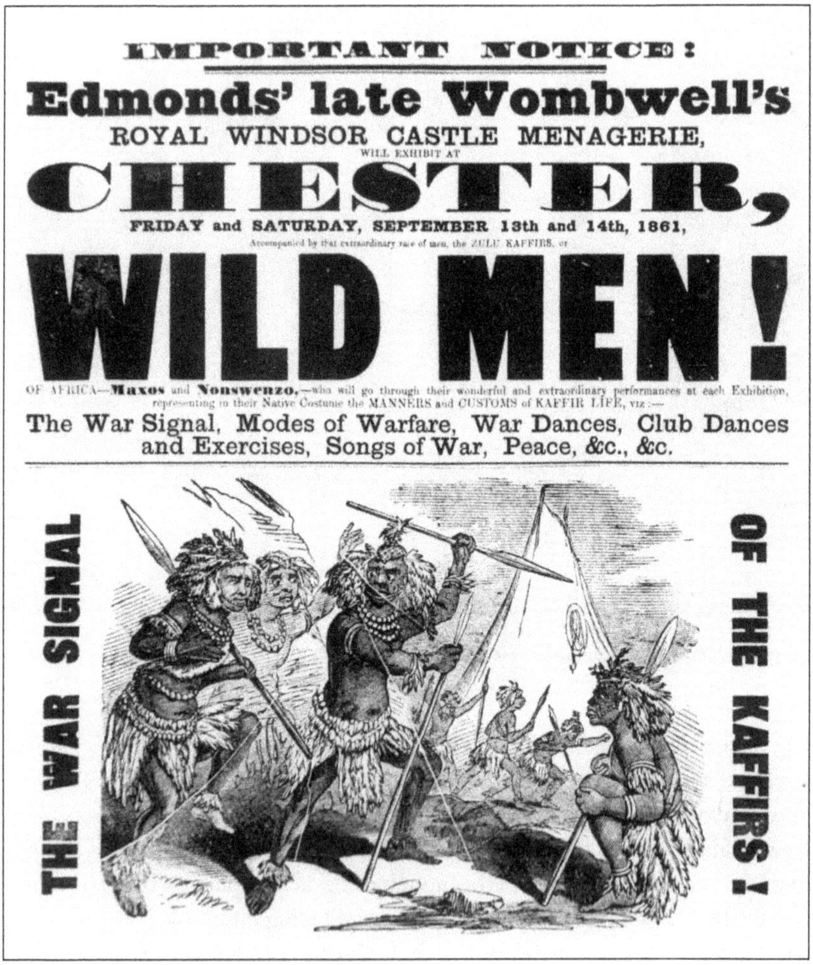

Figure 43. Poster of Wild Kaffirs in Chester, England, September 13, 1861. Reprinted by permission of the National Library of South Africa, Cape Town campus (AZF, 1990-9).

"Bunk" is a modern equivalent of "humbug," the term Barnum himself preferred to use when speaking of such deceptions. Barnum was a master of the technique of improving upon Nature with Art and then getting an audience to pay to see what he had created. He made extravagant claims for some of his featured attractions and in the next breath denied the truth of these claims, leaving spectators to decide for themselves whether the exhibit was honest or fraudulent. Barnum felt that since his shows always offered patrons plenty for their money, no one would take offense if he occasionally played a few practical jokes. In fact, he believed that the victims themselves enjoyed these jokes too. "The American people like to be humbugged," he said.[25]

One of Barnum's longest-lasting practical jokes was the fabrication of a creature he installed at the American Museum in 1860 as a biological conundrum. Zip, as he later came to be called, was originally heralded in newspapers, posters, and handbills as a nondescript, a Wild Boy, a Man Monkey, a Missing Link, and a "What-Is-It?"[26] "Is it a lower order of MAN? Or is it a higher order of MONKEY? None can tell! Perhaps it is a combination of both. It is beyond dispute THE MOST MARVELLOUS CREATURE LIVING. It was captured in a savage state in Central Africa, is probably about 20 years old, 4 feet high, intelligent, docile, active, sportive, and PLAYFUL AS A KITTEN. It has the skull, limbs and general anatomy of an ORANG OUTANG and the COUNTENANCE of a HUMAN BEING."[27] A pamphlet sold at the American Museum went into much greater historical and anatomical detail in describing this "most wonderful of all Nature's works":

> This nondescript was captured by a party of adventurers who were in search of the Gorilla. While exploring the River Gambia, near the mouth, they fell in with a race of beings never before discovered. They were six in number. They were in a PERFECTLY NUDE STATE, roving about among the trees and branches, in the manner common to the Monkey and Orang Outang. After considerable exertion, the hunters succeeded in capturing three of these oddities—two males and a female. All of them were forwarded to this country, but, unfortunately, two of them sickened and died on the voyage across. The present one is the only survivor. When first received here, his natural position was ON ALL FOURS; and it has required the exercise of the greatest care and patience to teach him to stand perfectly erect, as you behold him at the present moment. But a few weeks have elapsed, in fact, since he first assumed this attitude, and walked about upon his feet. If you notice, you will perceive that the WALK OF THE WHAT IS IT is very awkward, like that of a child beginning to acquire that accomplishment. When he first came his only food was raw meat, sweet apples, oranges, nuts, &c., of all of which he was very fond; but he will now eat bread, cake, and similar things, though he is fonder of raw meat or that which, slow cooked, is rare. If you notice the formation of this nondescript, you will observe that it is something very peculiar, indeed. The formation of the head and face combines both that of the native African and of the Orang Outang. . . . He has been examined by some of the most scientific men we have, and pronounced by them to

Figure 44. Carte de visite of Zip, the What-Is-It? Photo by John Wesley Nichols. From author's collection.

Figure 45. Poster of Zip, the What-Is-It? Reprinted by permission of Shelburne Museum, Shelburne, Vermont.

be a CONNECTING LINK BETWEEN THE WILD NATIVE AFRICAN AND THE BRUTE CREATION.[28]

Some publicity materials gave South Africa, not Central Africa or the Gambia, as Zip's aboriginal arboreal address; to Barnum the precise location didn't seem to matter so long as the capture of this primordial savage allegedly took place somewhere in Africa. For where else would a black apeman be likely to have been found?

William Henry Johnson, a microcephalic African American who played this role for decades, was described in J. Bryan's biography of Barnum as "a Negro boy whose cone-shaped skull tapered to a crown no larger than a baseball. He shaved his head daily but let a topknot grow, until he looked like a sea anemone. His skin was grotesquely wrinkled. He communicated by grimaces and grunts. If anyone handed him a cigar, he ate it."[29] For a number of years, Zip's true identity was a well-guarded secret, and even after the truth was known—at least to other circus veterans, several of whom mentioned the ruse in their memoirs[30]—Johnson's antics were so effective in conveying an image of intellectual incompetence that even those who were in on the joke genuinely believed him to be feebleminded, mentally retarded, or a complete idiot. However, an interview he gave to a newspaper reporter a few weeks before his death in 1926, when at the age of eighty-four he was still employed at Coney Island as "Old Zip," reveals that he was far from a numskull.[31] His famous last words, "Well, we fooled 'em a long time, didn't we?" may be true, even if apocryphal.[32]

But the important point about Zip is not his authentic pinhead nor his alleged empty head but rather the fact that he got ahead by pretending to be backward—that is, to be African. In the popular imagination, which Barnum understood and exploited better than any other businessman, Africanness was equated with brutishness, beastliness, imbecility. It is significant that Zip was presented as a creature lacking the most basic of human equipment: he was said to be "without a language."[33] This made him "unlike any other being on earth," a veritable missing link.[34] Only Africa, as conceived by the Western world, could have spawned such a monster.

According to one under-the-tent source, "Barnum engaged 'Zip' with the understanding that he would pay him one dollar a day as long as he could keep his mouth shut, but the pay would stop the minute Barnum caught him speaking to anyone. Whether this is true or not, 'Zip' has never spoken to anyone outside the showfolks, and to only three or four showfolks, and to them only a word or two at a time."[35] A lion tamer confirmed this in his autobiography, saying that Johnson "was 'made' for the part. Years of practice had made it easy for him to be mute when his manager or the proprietor of the show or strangers were around. But when alone with familiar faces he could chatter glibly enough and swear like a pirate."[36] Barnum's oldest circus clown also recalled that Zip "had sense enough to understand that if he talked that his value as a missing link would be considerably lessened; so he always refused to talk, except when among friends."[37] Taciturnity was the price he had to pay for job security.

Notice that in this creature Barnum very cleverly combined a number of stock idiosyncrasies with a few new ones. Zip was both a mute missing link and a wild man, but he was not so wild or brutish that he had to be chained, handcuffed, or confined behind bars. Rather, he was "playful as a kitten," and since he was only four feet tall and had a big, infectious smile, he became a great favorite among children. Here was a docile wild man, a miniature mutant, a domesticated savage. Later in his career he even took up the violin, scratching out unmelodic noises with great enthusiasm. Barnum, a nineteenth-century

Walt Disney, had created a family entertainment out of the stuff of nightmares. Zip was a new kind of freak—a happy, wholesome, harmless little monster.[38]

Harmless in one sense, perhaps, but not so harmless in another. To gullible spectators, particularly children, who had never seen anyone like him before, Zip may have represented brute reality in the depths of the "Dark Continent." In his cheerful way he nonetheless contributed to a destructive, negative image of Africa.

Johnson's careful adherence to his vow of silence doubtless helped to prolong his career in show business, and a very lucrative career it was. Indeed, he became a circus institution. From a dollar a day his salary rose until "his income was unparalleled, among all the Congress of Curious People,"[39] permitting him to acquire real estate in New Jersey. His fame was such that a New York bar as well as a Broadway play were named after him,[40] and he was given a cameo role, as Zip the freak, in a production at the New Amsterdam Theatre in the mid-1920s.[41] Even in his last years, "no fake freak ever earned as much money at Coney Island as Zip" because he continued to draw large crowds.[42] It was estimated at the time of his death that in his sixty-seven years in show business he had been seen "by more people than anybody that ever lived. The figure is close to a hundred million—nearly the population of the United States, as checked by circus attendance over Zip's period."[43] Given these impressive figures, we should not underestimate the influence he may have had on the American imagination.

Of course, Barnum was not the only circus entrepreneur to trade in black deception. Earlier showmen had used similar tactics before and had publicly admitted doing so in their memoirs. Indeed, there appears to have been a venerable circus tradition both in the United States and Europe of misrepresenting African peoples by recruiting "natives" locally. "Lord" George Sanger, in his autobiography, recalled how his father procured Tamee Ahmee and Orio Rio, "the savage cannibal pigmies of the Dark Continent," for one of his caravans:

> They were really two rather intelligent mulatto children, their mother being a negress and their father an Irishman. My father had got them from their mother in Bristol, and they were aged respectively ten years and nine years. Feathers, beads, and carefully applied paint gave them the necessary savage appearance, and the "patter" did the rest.
>
> "Ladies and Gentleman: These wonderful people are fully grown, being, in fact, each over thirty years of age. They were captured by Portuguese traders in the African wilds and are incapable of ordinary human speech. Their food consists of raw meat, and if they can capture

ZIP, ORIGINAL WHAT IS IT?
COPYRIGHT 1801

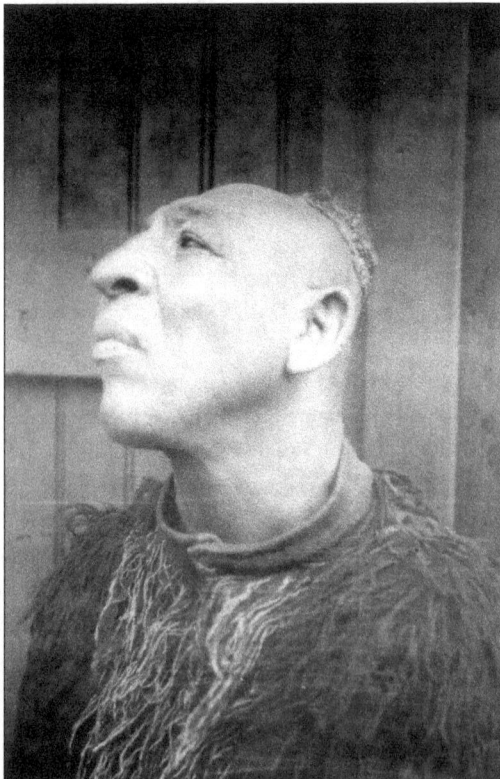

Figure 48. French biographical pamphlet on Zip. From author's collection.

a small animal they tear it to pieces alive with their teeth, eagerly
devouring its flesh and drinking its blood."

Thus was the tale told, and credulous country folk were mightily
impressed.[44]

Sanger also confessed to having perpetrated similar hoaxes himself, once by
imitating a rival's ploy of using local blacks to play Red Indians:

> We went into some dreadful slums [in Liverpool], where in half an
> hour I engaged eight wild men and two savage women. One of the
> men was, I think, the most awful-looking fellow I ever saw, so I made
> him chief of the tribe.
>
> A little red ochre for skin tint, some long, snaky black hair, feathers,
> skins, and beads did the trick properly, and I had as savage a lot of
> Ojibbeways to look at as ever took a scalp. They had some terrible-
> looking weapons, and learned to do war dances, to yell like fiends, and
> perform tribal ceremonies. . . . My! it was a swindle.[45]

Another circus man, relating similar escapades, recorded the plaint of an
African American from Baltimore who, finding himself penniless in Berlin, had
enlisted as an untamed arrival from Africa with a small American circus then
playing abroad, but he had quickly got fed up with it and escaped:

> You see, boss, I'se been working here, got ten dollars a week to play
> wild man. I was all stripped 'cept around the middle and wore a claw
> necklace; had to make out as if I couldn't talk. 'Twas mighty tiresome
> to howl and grin all day. Then times got hard. I had to eat raw meat
> and drink blood. The circus man, he stood off as if he was afraid of me
> and chucked meat on the floor to me. I had to lean over, pick it up in
> my teeth and worry it like I was a dog. It was horse meat and pretty
> tough, boss, but it brought crowds for a while. Then it got drefful cold
> for a nigger with no clothes on and they put a snake around my neck. I
> couldn't stand that, so I'se come to the hospital.[46]

Such confessions suggest that African Humbuggery, far from being P. T.
Barnum's exclusive invention, was a conventional form of sideshow fraud, a
widely used trick of the international circus trade. Zip belonged to a very large
family of counterfeit African freaks.

Some of the veteran Humbuggers played a variety of ethnic roles. One of
them, interviewed by police in Wisconsin, explained how he made a living:

"I've been in Barnum's band of brave, bold, but bad Bedouins. I've played Zulu, Kaffir, Malay, Indian and 'Greaser,' swallowed the sword for six months, ate fire, licked hot pokers with my tongue, danced on hot coals, chewed hot steel, breathed out fire from my nose, walked over razors, broke glass with my feet and played the human ostrich."[47]

In defense of Barnum it may be argued that he didn't always falsify reports of the individuals and groups he exhibited, and he may not have had a lower opinion of Africans than he did of other non-Western peoples. He was probably among the first to display real Pygmies, Hottentots, and Zulus in the United States, and he later incorporated Algerian Arab dancers and equestrians into his elaborate "Wild Moorish Caravan."[48] Except for Zip and a few other morphologically or culturally deviant individuals, the ordinary "Africans" he employed appear to have been presented no differently in his shows than were colorful foreigners from South America, India, the Far East, and Oceania. In 1885 the Great Barnum and London Nine United Shows featured an "Ethnological Tribal Congress of Strange, Savage, Heathen Nations, including Hindoos, Syrians, Burmese, Guatamalans, Afghans, Cannibals, Uj-Magr Gypsies, Tshandalas, Patagonians, Todars, Siamese, Aztecs, Singhalese, East India Nautch Dancing Girls, Buddhist Priests, Botocudoes, Nubians, Zulus, Australians, Mohammedans from the Sahara, Oceanic Idolaters, 'Miramba' Band, Moung-Bok, Arada, Savage Sioux, Indian Venus, Giants, Dwarfs, Fat Women, Phantom Men, Wild Quiche Midget, Armless Phenomena, Bearded Women, and other Prodigies."[49] African peoples, like strange peoples elsewhere, were living examples of the incredible variety of the human species. Barnum displayed them as specimens in a global zoo.

It was only at the outermost fringes of normality that he took liberties, confronting his audience with a mock conundrum like Zip, a creature that gave the appearance of being both man and monkey. Albinos, Wild Men from Borneo, Leopard Children, Aztec Lilliputians, and Two-Headed Nightingales hovered somewhere in the same uncertain twilight realm between the possible and the impossible. One of Barnum's close friends noted that "to engineer some grotesque and startling paradox into tremendous notoriety, to make something immensely puzzling with a stupendous sell as postscript, was more of a motive with him than even the main chance."[50] In the nineteenth century, Africa, a relatively unknown continent, offered Barnum and other showmen splendid opportunities for engineering stupendous paradoxes and thereby capitalizing on human curiosity. In the heart of this shady darkness resided the very soul of Humbug, P. T. Barnum's legacy to a young nation trying to come to terms with the troubling ambiguities of its own racial heterogeneity.

10

Africa's First Olympians

In the summer of 1904, when the third modern Olympiad was held in Saint Louis, Missouri, three runners from South Africa competed in the marathon. They were the only official African contestants, but several representatives from the Belgian Congo joined in preliminary games held a few weeks before the serious track and field competitions began. Such pioneers merit attention for their very presence as contestants in sporting events in the United States tells us a great deal not only about the history of the modern Olympic Games but also about American racial attitudes at the turn of that century.

One must remember that in 1904 St. Louis was commemorating the centenary of the Louisiana Purchase by hosting a lavish international exposition from April to October, so the Olympics, coming at the end of the summer, were merely one more attraction at this spectacular World's Fair. Every day over a hundred thousand people swarmed into the fair, but it is estimated that the largest crowd drawn to any of the Olympic events numbered no more than ten thousand.[1] The masses evidently were far more interested in walking down the mile-long Pike with its numerous international exhibition halls and amusements than they were in sitting in the sun to watch international athletic competitions.

But the real reason for the poor turnout may have been that the Olympic Games that year were not truly international. Only eleven other nations had bothered to send teams; France, host of the 1900 Olympiad in Paris, was not among them. England, another athletic powerhouse, also had no official representation. With these two tough competitors absent, the United States dominated virtually every major event, winning twenty-one of the twenty-two gold medals in track and field. In fact, the St. Louis Olympics were little more than a contest between rival amateur athletic clubs from various American cities. Even some of the best university teams in the country had chosen not to compete.

In these circumstances it was understandable that the Olympic organizers should wish to maximize participation as much as possible. Entry standards may have been relaxed to enable untried and untrained athletes to join in, or there may have been no entry standards at all. Certainly the marathon seems to have been open to all comers. Of the forty runners who signed up for this race (thirty-one of whom actually ran), at least half had never run in a marathon before. Among these first-timers was Felix Carvajal, a mailman from Cuba who turned up at the starting line wearing long trousers, a long-sleeved shirt, a beret, and heavy walking shoes; despite stopping on the course several times to joke and chat with spectators and once to recover from stomach cramps suffered from eating green apples along the way, he somehow managed to place fourth. Other neophytes included a contingent of ten Greeks working in the United States who felt compelled to defend their nation's honor. Greece, after all, had won gold and silver medals in the marathon at the first modern Olympiad in Athens in 1896. However, in St. Louis the best the fastest of them could do was to finish fifth, just behind the Cuban mailman.

South Africa's representatives were reported in the press to be "two Kaffirs from Zululand" named Len Tau and Jan Mashaini and "a man" (some accounts said "Englishman") named R. W. Harris from Aliwal South, Cape Colony.[2] All three were performing at the World's Fair in a big South African Boer War Exhibition that featured reenactments of famous battles between the Boers and British; more than six hundred veterans of that war, including Boer generals Piet Cronje and Ben Viljoen, took part in this military spectacle, which proved to be so popular an attraction that the two daily performances had to be supplemented with a third on weekends and holidays. About sixty Africans, ranging from Basutos on horseback to Zulus and Swazis in war dress, joined in these mock maneuvers and took care of the horses and wagons in off-hours.

The *St. Louis Post-Dispatch* said that Len Tau and Jan Mashaini (see fig. 49) had "served as dispatch runners for the English in the war with the Boers and were the fleetest in the service. On account of the vast area of the country covered these men were compelled to possess wonderful stamina as well as being fleet-footed."[3] The *St. Louis Daily Globe-Democrat* reported that they "can travel at a fast pace all day" and had already proven their mettle in shorter races.[4] However, these "native mail carriers" had never competed in a

Figure 49. Photo of Len Tau and Jan Mashaini, South African marathon runners, 1904. Reprinted by permission of the Missouri History Museum, St. Louis (Image no. 15742).

marathon before, so, as one journalist put it, "their lasting qualities are un-known quantities."[5]

R. W. Harris, on the other hand, was acclaimed as "the best long-distance runner of the country from which he hails."[6] He was said to be "well-built" and "better known in his own country as a middle-distance runner, than a mile runner," but he too was a "novice" who had never before been tested in a marathon.[7] However, he was training hard for the race, and some papers mentioned him as a very serious contender for a medal.[8]

The race started at three o'clock on a very hot afternoon at the end of August. The temperature registered 90°F (32°C) in the shade, and the road conditions were far from ideal. After completing five laps around the stadium track, the runners set out on a hilly rural course that alternated between ankle-deep dust and cracked stones. They were accompanied by men on horseback, trainers on bicycles, and doctors in automobiles. One eyewitness reported that "the roads were so lined with vehicles that the runners had to constantly dodge the horses and wagons. So dense were the dust clouds on the road that frequently the runners could not be seen by the automobiles following them."[9] Moreover, there was only one place along the road where the athletes could obtain fresh water, and this was at a well twelve miles from the start; some of the foreign athletes experienced intestinal disorders after drinking this water. Charles J. P. Lucas, who wrote a book titled *The Olympic Games, 1904*, claimed that "the course through St. Louis County was the most difficult a human being was ever asked to run over."[10] David E. Martin and Roger W. H. Gynn, authors of a history of marathon running, called the course "probably the most devastating marathon environment ever seen: certainly no race prior to it, and very likely no race staged ever since, could match it for brutality of conditions."[11]

Needless to say, many runners could not complete the distance. Some of them dropped out after only a few miles. Others plodded on only to fall ill or to develop debilitating cramps farther on. The "man" from South Africa, R. W. Harris, gave up after covering about half the course. A Californian named Garcia kept going for seventeen of the twenty-six-plus miles but collapsed when afflicted by a severe internal hemorrhage brought on by swallowing so much dust that his stomach membrane eroded away; two spectators in an automobile saved his life by rushing him to a nearby military hospital. The man who won the race, veteran marathoner Thomas J. Hicks of Massachusetts, was ready to quit at the eighteen-mile point but was encouraged to go on by his handlers, who tried to refresh him with warm sponge baths and a Spartan diet of egg whites, brandy, and doses of strychnine to dull the pain. He arrived at the finish line so thoroughly doped and exhausted that he could not stand up to receive his trophy. His time was an unimpressive three hours, twenty-eight minutes, and fifty-three seconds—fully half an hour off the Olympic record set in Athens eight years earlier.

Len Tau and Jan Mashaini trotted in some time later, finishing ninth and twelfth, respectively, in the field of fourteen runners who actually completed the course. Commentators said that Len Tau would have done better had he not been chased nearly a mile off course by an angry dog.[12] He ended up running a longer distance than the others but still managed to outlast two-thirds of the starters. Of course, in a race of this sort it was an accomplishment merely to reach the end. Len Tau and Jan Mashaini, Africa's first Olympians, displayed extraordinary courage, stamina, and athletic ability by surviving a grueling ordeal undertaken in the worst of conditions. Without the benefit of formal training, of attendants, of warm sponge baths, sustenance, or drugs, they ran faster and farther than many of the best long-distance runners of their day. Their achievements should not be forgotten.

But some would say that they should not be credited as the first Africans to compete in Olympic events because a few weeks earlier, on August 11 and 12, a small preliminary competition had been organized in St. Louis to test the athletic prowess of a number of non-Western peoples being exhibited at the World's Fair. Sponsored by the Anthropology Department at the exposition, these "Anthropological Games" pitted American Indians against Japanese Ainus, Filipinos against Syrians, and giant Patagonians against Pygmies, the object being to "decide for all time whether or not the members of these tribes are equal to those of civilized nations in feats of strength, endurance and quickness."[13] Trials were held in many of the standard track and field events—100-yard dash, quarter-mile, mile, 120-yard hurdles, shot put, javelin, high jump, broad jump—but there were also contests in such unconventional athletic specialties as pole climbing, baseball kicking, and bolo throwing. On the first day of this Olympic sideshow Africa was represented by the Pygmies, on the second day by both the Pygmies and the "Kaffirs."

The Pygmies were regarded as a prize catch by the Anthropology Department. It was claimed that they were the first group of their kind ever to be exhibited in the United States, and several "recognised authorities" pronounced that they undoubtedly were specimens of "the lowest order of mankind, intermediate between man and ape."[14] It was even rumored that one of them, whose teeth were filed to sharp points, was a genuine cannibal. Naturally such exotic creatures attracted a great deal of attention.

The Pygmies tolerated most of the gaping with good humor, sometimes mischievously playing upon the naive misconceptions of the crowd. The "cannibal," for instance, a young man named Ota Benga, pretended to suffer hunger pangs whenever he saw a plump black American pass by.[15] And on

Figure 50. Photo of Pygmies at the 1904 World's Fair in St. Louis. Photo by Official Photographic Company. Reprinted by permission of the Missouri History Museum, St. Louis (Image no. 16492).

those rare occasions when the whole group of Pygmies were permitted to stroll along the Pike viewing the other exhibits, one of them, according to the *St. Louis Daily Globe-Democrat,* "would suddenly fall upon somebody's arm and, simulating a wild champing of it from wrist to shoulder, say, 'Me cannibal! You cannibal? What you eat?'"[16] They also learned to capitalize on their novelty value, insisting on high fees whenever photographs were taken. One reportedly "learned to hold out his hand to visitors and say 'Gim nick, show teef.'"[17] In his official report on "Anthropology Days at the Stadium," James E. Sullivan complained: "The Pigmies from Africa were full of mischief. They took nothing whatever seriously, outside of their own shinny game and the tree climbing."[18]

On the first day of the Anthropological Games the Pygmies did not fare very well. They were outstripped by the American Indians in the running events and by the Patagonians in the throwing events, but they had fairly good qualifying times in the pole climb, partly because no other groups deigned to compete in it. The only competitors the Pygmies consistently outclassed were the Negritos, a people from the Philippines even smaller than themselves. On the next day, however, when the final heats were held, the Negritos did enter the pole climb and finished first and third. The Pygmies were disappointed to come

Figure 51. Photo of Pygmies at the 1904 World's Fair in St. Louis (Ota Benga on far right). Photo by Gerhard Sisters. Reprinted by permission of the Missouri History Museum, St. Louis (Image no. 24755).

in second, but they cheered up a bit when they earned another second place in throwing the javelin for accuracy, the only other event in which they won any points. A local newspaper reported: "They experienced several false starts in the running events, but were quick to laugh and make fun of other competitors when they too made false starts. The pygmies did not fare well in the jumping events, not just because of their size, but because they went into convulsions when a Japanese took a tumble in his attempt at the long jump."[19]

To keep the crowd-pleasing Pygmies in the spotlight, officials at the Anthropological Games organized a special event for them alone—a mud fight. Spectators were told that this was a "native pastime" in the Congo, with one side winning when the other gave up the fight and quit the field.[20] The Pygmies were divided into two teams, and at the starter's signal they began pelting each other with soft, sticky clay. One of the contestants withdrew after being hit in the eye, and his team was soon routed. A dispute then arose, the losers asserting that the ammunition for the contest had been distributed unfairly. This animated debate, like the mud fight itself, was said to have "created amusement among the spectators."[21]

Meanwhile, in another part of the stadium fourteen competitors had lined up for the mile run, and when the race got underway, the "Zulus" Len Tau and Jan Mashaini rushed out to an early lead.[22] One newspaper reported that Len Tau

> set a killing pace for the first lap, running like an old-time professional, and followed by his countryman, but the Indians with their usual cunning, laid back and avoided the early pace. At one time the Kaffir had a lead of 20 yards, but kept continually looking backward, and thereby lost much ground. Coming into the stretch the Kaffir was leading, but very tired, and a Syrian, Yousouf Hans, who held second place, came along and passed the Kaffir, following the Indian, Black Whitebear, across the tape with the Kaffir third. Had the Syrian started earlier he would have beaten the Indian, as he was the freshest at the finish, despite the fact that Black Whitebear had a record in school of 4:50 for the mile.[23]

His winning time in St. Louis, however, was 5:38, hardly a threat to the Olympic record.

The results of the Anthropological Games were not such as to inspire confidence in the athletic abilities of those groups that participated in them. Most commentators admitted being unimpressed and disappointed. The official history of the St. Louis World's Fair noted that "in actual competition the representatives of the savage and uncivilized tribes proved themselves inferior athletes, greatly overrated."[24] Dr. W. F. McGee, head of the Anthropology Department at the World's Fair, nonetheless "stated that he was pleased with the outcome of the meet and was satisfied that the white man leads the world."[25] Indeed, this appears to have been the point that the organizers of this Olympic parody were striving to prove. The whole spectacle serves to illustrate Raymond Corbey's later observation that at world's fairs, colonial natives and Western citizens figured "as characters in the story of the ascent to civilization, depicted as the invisible triumph of higher races over lower ones and as progress through science and imperial conquest."[26]

But there were some who refused to accept the conclusion that Western athletes were innately superior to non-Western ones. Baron Pierre de Coubertin, founder of the modern Olympic Games and first president of the International Olympic Committee, denounced the Anthropological Games as an "outrageous charade" that would "of course lose its appeal when black men, red men, and yellow men learn to run, jump and throw and leave the white men behind them."[27] The past century of Olympic competition has proved him right. Len Tau, Jan Mashaini, and the Pygmies may not have won any major medals at St. Louis in 1904, but they achieved a much greater victory for Africa and the rest of the world by helping to draw attention to the need to make future Olympic Games more truly international.

Conclusion

What can be said of the performers who participated in these shows? Should they have lent their talents to this kind of enterprise? Should they have allowed their persons to be used to the detriment and disgrace of their race? Should they have contributed to misleading stereotypes about Africa, about black peoples elsewhere, about themselves? Should they have collaborated in their own exploitation and degradation? Why didn't they try to put a stop to this type of racial slander, this pernicious kind of ethnic slur? These are troubling questions, and without more information about the actual motives of these performers, it is difficult to attempt to answer them justly.

Of course, some of the earliest black show people were captives or slaves and therefore didn't have much to say about how they were used by their owners and exhibitors. Sartjee Baartman is a case in point. Though she testified in court that she had "no complaint to make against her master [and] is perfectly happy in her present situation," it appears likely that she had been coached and perhaps even coerced by her master Hendric Cezar to make such a statement.[1] Yvette Abrahams has argued persuasively that "if [she] had been a slave and she thought such an acknowledgement would [have] brought her into trouble, she would most certainly have lied," especially since "she was a woman alone, far from her people, and quite probably felt intimidated" when being questioned in Dutch by white men from a different culture. In such a predicament, she "would have done her utmost to discover what her interlocutors wished to hear, which responses would get her into least trouble, and which might conceivably ameliorate her situation."[2] An obedient slave, she chose to avoid telling the truth about the tawdry circumstances of her employment.

Yet it is clear from evidence produced by some of those who witnessed her performances that she sometimes did have complaints about the conditions in which she was forced to work. Once when she was ill and didn't want to dance, Cezar threatened her with a long piece of bamboo to compel her compliance. But when a gentleman in the audience laughed derisively as she was playing on an instrument resembling a guitar, she took this as an insult and tried to strike him before being restrained by Cezar.[3] Sartjee evidently was unwilling to tolerate abuse from those she was endeavoring to entertain. She had enough pride and agency to take such matters into her own hands. She was not the sort of person to suffer indignities from strangers passively.

The same could be said of the Bosjesmans, who also occasionally created problems for their manager, J. S. Tyler, when they felt mistreated by spectators. One evening in Birmingham a large crowd began to hoot and pelt them with mud when they arrived at the building where they were to perform: "This attack at once rude and certainly unprovoked, raised the ire of the Bosjesmans, who regardless of the consequences, rushed upon the populace by whom they had been assailed, and began to use their clubs, and were preparing their bows and armour for downright mischief, when the exhibitor and his assistant interposed, and prevented, doubtless, some serious infliction."[4] In London a few months later, during the course of Mr. Tyler's lecture, "the Bushmen took offence at some gesture made by one of the audience, and after talking together, commenced so furious an attack on Mr. Tyler and his assistant, that it required the assistance of six policemen to bring them into subjection, and to prevent any further mischief, they were obliged to be taken to their lodgings in Camberwell, in separate carriages, each accompanied by two policemen."[5] And in Devizes, a man in the audience

> caught the eye of one of the male bushmen, and riveted his attention by making grimaces and shaking his face at him in a menacing manner. The Bosjesman eyed him intently, and evidently with rising indignation. His eyes glared, his nostrils dilated, and his whole frame became strongly agitated. . . . This continued for some seconds; at last the savage, unable to endure the irritation any longer, suddenly drew an arrow to its point, and let fly at the head of his foolish tormentor. Fortunately it missed the man. The arrow struck his hat, piercing it through. Then, apparently in a frenzy of passion, he sprang, like an ourang-outang, from the platform among the company; and the rest of his companions were preparing to follow him, when the lecturer . . . immediately rushed

forward and knocked the foremost down. A struggle ensued; some
keepers came to Mr. Tyler's assistance, and it was with great difficulty
the Bosjesman could be prevented from rushing on his assailant.[6]

However, such outbursts were rare. The Bosjesmans reacted this way only
when provoked beyond endurance by people intent on testing their savage
wildness and lack of self-restraint. Normally they were very well behaved. Un-
civil spectators angered them, prompting attempts at reprisals. James C. Scott,
in a study of domination and resistance, has pointed out that "any indignity is
compounded greatly when it is inflicted in public. An insult, a look of contempt,
a physical humiliation, an assault on one's character and standing, a rudeness
is nearly always far more injurious when it is inflicted before an audience."[7]
Sartjee Baartman and the Bosjesmans responded to such provocations by
lashing out at their tormentors.

The Zulu Kaffirs at Hyde Park Corner chose another method of dealing
with a problem they faced. When they had a major disagreement with their
manager, C. H. Caldecott, they agreed to settle the matter in court. Here is a
transcript of the legal proceedings that ensued:

> [Mangos], the chief of the Zulu Kaffirs at present exhibiting at the St.
> George's Gallery, Knightsbridge, was brought before the magistrate,
> charged under the following circumstances:—Some difficulty arose as
> the mode of making the accused acquainted with the evidence against
> him, which was ultimately effected by a double interpretation, a gentle-
> man turning the English into Dutch, and a Kaffir, who understood the
> latter, acquainting the defendant with what was said, and *vice versa*
> when it came to his turn to speak. Mr. Charles Henry Caldicott [*sic*],
> son of a merchant at Port Natal, said that his father brought the Zulu
> Kaffirs, at present exhibiting at the St. George's Gallery to this country
> with him, and left them in his charge. Defendant was the chief of the
> Kaffirs. On Tuesday afternoon defendant and four of the others went
> out without complainant's leave into the Park. He sent for them, but
> they refused to return, until a policeman, who was sent for them, brought
> them back. When they arrived at the door of the exhibition they would
> not go in, but stood about the door, and when the defendant was
> spoken to he was very impertinent, and would not listen to what he
> said. As a great number of persons, attracted to their appearance,
> gathered round the door, complainant and some friends tried to
> push them in and close the door, as their remaining outside caused a
> great annoyance to the neighborhood. Defendant then threatened

complainant, telling him to look out (in Kaffir), and lifting up his fist, told him he would strike him. Complainant tried to induce them to be calm and go in, when defendant came close up to him, and struck him on the shoulder with his hand; it was done in a very threatening way, but did not hurt him. Defendant then drew his hand across his face. Three or four of complainant's friends got before defendant, and prevented him, or he would have struck him again. Defendant and his party then went up stairs into the gallery, and armed themselves with their clubs; and thinking that the lives of the other Kaffirs, who had sided with him, would not be safe [Caldecott] gave the defendant into custody. The above having been interpreted to the defendant, he was in due form asked what he had to say in reply. Defendant having uttered a few words, the English interpreter observed, "He wishes to know why he was pushed and struck for going out." Mr. Broderip to Mr. Caldicott—Has he signed any agreement or contract to give you power over him? Mr. Caldicott produced an agreement signed by the defendant and the others on the 30th of November, 1852, and duly certified by Mr. J. Shepstone, diplomatic agent, to the effect that Mr. Caldicott should pay their passage to England, clothe, maintain, and allow them a certain sum per month, and land them again at Port Natal within 18 months, unless a further agreement should be made by mutual consent, for which they agreed to serve him faithfully during the said period, by performing all such native dances and other customs as might be required for the purposes of exhibition or otherwise. Mr. Caldicott pointed out to the magistrate that if they were permitted to go abroad at their own pleasure, without control, the consequences to the public might be most serious. Mr. Broderip gave Mr. Caldicott every credit for carefully looking after them, but still the question was, whether he had any power to prevent their going in and out at pleasure, so long as they "performed such native dances and other customs for exhibition;" their agreement was strictly confined to that. Mr. Broderip remarked that neither complainant nor his father had any power over these men except that given in the agreement, and they had no other power to coerce them. What complainant wished was very proper, and with a due regard to the public; but the question was, whether he was legally justified in putting restrictions upon them. He had better, perhaps, have not been so strict with them on this occasion. Mr. Broderip, addressing the interpreters, said—Tell the defendant that if he strikes anybody he will be punished according to our law. If he has any complaint of the way he is treated, and violent hands are laid upon him, they must let him come here and complain. Will he undertake to behave well in future, and not be violent, but come here if he has any complaint? The interpreter having communicated this, announced as his reply, "that he was very sorry, and that he would not do it again; but if a man pushed him he must push again.["] Mr. Broderip—Tell him he must not push again, but that the man who pushes wrongfully will be brought here and punished. He was then discharged.[8]

Qureshi cites an earlier case that year in which a Zulu chief named Larcher sued his manager in a London court in a dispute over pay, whereupon an arbitrator was appointed to resolve the matter to the satisfaction of both parties.[9] Mangos and Larcher, like Sartjee Baartman, had British justice on their side, protecting their rights. Millie-Christine had also benefited from the intervention of a compassionate judge who returned her to her mother instead of recognizing the claims of legal ownership put forward by her unscrupulous manager. In Baartman's case, the protection of the court did not work in her favor for it put her back in the grasp of Hendric Cezar, but at least it honored the testimony she provided and treated her as a free and equal member of society and, as such, entitled to respect under the law of the land. Millie-Christine's case also had ironic consequences for it returned her, as well as her mother, to a condition of slavery in the United States. But it is significant that in all these court proceedings involving "African" entertainers in England in the early and middle years of the nineteenth century, the fundamental rights of the allegedly uncivilized performers were not violated. Even the Bosjesmans' warlike acts were never prosecuted, for it was clear that they were victims responding in self-defense to loutish taunts and threats calculated to provoke them. In every instance the visiting show people were protected and given due stature under the law as beings with full human rights. Spectators might laugh at such creatures, but the courts did not.[10]

The children involved in this kind of show business—for example, the Earthmen, Millie-Christine, and the infants among the Bosjesmans and Zulu Kaffirs—tended to win over audiences more readily than the adults did. Audiences were delighted with their antics and often rewarded them with small gifts—coins in particular. The babies were usually described as more attractive than their parents, and there were hopes expressed that their exposure to Western ways and a modicum of education would enable them to grow up civilized and Christianized. Their managers fed public interest in the future of such children by claiming that Millie-Christine, for instance, was being exhibited "for the purpose of purchasing the freedom of their parents and brothers and sisters, to whom they will be united when manumitted,"[11] and that the Earthmen,

Martinus and Flora, "are now being exhibited with the praiseworthy view of raising a fund for their education";[12] "'serious' people have the satisfaction of knowing that they are to go back when a few years older, as missionaries, or as assistants to missionaries, for the conversion of Earthmen in general."[13] It was further reported that "some care has been taken to keep them from stimulating fluids, with the exception of tea and coffee. They are generally abstemious, and their single failing is an inordinate craving for cigars."[14] Such details increased interest in these little people and provided a laudable motive for attending their exhibitions.

There were other African performers who were protected by individuals who took a special interest in their welfare. One such lucky star was Franz Taaibosch, better known as "Clicko, the Wild Dancing South African Bushman," who was rescued from an exploitative manager in Cuba and transferred to the Ringling Bros. and Barnum & Bailey Circus in the United States by Frank Cook, the legal agent for that circus. Cook not only liberated him from degrading working conditions and provided him with steady employment in the circus as well as in dime museums in North America from 1917 to 1937, but he also became Clicko's legal guardian and housed him at home when the circus was not on tour. When Cook died in 1937, his wife and daughters "inherited" Clicko and cared for him until he passed away three years later.[15]

Zip was another who benefited from the protection of a circus employee — namely, Captain O. K. White, who became his guardian, manager, friend, and adviser for thirty-five years. When Zip passed away, White was so grief-stricken that he collapsed at the funeral and died a few days later.[16] Robert Bogdan reports that "White had established a fund for [Zip] until his death if he had wished to give up the life of a freak."[17] Zip was also said to be one of P. T. Barnum's particular favorites. When Barnum died in 1891, he "left to the 'what-is-it' a big strip of land on his Bound Brook (N. J.) ranch. Here Zip would go in the winter season."[18]

Of course, the majority of black performers were not this fortunate, and some of them were treated abominably. One reads of South African choirs touring England and the United States in the 1890s that were abandoned and swindled of their earnings by white managers and agents,[19] of "a troupe of thoroughly traditional rural-traditional dancers" connected with the Savage South Africa spectacle at Earls Court in London in 1899 and in Saint Louis in 1904 being left by their promoter at a Boer War show on Coney Island,[20] and of the Pygmy Ota Benga being installed in a monkey cage at the Bronx Zoo. Many of these abandoned performers were never repatriated to their homelands in Africa, and, sadly, Ota Benga eventually committed suicide in the United States.[21] So did Steaurma Jantjes, a Hottentot who was one of five

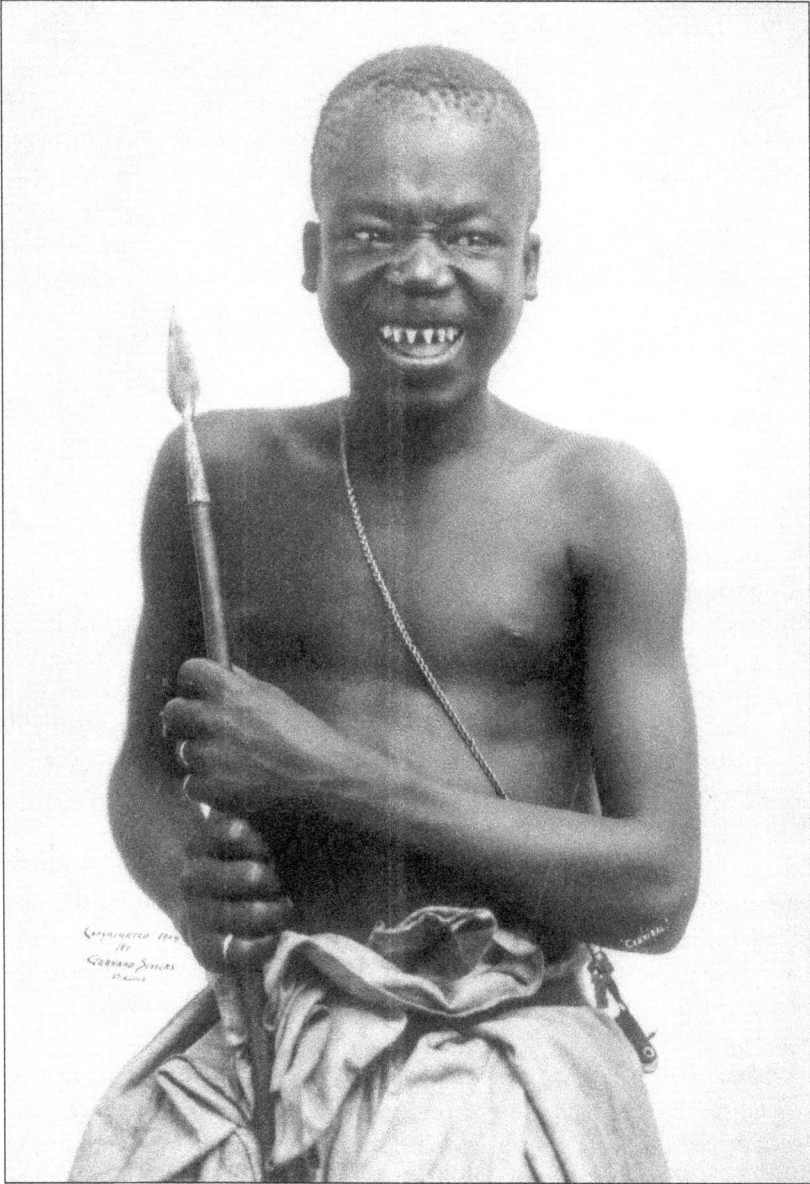

Figure 52. Photo of Ota Benga, one of the Pygmies at the 1904 World's Fair in St. Louis. Photo by Gerhard Sisters. Reprinted by permission of the Missouri History Museum, St. Louis (Image no. 28117).

"Wild African Savages" from South Africa exhibited at the Aquarial and Zoölogical Gardens in Boston and at Barnum's American Museum in New York in 1860–61.[22]

When performers like these died abroad, their bodies often were turned over to the scientific community for examination and dissection. As we have seen, this happened to Saartje Baartman in Paris, with Baron Georges Cuvier writing a scholarly paper on her anatomical peculiarities, preserving her brain, pudenda, skeleton, and other parts for further research, and preparing a cast of her body for public examination. A "Zulu Kaffir" who performed in London in 1853 had been told that one of his fellow performers who died subsequently on tour in Berlin "was only buried because we were there, and that he was afterwards taken out and cut up, to see if he was made inside like the white people."[23] Also, Steaurma Jantjes's exhibitor, James Cutting, "bequeathed the young man's body to Jeffries Wyman . . . [who] performed the dissection himself, and later reported his measurements before the Boston Society of Natural History, comparing them to previous studies, including that of Sara Baartman. . . . Dr. Wyman also made a plaster bust of Steaurma's head, which in 1866 passed into the collections of the new Peabody Museum of Ethnology, of which Wyman was the first president" (see fig. 53).[24] Much the same happened when Flora, the female Earthman, died in London in 1864. Her body was sent to the Royal College of Surgeons in London, where it was dissected by W. H. Flower and James Murie, who reported, among other observations, that "the external organs of generation corresponded in the main with the description given by Cuvier."[25] They also took care to preserve her skeleton at the Museum of the Royal College of Surgeons.

These examples show that in the nineteenth century show business and biological science benefited from a symbiotic relationship, one that enabled each to reinforce efforts by the other to find and disseminate new information about the human species, without necessarily pondering too closely some of the ethical questions raised by the methods employed to acquire such knowledge. African bodies were considered fair game in the quest for a broader understanding of the range of human variation.

Most of the performers we have discussed were active mainly in England and the United States, but some of them, as well as several followers representing basically the same ethnic groups, were seen and studied in other European countries too. Sartjee Baartman appeared in Ireland[26] and France,[27] and other Hottentot women were on display in at least Scotland[28] and Germany[29] later in the century. Bosjesmans were transported to the Netherlands[30] and France,[31] and the Zulu Kaffirs, as reported by one of their troupe when he got back to South Africa, toured France, Belgium, Germany, and Prussia; in Berlin they

Figure 53. Death mask of Steaurma Jantjes, a Hottentot exhibited in Boston and New York, 1861. Reprinted by permission of the President and Fellows of Harvard College, Peabody Museum of Archaeology and Ethnology, PM# 67-1-50/57477.0 (digital file# 80310001).

were included in a farce (see fig. 54) staged by two comedians, Schultze and Müller.[32] Wherever these travelers went, they left not only vivid impressions in the minds of those who saw them but also durable traces in the popular and scientific media of the day. They were long-lasting sensations.

There is no point in blaming them for having participated in this international traffic in negative image formation. Some of them were innocent victims

Figure 54. Cover of a farce involving the Zulu Kaffirs in Germany. © The British Library Board. Reprinted by permission of the British Library (Rudolph Hahn, *Schultze und Müller unter den Zulu-Kaffern*, 1854, 12350. bbb.44.[2]).

Figure 55. Sketch of a later troupe of Zulus at the Folies-Bergère in Paris, 1878. From author's collection.

Figure 56. Caricature by George Cruikshank of "Giraffes—Granny-Dears and Other Novelties," 1836, in which Africans are the observers rather than the observed. From author's collection.

who had been lured into such employment by promises of wealth and adventure. Others may have been curious to see some of the rest of the world, especially places where white people lived. And of course the real freaks (conjoined twins, pinheads, giants, dwarfs, people with too many limbs or too few) and possibly also some of the bogus wonders (missing links, pseudo-Zulus, wild men) may have had no other opportunities to earn an adequate living. A few of these latter imposters, attuned perhaps to the tradition of black minstrelsy, simply may have enjoyed "puttin' down ole massa" through the medium of disguised entertainment; in other words, there may have been a submerged satirical edge to some of these performances that was deeply satisfying psychologically to the performers.[33] It may have been great fun for them to try to scare the wits out of a sideshow audience by pretending to be a man-monkey, a bloodthirsty warrior, a cannibal, a wild man, or an uncivilized brute. Show business could have afforded a creative outlet for their feelings of frustration and aggression.

For at least one thing is clear from the written records on these performances: many of the performers were extremely good at their work. They entered into the spirit of their roles fully and sometimes went beyond the call of duty by sustaining their acts after working hours were over. Reviews show that the Bosjesmans, Earthmen, Zulu Kaffirs, and even some of the pseudo-Zulus won applause because they were regarded as talented actors. There is even a bit of evidence to suggest that the Hottentot Venus became an effective performer. A century later Clicko the Dancing Bushman, Zip the "What-Is-It?," and the irrepressible Pygmies at the St. Louis World's Fair certainly knew how to hold a crowd. These "circus Africans" were often natural entertainers who possessed the ability to excite audiences when they stepped into a ring, onto a platform, or upon the boards of a theater stage.

Yet despite their highly professional accomplishments, despite the creative energy that may have been expressed in their singing, dancing, shouting, and miming, despite the fame and fortune a few underprivileged individuals may have won by participating in such savage spectacles, and despite the efforts of theater managers in London and New York to revive this brand of entertainment in more recent times by staging degrading South African musicals, let us hope that these waning traditions of black performance that denigrate Africa and Africans will soon disappear from the Western world. Racist show business ought to be civilized off the face of the earth.

Notes

Introduction

1. See the chapter titled "The Invention of the Three Human Races" in Peter Rigby's *African Images: Racism and the End of Anthropology*, 26–30, for an analysis of the tendency among some contemporary physical anthropologists and sociobiologists, especially geneticists, to persist in relying upon an "old-fashioned" hierarchical tripartite classification of mankind into color-coded races, now reconceived in yellow, white, and black order.

2. C. White, *An Account of the Regular Gradation*, 83.

3. Lawrence, *Lectures on Physiology*, 363.

4. Quoted in Coleman, *Georges Cuvier, Zoologist*, 166.

5. Pickering, *Stereotyping*, 109–10.

6. Cuvier, "Extrait d'observations," 259–74, reprinted in Geoffrey-Saint-Hilaire and Cuvier, *Histoire naturelle des mammifères*, 211–22.

7. Such performers are discussed in Lindfors, *Africans on Stage*.

8. Knox, *The Races of Man*, 6.

9. Stepan, *The Idea of Race in Science*, 1.

10. See, e.g., Bolt, *Victorian Attitudes to Race*; Curtin, *The Image of Africa*; Fryer, *Staying Power*; Lyons, *To Wash an Aethiop White*; Shyllon, *Black People in Britain*; Walvin, *Black and White*.

11. Walvin, *Black and White*, 160, adds to this catalogue of racial characteristics by pointing out that at the end of the eighteenth century "the Negro was held to be peculiarly sexual, musical, stupid, indolent, untrustworthy and violent."

12. See also Killam, *Africa in English Fiction*, and Brantlinger, *Rule of Darkness*.

13. See Gould, *The Mismeasure of Man*.

14. For instance, Altick, *The Shows of London*; P. Blanchard, *Human Zoos*; Ewen and Ewen, *Typecasting*; Goodall, *Performance and Evolution*; Jahoda, *Images of Savages*; Karp and Lavine, *Exhibiting Cultures*; Poignant, *Professional Savages*; Qureshi, *Peoples on Parade*; Ryan, *Picturing Empire*.

15. For instance, Bogdan, *Freak Show*; Durbach, *Spectacle of Deformity*; Fiedler, *Freaks*; Thomson, *Freakery*; Tromp, *Victorian Freaks*.

16. For studies of indigenous British blacks, see Gerzina, *Black Victorians/Black Victoriana*; J. Green, *Under the Imperial Carpet*; Marsh, *Black Victorians*; Scobie, *Black Britannia*.

Chapter 1. Courting the Hottentot Venus

1. For further information on her career, see Holmes, *The Hottentot Venus*, and Crais and Scully, *Sara Baartman and the Hottentot Venus*. These and other sources differ in spelling Baartman's first name and her keeper's surname. I have retained the spellings used in the sources I cite.

2. *Times*, November 26, 1810, 3.

3. Mathews, *Memoirs of Charles Mathews*, 137.

4. A Constant Reader, "The Female Hottentot," *Examiner*, October 14, 1810, 653.

5. The first of these, signed "An Englishman," appeared in the *Morning Chronicle*, October 12, 1810, 3.

6. Ibid., October 13, 1810, 3.

7. Humanitas, "Female Hottentot," *Morning Chronicle*, October 17, 1810, 3. Following the letter by "A Constant Reader" in the *Examiner* (cited in note 4), the editor added that Cezar's "assertions" in the press "must be listened to with caution, as we have been informed that on her first arrival in London, she was offered for sale by Capt. Cezar."

8. Humanitas, "Female Hottentot," *Examiner*, October 21, 1810, 669. This may be the same "Humanitas" (possibly Zachary Macaulay?) who wrote the letter to the *Morning Chronicle* (cited in note 5) a few days earlier.

9. A Man and a Christian, "The Hottentot Venus," *Morning Post*, October 18, 1810, 3.

10. *Morning Chronicle*, October 23, 1810, 4.

11. See, e.g., Humanitas, "Female Hottentot," *Morning Chronicle*, October 25, 1810, 3, and White Man, "Hottentot Venus," *Morning Post*, October 29, 1810, 3.

12. *Examiner*, October 28, 1810, 681.

13. All the remarks by Macaulay, Babington, and Van Wageninge quoted here are taken from the Affidavit filed at Chancery Lane (Public Record Office No. KB1/36, pt. 2). It is worth noting that Lord Caledon subsequently denied having a hand in the matter. In a letter to the Earl of Liverpool dated March 1, 1811, he said, "It having been stated in a recent trial before Lord Ellenborough that a female Hottentot had been carried out of this Colony with my knowledge and consent, it is due to the high situation I have the honor to hold, for me to acquaint Your Lordship that I was wholly ignorant of the

transaction until long after her departure, and that she never did apply for or receive a permission to leave the Colony." Theal, *Records of the Cape Colony*, 503.

14. Bullock's affidavit (Public Record Office No. KB1/36, pt. 2).

15. *Bell's Weekly Messenger*, November 25, 1810, 376. Other accounts of the first day in court may be found in the *Morning Chronicle*, November 26, 1810, 3; *Times*, November 26, 1810, 3; *Observer*, November 25, 1810, 3; and *Morning Post*, November 27, 1810, 3.

16. *Morning Chronicle*, November 26, 1810, 3.

17. Affidavit signed by S. Solly and Geo. Moojen (Public Record Office No. KB1/36, pt. 2), and quoted by Strother, "Display of the Body Hottentot," 41.

18. Affidavit signed by A. J. Guitard (Public Record Office No. KB1/36, pt. 2).

19. Reports of the second day in court can be found in the *Times, Morning Chronicle, Morning Herald, Sun,* and *Courier* of November 29, 1810; *Westminster Journal, Old British Spy,* and *Evans and Ruffy's Farmer's Journal* of December 1, 1810; and *Bell's Weekly Messenger, Examiner, News, National Register, Johnson's Sunday Monitor,* and *British and London Recorder* of December 2, 1810. The case was also widely reported in provincial newspapers, most of which gleaned their stories from the London press. An official summary of the case appears in East, *Reports of Cases Argued*, 194–95, and this is discussed briefly in "Show Girl—Old Style," 545.

20. *Morning Post*, November 29, 1810, 3.

21. *Morning Chronicle*, November 29, 1810, 3. For an account of the lawsuit that attributes a less noble motive for Macaulay's intervention, see the chapter "Before the Law" in Crais and Scully, *Sara Baartman and the Hottentot Venus*, 82–102.

22. *Morning Herald*, November 29, 1810, 3.

23. "Political Periscope," 192.

24. This ballad has been bound between pages 102 and 103 in volume 1 of Lysons's unpublished scrapbook of "Collectanea: or, a Collection of Advertisements and Para-graphs from the Newspapers, Relating to Various Subjects" in the British Library (1881.b.6), and is reprinted in Toole-Stott, *Circus and Allied Arts*, 334–36. It had appeared in the *Bristol Mirror*, September 28, 1811, 4.

25. Verneau, "Le centième anniversaire," 178. I am grateful to Martin Sonenberg for translating this passage.

26. For an English translation of this play, see Sharpley-Whiting, *Black Venus*, 127–64.

27. Crispe, *Reminiscences of a K.C.*, 2. The John Johnson Collection at the University of Oxford holds a poster hand-dated June 1836 describing Ferguson's Extraordinary Exhibition of Nature and Art and Grand Promenade in London that identifies this woman as Miss Kaitus Vessula from the Cape of Good Hope, "the second female of this peculiar tribe that was ever introduced into this country. In addition to her very particular formation, THIS LADY exhibits the most remarkable feats of strength." Aberdeen University Library holds a similar poster (Circus bills 54) featuring this performer, who was being exhibited alongside a Beautiful Spotted Indian, a White Negress, a Boa Con-strictor, and an Infant Crocodile.

28. Thackeray, *Vanity Fair*, 185.

29. Swinburne, *Studies in Prose and Poetry*, 138–39. I am grateful to the late Joseph Jones for this reference.

30. Cuvier, "Extrait d'observations," 259–74, reprinted in Geoffroy-Saint-Hilaire and Cuvier, *Histoire Naturelle des Mammifères*, 211–22.

31. Gould, "The Brain Appraisers," 86.

32. Gratiolet, *Mémoire*, 65–67.

33. J. Marshall, "On the Brain of a Bushwoman," 500–58.

34. Racinet, *Le Costume Historique*, 255.

35. Mbeki, quoted in Qureshi, "Displaying Sara Baartman," 251.

36. Book description on back cover of Gordon-Chipembere, *Representation and Black Womanhood*.

37. Willis, *Black Venus 2010*; Badou, *L'énigma de la Vénus Hottentote*.

38. Chase-Riboud, *Hottentot Venus*; Clarke, *They Call Me Hottentot Venus*; Franco, *Exile Child*.

39. Parks, *Venus*; Taub and Siocnarf, "The Hottentot Venus."

40. Alexander, *The Venus Hottentot*; Gray, *Hottentot Venus and Other Poems*; Frankel, *Hottentot Venus*.

41. Maseko, *The Life and Times of Sarah Baartman* and *The Return of Sarah Baartman*.

42. See, e.g., the contributions of Abrahams; Altick; Boëtsch and Blanchard; Blanckaert; Brandes; Dell; Drimmer; Ewen and Ewen; Fausto-Sterling; Fauvelle-Aymar; Gilman; Gordon; Gould; L. Green; Hoad; Hobson; Kirby; Kushner; Magubane; Master; Mitter; Netto; Prestney; Qureshi; Ritter; Samuelson; Schiebinger; Scully; Sharpley-Whiting; A. Smith; Sòrgoni; Strother; Thomson; Tobias; Upham; Vlasopolos; Wiss; Youé; and Young.

Chapter 2. The Bottom Line

1. Walvin, *Black and White*, 46–47.

2. See, e.g., Equiano, *The Interesting Narrative*; Sancho, *Letters of the late Ignatius Sancho*; Cugoano, *Thoughts and Sentiments*.

3. Walvin, *Black and White*, 71–72. See also Edwards and Walvin, *Black Personalities*.

4. *Morning Post*, September 20, 1810, 2.

5. George, *Catalogue*, 8, no. 10530, 410. For detailed information about Grenville during this period, see Roberts, *The Whig Party*.

6. "The Hottentot Venus and the Grenvilles," *Satirist, or, Monthly Meteor*, November 1, 1810, 424–27, and "The Hottentot Venus and the Grenvilles (Further Particulars)," *Satirist, or, Monthly Meteor*, December 1, 1810, 550–54.

7. This colored aquatint is discussed and reproduced in black and white by Kirby, "The Hottentot Venus," 57. In a later article, "More about the Hottentot Venus," 126, Kirby identified the artist as Frederick Christian Lewis. In *Sara Baartman and the Hottentot Venus*, 74, Crais and Scully report that "Lewis was not only famous [for his aquatints]: he was also well connected and worked on commission for members of the royal family." George, *Catalogue*, 8, 959, says Lewis's aquatint of Baartman was published by Hendrick

[*sic*] Cezar on September 18, 1810. A. Smith, "Still More about the Hottentot Venus," discusses the caricatures of Saartjee held at the Africana Museum in Johannesburg.

8. George, *Catalogue*, 8, nos. 11578 and 11578A, 948.

9. Ibid., 8, no. 11602, 959.

10. Ibid., 8, no. 11577, 947–48.

11. Ibid., 8, no. 11580, 949–50.

12. Ibid., 9, no. 11748, 38–39.

13. Lysons, "Collectanea," vol. 2.

14. George, *Catalogue*, 10, no. 14449, 338.

15. Ibid., 9, no. 11763, 45–46.

16. Ibid., 9, no. 11765, 47–48.

17. Ibid., 9. no. 12749, 654–56.

18. Ibid., 9, no. 12799, 695–96.

19. Ibid., 9, no. 13249, 910–12. This appears to be a parody of James Gillray's "The Union Club"; see George, *Catalogue*, 8, no. 9699, 4–6. Patten, *George Cruikshank's Life, Times, and Art*, 1:84, notes that Cruikshank "tried to outdo Gillray's unbridled virulence" by adopting "a similar ferocity of image." Marcus Wood, *Radical Satire and Print Culture*, 50, calls this print a "rabidly anti-abolitionist satire." Baudelaire, quoted in Bryant's *The Comic Cruikshank*, 95, identified Cruikshank's "inexhaustible abundance of grotesque invention" as his distinctive quality as a caricaturist.

20. George, *Catalogue*, 9, no. 12702, 627–28.

21. Ibid., 10, no. 14637, 409–10.

22. Facsimile of Transportation Cards (1811) published in 1978 by Harry Margery, Limpne Castle, Kent, in association with Guildhall Library, London.

23. George, *Catalogue*, 9, no. 13043, 834–35.

24. For information on these, see the Bibliothèque Nationale, *Collection de Vinck*, vol. 5, nos. 9266–68.

25. See Cuvier, "Extrait d'observations," 259–74, reprinted with two illustrations in Geoffroy-Saint-Hilaire and Cuvier, *Histoire naturelle des mammifères*. These paintings are reproduced in Honour, *The Image of the Black*, vol. 4, pt. 2, 52–53.

Chapter 3. Ira Aldridge at Covent Garden

1. Fryer, *Staying Power*, 235.

2. Egan, *Pierce Egan's Anecdotes*, 151.

3. The best summary of Aldridge's full career remains Marshall and Stock, *Ira Aldridge*. See also Mortimer, *Speak of Me as I Am*, as well as Lindfors, *Ira Aldridge: The Early Years, 1807–1833*, and *Ira Aldridge: The Vagabond Years, 1833–1852*, and the essays collected in Lindfors, *Ira Aldridge: The African Roscius*.

4. This count is based on retrievable documents such as playbills, press notices and reviews, letters, and theater histories, but since Aldridge appeared in many places that did not produce or preserve such documents, it is likely that these numbers do not accurately reflect the full extent of his theatrical activities during these years. He probably visited

many more cities and towns, took part in their productions, and performed with more actors and actresses than are represented here.

5. For informed accounts of this skit, see Marshall and Stock, *Ira Aldridge*, 40–44; MacDonald, "Acting Black," 231–49; and Evans, "Ira Aldridge," 165–87.

6. *Figaro in London*, September 22, 1832, 68. At that time the name Roscius, alluding to the eminent Roman actor of tragedy and comedy, Quintus Roscius Gallus, was often applied to young actors who displayed precocious talent.

7. Before founding *Figaro in London* à Beckett had attempted to publish a satirical scandal sheet, *The Cerebus; or, the Hell Post*; a weekly journal of ephemera, *The Censor*; and a weekly, *Literary Beacon*; but these ventures failed. During the next two years, while editing *Figaro in London*, he tried to launch several additional popular pulp magazines— *The Thief*, *The Comic Magazine*, *T. Dibdin's Penny Trumpet*, *People's Penny Pictures*, *The Ghost*, *The Terrific Penny Magazine*, *The Wag*—but none of these caught on with the public. For further details on à Beckett's life and literary career, see Schlicke, "À Beckett," 1:58–59; Lemon, *Mr. Punch*; Spielmann, *The History of "Punch"*; Mayhew, *A Jorum of "Punch"*; and à Beckett, *The Becketts of "Punch."* Further discussion of his journals can be found in North, *The Waterloo Directory of English Newspapers and Periodicals, 1800–1900*. For additional information on *Figaro in London*, see Ellis, "The Dramatist and the Comic Journal in England."

8. "Address," *Figaro in London*, December 10, 1831, 1.

9. Fox, "Political Caricature," 226.

10. "Preface," *Figaro in London* 1 (1832): i.

11. Spielmann, *History of "Punch,"* 273; Schlicke, "À Beckett," 1:58.

12. This statement appears in his counterattack on the *Tatler*, which had sought to defend an actress whom à Beckett had censured. See *Figaro in London*, October 6, 1832, 177–78, and October 13, 1832, 180.

13. Ibid., January 12, 1833, 7.

14. Nicholson, *The Struggle for a Free Stage*, 364n1.

15. *Figaro in London*, August 11, 1832, 144.

16. Ibid., October 27, 1832, 188.

17. Ibid., November 24, 1832, 204.

18. Ibid., December 8, 1832, 212.

19. The *Satirist*, January 27, 1833, 454, had reported that "Young Kean and the African Roscius are about to appear at Covent Garden," so Laporte apparently hired them at approximately the same time, perhaps with the intention of having them perform together.

20. E. F. Yunge, *Memoirs, 1843–1863*, translated from Russian and quoted in Marshall and Stock, *Ira Aldridge*, 104.

21. *Times*, March 5, 1833, 6.

22. Cole, *The Life and Theatrical Times*, 1:204–5.

23. According to the "Diary of Covent Garden Theatre containing the daily receipts and expenditure, the titles of plays performed, etc.," a manuscript held at the British Library (Add. ms. 23162), *Merchant of Venice* and two afterpieces earned £150 8s on March 21, 1833, while *Othello* and two afterpieces earned £289.5 on March 25, 1833.

24. The manuscript of this oratorio, adapted by Michael Rophino Lacy from works by Rossini and Handel, is included among the plays submitted to the Lord Chamberlain's office that are held at the British Library (Add. ms. 42920.10). Allardyce Nicoll, *A History of Early Nineteenth Century Drama*, 474, does not list this play under Lacy's name but records it in his handlist of plays by unknown authors.

25. Covent Garden playbill, April 8, 1833.

26. *Figaro in London*, April 6, 1833, 56.

27. This handbill, held in Harvard University's Theatre Collection, is reprinted in full in Marshall and Stock, *Ira Aldridge*, 118. Its author more than likely was Laporte himself, who was then a member of the Garrick Club.

28. *Figaro in London*, April 13, 1833, 60.

29. *Literary Test*, January 1, 1832.

30. *Dramatic Mirror*, May 10, 1847, 35.

31. *Age*, March 31, 1833, 102.

32. Ibid., April 7, 1833, 110.

33. *Sunday Herald*, April 7, 1833, 3.

34. *Town Journal*, April 7, 1833, 110.

35. *Age*, April 14, 1833, 118.

36. See, e.g., *Bell's Weekly Messenger*, April 14, 1833, 116; *Satirist*, April 14, 1833, 542; *Gentleman's Magazine of Fashion, Fancy Costumes, and the Regimentals of the Army*, May 1, 1833, 20.

37. *Times*, October 11, 1825, 3.

38. *Atlas*, April 11, 1833, 226; *English Chronicle*, April 11, 1833, 4; *Globe and Traveller*, April 11, 1833, 2; *Morning Post*, April 11, 1833, 3; *Town Journal*, April 14, 1833, 118; *Spectator*, April 13, 1833, 328.

39. *Observer*, April 14, 1833, 5; *Globe and Traveller*, April 11, 1833, 2; the direct quotes are taken from the *Morning Chronicle*, April 11, 1833, 2, and the *Morning Post*, April 11, 1833, 3, respectively.

40. *English Chronicle*, April 11, 1833, 4; *Morning Chronicle*, April 11, 1833, 2; *Town Journal*, April 14, 1833, 118; the direct quotes are taken from the *Globe and Traveller*, April 11, 1833, 2, and the *Observer*, April 14, 1833, 4, respectively.

41. *British Traveller*, April 11, 1833, 3 (reprinted in *Baldwin's London Weekly Journal*, April 13, 1833, 3).

42. *English Chronicle*, April 11, 1833, 4 (reprinted in the *Morning Herald*, April 11, 1833, 3); *Bell's Weekly Messenger*, April 14, 1833, 116.

43. *Town Journal*, April 14, 1833, 118.

44. *Morning Chronicle*, April 11, 1833, 2.

45. *Satirist*, April 14, 1833, 542; *Morning Post*, April 11, 1833, 3; *Town Journal*, April 14, 1833, 118.

46. *Atlas*, April 11, 1833, 226.

47. *Morning Chronicle*, April 11, 1833, 2.

48. *Satirist*, April 14, 1833, 542.

49. *Atlas*, April 11, 1833, 226; *Literary Gazette, and Journal of the Belles Lettres*, April 13, 1833, 236; *Spectator*, April 13, 1833, 328; *Age*, April 14, 1833, 118.

50. *Globe and Traveller*, April 11, 1833, 2; *News*, April 14, 1833, 118.

51. *English Chronicle*, April 11, 1833, 4 (reprinted in the *Morning Herald*, April 11, 1833, 3); *Courier*, April 11, 1833, 3.

52. *Theatrical Observer; and Daily Bills of the Play*, April 11, 1833, 1.

53. *English Chronicle*, April 11, 1833, 4 (reprinted in the *Morning Herald*, April 11, 1833, 3); *Times*, April 11, 1833, 3 (reprinted in the *Sun*, April 11, 1833, 3); *Sunday Times*, April 14, 1833, 3.

54. *Bell's Weekly Messenger*, April 14, 1833, 116.

55. *Morning Chronicle*, April 11, 1833, 2.

56. Ibid.; *British Liberator*, April 14, 1833, 1.

57. *Sunday Times*, April 14, 1833, 3.

58. *Courier*, April 11, 1833, 3; *Morning Post*, April 11, 1833, 3.

59. *Town Journal*, April 14, 1833, 118.

60. *Literary Gazette, and Journal of the Belles Lettres*, April 20, 1833, 252.

61. *English Chronicle*, April 11, 1833, 4.

62. *Theatrical Observer; and Daily Bills of the Play*, April 11, 1833, 1.

63. *Morning Chronicle*, April 11, 1833, 2.

64. *Atlas*, April 11, 1853, 226.

65. *Guardian and Public Ledger*, April 11, 1833, 3 (the same review appeared in the *Standard*, April 11, 1833, 1); *London Packet and Chronicle*, April 10–12, 1833, 4; *British Traveller*, April 11, 1833, 3; *Baldwin's London Weekly Journal*, April 13, 1833, 3.

66. See, e.g., *Atlas*, April 11, 1833, 226; *Morning Chronicle*, April 11, 1833, 2; *British Liberator*, April 14, 1833, 1; *Sunday Herald*, April 14, 1833, 3.

67. *National Omnibus and General Advertiser*, April 19, 1833, 29.

68. *Atlas*, April 21, 1833, 242.

69. *Courier*, April 11, 1833, 3; *Morning Post*, April 11, 1833, 3.

70. *Guardian and Public Ledger*, April 11, 1833, 3 (the same review appeared in the *Standard*, April 11, 1833, 1); *London Packet and Chronicle*, April 10–12, 1833, 4; *British Traveller*, April 11, 1833, 3; *Baldwin's London Weekly Journal*, April 13, 1833, 3.

71. *Literary Gazette, and Journal of the Belles Lettres*, April 20, 1833, 252. See also a similar remark in the inscription under a print of Aldridge as Othello among the unpublished letters collected and arranged by G. B. Smith at the Garrick Club; here his death scene is praised as "particularly good," an assessment that accords with what was said in a review of his debut at the Royalty Theatre eight years earlier when his enactment of Othello's death was hailed as "one of the finest representations of physical anguish we ever witnessed." See the *Public Ledger and Daily Advertiser*, May 13, 1825, 4.

72. *Age*, April 14, 1833, 118.

73. The negative review in the *Times*, April 11, 1833, 3, was reprinted in the *Sun*, April 11, 1833, 3. The *New Court Journal and Gazette of the United Services*, April 13, 1833, 39, like *Figaro in London*, condemned the show even before seeing it.

74. *Athenaeum*, April 13, 1833, 236.

75. *National Standard, and Journal of Literature, Science, Music, Theatricals and the Fine Arts*, April 20, 1833, 248.

76. This is an interesting defense considering that ten days earlier the *Atlas* had also expressed uneasiness about "a questionable familiarity" between actor and actress in "the whole scene previous to the murder of Desdemona." See the *Atlas*, April 11, 1833, 226.

77. *Atlas*, April 21, 1833, 242.

78. *Bell's Weekly Messenger*, April 14, 1833, 116; *New Court Journal and Gazette of the United Services*, April 13, 1833, 39. The latter refused to go to see Aldridge perform on grounds that his appearance at Covent Garden "amounts to something very considerably less excusable than the ridiculous" for "he cannot, in the nature of things, be qualified to meddle with the sublimities of Shakspeare."

79. *Sunday Herald*, April 21, 1833, 3. However, a week earlier this paper had criticized Aldridge's "inability and impudence" as an actor and had recommended that he "be forthwith emancipated from the thraldom of his engagements." See *Sunday Herald*, April 14, 1833, 3.

80. *Morning Post*, April 11, 1833, 3.

81. *Town Journal*, April 14, 1833, 118.

82. *Atlas*, April 11, 1833, 226; *Globe and Traveller*, April 11, 1833, 2; *Courier*, April 11, 1833, 3.

83. *Morning Chronicle*, April 11, 1833, 2.

84. *Morning Herald*, April 11, 1833, 3 (reprinted in *English Chronicle*, April 11, 1833, 4). The *Sunday Times*, April 14, 1833, 3, also referred to it as a "specimen of Senegal blarney," and the *Satirist*, April 14, 1833, 542, dismissed it as a "little exhibition of Senegal humbug."

85. *Atlas*, April 11, 1833, 226.

86. The same statement was made in the *Morning Chronicle*, April 13, 1833, 3, and in the *Globe and Traveller*, April 13, 1833, 3.

87. The same news had been spread in the *Court Journal*, April 13, 1833, 249; *Morning Chronicle*, April 11, 1833, 2; and *Spectator*, April 13, 1833, 328; but the *National Standard, and Journal of Literature, Science, Music, Theatricals, and the Fine Arts*, April 27, 1833, 254, reported that "there was nothing in his [second] performance that tended to establish himself with the public, as a fit representative of Othello."

88. Covent Garden playbill, April 11, 1833, British Library.

89. *Times*, April 16, 1833, 4.

90. *National Omnibus; and General Advertiser*, April 26, 1833, [37].

91. Ibid., 19 April 1833, 28. See also *Bell's Life in London*, April 14, 1833, 2, which said, "An influenza epidemic has been raging in the Metropolis during the past fortnight, from which scarce a family has escaped."

92. *Bell's Life in London*, April 21, 1833, 2.

93. *Theatrical Observer; and Daily Bills of the Play*, April 15, 1833, 1; *Ladies' Penny Gazette*, April 20, 1833, 207; *Weekly True Sun*, April 21, 1833, 3.

94. *National Omnibus; and General Advertiser*, April 12, 1833, 24; *News*, April 14, 1833, 118; *Bell's Weekly Messenger*, April 14, 1833, 116.

95. "Diary of Covent Garden Theatre containing the daily receipts and expenditure, the titles of the plays performed, etc." held at the British Library (Add. Ms. 23162).

96. *Times*, April 11, 1833, 3; *Sun*, April 11, 1833, 3.

97. *National Omnibus; and General Advertiser*, April 26, 1833, 38. Ironically, this paper's first reaction to Aldridge playing Othello had not been favorable, noting only that this "genuine nigger" was "too respectable to laugh at, and not clever enough to be admired," but on seeing him in the role a second time, the *National Omnibus* championed him as "a practised actor . . . equal to any on the stage." See the issues dated April 12, 1833, 24, and April 19, 1833, 29, for expression of these contrasting opinions.

98. *Times*, April 11, 1833, 3.

99. *National Omnibus; and General Advertiser*, April 19, 1833, 29. Another black role in which Aldridge was popular at this stage in his career was that of Gambia in Morton's *The Slave*.

100. *Figaro in London*, April 20, 1833, 64.

101. *National Omnibus; and General Advertiser*, April 26, 1833, 38.

102. *Figaro in London*, April 27, 1833, 68.

103. Ibid., May 4, 1833, 72.

104. Grant, *The Metropolitan Weekly and Provincial Press*, 3:14, states that the editors of the *Age* and the *Satirist* "were making an income of from 5000£. to 6000£. a year" by threatening to publish scandalous facts about prominent people in society unless they agreed to pay a stipulated sum.

105. *Age*, April 7, 1833, 110.

106. Walvin, *Black and White*, 140.

107. Ragatz, *The Fall of the Planter Class*, 427–29, cited by Waters, "Ira Aldridge," 5. See also Waters's *Racism on the Victorian Stage*.

108. The "Minutes of the Literary Committee of the Society of West India Planters and Merchants," a microfilm copy of which is held at the Commonwealth Institute in London, reveals that the committee also rewarded provincial papers such as the *Edinburgh Evening Post*, *Edinburgh Observer and New North Briton*, *Glasgow Courier*, Liverpool's *Albion*, and the *Dumfries Courier* for publishing articles favorable to proslavery interests. Publications such as *Blackwood's Magazine*, *New Monthly Magazine*, *Watchman*, and *Christian Remembrancer* were on the committee's payroll as well. The first page of the Literary Committee's Minutes states that the committee was established on June 30, 1823, "for the purpose of taking such measures as [the members] shall find expedient for the Protection of the Interests of the West India Colonies through the Press."

Chapter 4. Clicks and Clucks

1. To preserve the flavor of nineteenth-century discourse, I use the older Dutch spelling of the term "Bosjesman" throughout this chapter.

2. *South African Commercial Advertiser*, June 27, 1846, 4.

3. *Liverpool Mail*, November 14, 1846, 3.

4. *Birmingham Journal*, April 24, 1847, 5.

5. Quoted in *History of the Bosjesmans*, 19, a booklet sold at later shows. Lichtenstein's *Reisen im südlichen Afrika*, first published in English translation by H. Colburn in

London (1812–15), was subsequently reissued in English by the Van Riebeeck Society in Cape Town (1928–30).

6. *Literary Gazette, and Journal of the Belles Lettres*, May 22, 1847, 388.

7. In contrast, see the photos taken during the Denver African Expedition of 1925, which Gordon, in *Picturing Bushmen*, 3, regards as "the first attempt on a large scale to present a systematically romanticized image of bushmen." In addition, see the many images and articles included in Skotnes, *Miscast*, a volume published to accompany a Bushman exhibition held at the South African National Gallery in 1996.

8. *Pictorial Times*, June 12, 1847, 376; *Sportsman's Magazine*, July 10, 1847, 319. Although the sketch is the same in both papers, the *Pictorial Times* identifies the figure in the background as Dr. Robert Knox, while *Sportsman's Magazine* reports he is Mr. J. S. Tyler. *Illustrated London News*, June 12, 1847, 381, printed a similar sketch (see fig. 19) and identified the gentleman in the background as Tyler. Knox, an Edinburgh anatomist who had been involved in the notorious Burke and Hare "resurrectionist" scandal, gave an anthropological lecture as part of the show; Tyler, who also lectured, was the manager who accompanied the Bosjesmans on their tour and had prepared an eight-page leaflet (*The Bosjesmans. A Lecture on the Mental, Moral, and Physical Attributes of the Bush Men. With Anecdotes by Their Guardian*) that was sold as part of the show. Qureshi, in *Peoples on Parade*, 113–14, discusses the lectures given by these exhibitors, noting that Knox's "reflected both his racism and anticolonialism," while Tyler's described such creatures as "pigmies" resembling "the higher tribes of asses [that hardly bore] a comparison with even the worst specimens on the human species found elsewhere." For more on Knox's career and racial ideas, see Curtin, *The Image of Africa*.

9. This poster (see fig. 20) is preserved in the John Johnson Collection of Printed Ephemera, Bodleian Library, University of Oxford.

10. Prichard, *The Natural History of Man*, plates xvii and xviii.

11. Traill, "The Languages of the Bushmen," 138.

12. Ibid., 139.

13. *Liverpool Mail*, November 14, 1846, 3. This remark was repeated almost verbatim in the *Liverpool Courier*, November 18, 1846, 6, and again in a review of the show published more than a year later in Dublin in *Saunders's News-Letter*, December 16, 1847, 2.

14. *Liverpool Chronicle*, December 5, 1846, 5.

15. *Birmingham Advertiser*, May 6, 1847, 2.

16. *Midland Counties Herald, Birmingham and General Advertiser*, April 22, 1847, 63.

17. *Glasgow Examiner*, June 24, 1848, 2.

18. *Douglas Jerrold's Weekly Newspaper*, May 22, 1847, 636. This comment was repeated verbatim in a review of the show published in Dublin's *Evening Packet*, December 28, 1847, 3.

19. *Spectator*, June 12, 1847, 564.

20. *Era*, June 6, 1847, 11.

21. *Manchester Guardian*, March 10, 1847, 5.

22. *Glasgow Examiner*, July 1, 1848, 2.

23. *Manchester Express*, March 9, 1847, 3.

24. *Warder,* January 22, 1848, 5.

25. *Plymouth Times,* August 3, 1850, 3.

26. *Morning Post,* May 19, 1847, 6.

27. *Cork Southern Reporter,* February 17, 1848, 2.

28. *Observer,* June 21, 1847, 6.

29. Livingstone, *A Popular Account of Missionary Travels,* 35.

30. Dickens, "The Noble Savage," 337–39, reprinted in Dickens, *Reprinted Pieces,* 197–202. Altick, in "Borrioboola-Gha," 157–59, has suggested that Dickens's recollection of the odious Bushmen he had seen in 1847 informed the tableau of the miserable bricklayers he graphically depicted five years later in *Bleak House,* the major difference being that "repugnance was replaced by implicit compassion." Moore, in "Reappraising Dickens's 'Noble Savage,'" 241, suggests that Dickens's publication of Arthur Whaley Cole's "'Cape' Sketches" in *Household Words* may have influenced his opinions of South African native peoples. Cole, like some of the British spectators at performances of the Bosjesmans, had described their language as "probably the most hideous language in the world, and the least articulate. . . . It is more like the chattering of apes than the tongue of man." See *Household Words* 2, no. 31 (1851): 118.

31. Dickens, "The Noble Savage," 337–39; Altick, "Borrioboola-Gha," 197, 202.

32. This is described in Stepan's *The Idea of Race in Science.* The same phenomenon in the United States is the subject of Stanton's *The Leopard's Spots.* For a well-substantiated debunking of this racist branch of science, see Gould, *The Mismeasure of Man.*

33. *Critic, London Literary Journal,* September 1853, 476.

34. *Illustrated London News,* November 6, 1852, 372; *London Journal and Weekly Record of Literature, Science and Art* 17 (1853): 325; *Illustrated Magazine of Art* 1 (1853): 445.

35. *Illustrated London News,* November 6, 1852, 371.

36. *Court Journal,* May 7, 1853, 300.

37. *Morning Post,* May 9, 1853, 3.

38. Regent Gallery handbill, hand-dated August 22, 1853, in the John Johnson Collection, University of Oxford.

39. Latham, "Ethnological Remarks," 149. When Flora later appeared at Barnum's American Museum in 1860, publicity materials elaborated on distinctive characteristics of Earthmen with an exuberant imaginative flair:

> The Earthman has no friends. He lives in a large, unvarying circle of enemies, from whom his only escape is invisibility, and this he accomplishes by burrowing holes into the ground, and there finding shelter beyond the reach of man or beast. It is this singular habit from which the name of "Earthmen" is derived. A colony of them resembles a gigantic warren of rabbits. Along the precipitous sides of a range of mountains the sunny border of which lies by a stream of fresh water, and high up from its banks thousands of holes are constructed, which extended back into the mountain, sometimes as far as three miles, and continuous passages from which penetrate from one mountain to another, upwards of twenty miles. These holes are so numerous and intricate, that in the course of time [whole] mountains become honey-combed, and a colony of Earthmen, who

have been hunted from one side of a mountain will speedily reappear on the other.

Quoted in Bogdan, *Freak Show*, 188–89. This description appears to have been adapted from an equally colorful one in a booklet published earlier in London, *History of the Earthmen*, a copy of which is held at Princeton University Library.

40. Conolly, *The Ethnological Exhibitions of London*, 27–28.

41. For an account of these years, see Qureshi, *Peoples on Parade*, 141–43.

42. *Illustrated London News*, November 6, 1852, 372; *London Journal and Weekly Record of Literature, Science and Art* 17 (1853): 325.

43. *Brighton Guardian*, October 5, 1853, 5.

44. *Brighton Examiner*, October 11, 1853, 5.

45. Regent Gallery handbill, hand-dated August 22, 1853, in the John Johnson Collection, University of Oxford.

Chapter 5. Charles Dickens and the Zulus

1. Caldecott, *Descriptive History of the Zulu Kafirs*, 4–5. All quotations are taken from this source.

2. Shaka's real and imagined exploits as a military leader and founder of the Zulu nation continue to engage the attention of modern historians. See, e.g., recent books by Daphna Golan, Carolyn Hamilton, and Dan Wylie.

3. *Examiner*, July 9, 1853, 439.

4. Latham, "Ethnological Remarks," 149–50.

5. See the entry on Charles Marshall in the *Dictionary of National Biography*, vol. 16 (London: Smith, Elder, 1893), 235–36.

6. *Times*, July 25, 1853, 1.

7. *Final Close of the St. George's Gallery, Hyde Park Corner, Piccadilly. Zulu Kafirs. Last Few Days in London* (London: n.p., 1853). This pamphlet reprinted reviews from the *Morning Chronicle*, July 25, 1853; *Morning Post*, June 15, 1853; and *Times*, May 18, 1853.

8. *Times*, May 16, 1853, 4.

9. Ibid., May 18, 1853, 8.

10. *Atheneaum*, May 28, 1853, 650.

11. *Spectator*, May 21, 1853, 485.

12. *Illustrated London News*, May 21, 1853, 399.

13. Ibid., May 28, 1853, 409.

14. Letter to John Leech, May 23, 1853, in Dexter, *The Letters of Charles Dickens*, 2:462–63.

15. Crotch, *The Touchstone of Dickens*, 85.

16. A noteworthy exception is Moore, "Reappraising Dickens's 'Noble Savage,'" 239, who argues that the tone of the piece, "completely at odds with anything he had written in the past, and, indeed, anything else he was writing at the time . . . [was] an attempt to sever any perceived connection between himself and Mrs. [Harriet Beecher] Stowe once and for all." However, a few pages later, 242, she acknowledges "Dickens's

growing tendency toward racism in the 1850s." According to Sheila Smith, *The Other Nation*, 80–81, the "complacent prejudice" and "narrow-minded arrogance" Dickens displayed in "The Noble Savage" may have been influenced to some extent by Thomas Carlyle's earlier racist essay on "The Nigger Question," causing him to write with "uncontrolled hysteria" about the Zulus and Bushmen.

17. "The Noble Savage," *Household Words*, June 11, 1853, 337. All quotations are taken from this source. The essay later appeared in Dickens's *Reprinted Pieces*, 197–202.

18. Isaacs, *Travels and Adventures in Eastern Africa*, 294–96.

19. Ibid., 297–98.

20. Pickering, *Stereotyping*, 149–50.

21. *Times*, February 24, 1961, 17.

22. Ibid., April 4, 1972, 6.

23. See the reviews in the *Times*, August 25, 1975, 7, and the *Sunday Times*, August 3, 1975, 4.

24. *Times*, November 20, 1975, 10.

25. *Sunday Times*, November 23, 1975, 35.

26. *Time*, January 24, 1977, 56. The fourth Zulu musical of the 1970s was panned by the press; see, e.g., the *Times*, January 6, 1977, 11, and *Sunday Times*, January 9, 1977, 37.

27. Dickens, "The Niger Expedition," 133.

28. For further examples of racist misrepresentations of Zulus in America see Vinson and Edgar's splendid survey, "Zulus Abroad." They conclude: "In America, persistent portrayals (largely by whites) of the Zulu as cannibals, as caged animals eating raw meat, as freaks living among double-headed women and racing against horses, and as savage Zulu warriors re-enacting European military conquests over Africans, certainly reinforced Dickens' sentiments in the minds of many Americans" (61–62).

Chapter 6. A Zulu View of Victorian London

1. "A South African Native's Picture of England," 126–38.

Chapter 7. Dr. Kahn and the Niam-Niams

1. These details are recorded in Kahn, *Catalogue*.

2. *Manchester Courier*, December 13, 1851.

3. Kahn, *Catalogue*, iv.

4. Altick, *The Shows of London*, 340–41.

5. Sexton, "Anatomical View of the Question," 6.

6. For a summary of the literature on this subject, see Bondeson, *A Cabinet of Medical Curiosities*, 170–85.

7. Burnett, *On the Origin and Progress*, 1:257–69.

8. Boswell, cited in Cloyd, *James Burnett*, 105.

9. du Couret, *Voyage au pays des Niam-Niams*; de Castelnau, *Renseignements sur l'Afrique Centrale*. The French reaction is described in Penel, *Homo Caudatus*.

10. Kahn, *Men with Tails*, iii–iv.

11. Ibid., 6–7.

12. *Lancet*, November 1854, 381.

13. *Literary Gazette, and Journal of Science and Art*, October 28, 1854, 919.

14. Kahn, *Catalogue*, 16.

15. *Literary Gazette, and Journal of Science and Art*, October 28, 1854, 920. In his "anthropological investigation into the contemporary mythical science of race, as found among white (European) male scientists," Peter Rigby identifies du Couret, de Castelnau, and their scientific colleagues in Paris who spread the legend about Niam-Niams as total charlatans. See Rigby, *African Images*, 5–9.

16. Conolly, *The Ethnological Exhibitions of London*, 37. For more on the scientific commentary on the Niam-Niams, see Jahoda, *Images of Savages*, 114–21, 252–53. Baxter and Butt, *The Azande*, 12, report, "The name *Niam-Niam* is still sometimes used of the Azande. . . . It has been used since the time of the mediaeval African geographers to describe vaguely those people inhabiting the cannibal belt of Central Africa. . . . If the term is thus extended to include tribes which are only similar in so far as they happen to be cannibals, it becomes too vague to be useful. The name *Niam-Niam* is now archaic and, though much used in early works, should be dropped from modern descriptive writing."

17. Such tales continue. Barnes, in his autobiography, *Master Showman*, 236, tells the following story with a straight face:

> I had heard of a tribe of long-tailed men in a certain part of Africa. It seemed to me that a specimen would make a good side-show feature, and I sent a man to Africa to capture one of the men. After many trials and struggles he succeeded, and brought one to the United States. The captive was placed in quarantine at Alcatraz Island, in the Bay of San Francisco, where I went to inspect him.
>
> The long-tailed specimen proved to be a hideous-looking negro, with a tail something more than a foot long. He was too shocking in appearance, I considered, to exhibit in a side-show, and I gave orders that he should be sent back to his home in Africa. No doubt he would have proved a wonderful attraction, but his appearance was so repulsive that I didn't want to have him around; he would have been distasteful to some of the spectators, and I have made it a policy never to display anything in the show that would offend good taste.

Chapter 8. The United African Twins on Tour

1. The page numbers cited hereafter refer to this twenty-six-page pamphlet, the cover of which reads *The Greatest Wonder of the World: Millie Christine, The Two-Headed Lady, The Most Wonderfully Made of God's Creatures. Complete History, Together with Reports of Medical Examinations of This Marvel of Mankind. With Compliments of The Great Inter-Ocean Largest and Best Show On Earth. John B. Doris, —Proprietor. Wherein Millie Christine will hold Semi-Daily Receptions Without Charge!* No bibliographical details are given, but internal evidence reveals that Doris published this edition of Millie-Christine's biography in 1883. I am grateful to

Howard Tibbals for allowing me to consult a copy of it in the Harold Dunn collection of circus memorabilia. Kunzog, "Millie Christine," 3–7, relied on the Doris biography and a London herald to reconstruct part of Millie-Christine's career in England, but without access to British newspapers he could not fill in gaps in the biographical record or check the accuracy of a number of important details. For more extensive information on Millie-Christine's early life and later career, see the biography by Martell, *Millie-Christine*, which corrects some of the errors in the Doris biography and adds many new details. The principal nineteenth-century biographical sources on Millie-Christine are reprinted in Frost, *Conjoined Twins*. There is also a brief biographical sketch on her in Drimmer, *Very Special People*, 55–61.

2. Millie-Christine, *History and Medical Description*. I am grateful to Howard Tibbals for allowing me to consult a copy of this thirty-two-page pamphlet in the Harold Dunn collection of circus memorabilia.

3. *Liverpool Mercury*, July 27, 1855.

4. Ibid.

5. Ibid., July 31, 1855.

6. *Liverpool Chronicle*, July 28, 1855. A pair of "Aztec Lilliputians" had been exhibited in the British Isles a few years earlier. They had been identified as frauds by the secretary of the Ethnological Society of London. See Latham, "Ethnological Remarks," 149–50.

7. *Liverpool Mail*, July 28, 1855.

8. *Liverpool Courier*, August 1, 1855.

9. *Albion*, August 6, 1855.

10. *Dundee Courier*, August 22, 1855.

11. *Dundee, Perth and Cupar Advertiser*, August 31, 1855.

12. *Dundee and Perth Saturday Post*, September 1, 1855.

13. *Dundee Courier*, September 5, 1855.

14. *Dundee, Perth and Cupar Advertiser*, September 4, 1855.

15. *Era*, September 9, 1855.

16. Ibid.

17. Ibid. See also the *Times*, September 17, 1855.

18. *Aris's Birmingham Gazette*, December 29, 1856.

19. *Birmingham Mercury*, January 10, 1857.

20. Ibid.

21. *Birmingham Daily Press*, January 6, 1857.

22. *Birmingham Mercury*, January 10, 1857.

23. Ibid.

24. *Western Democrat*, March 24, 1857. A female abolitionist who arrived in Charlotte a few weeks later could not find a place to lecture and moved on to Lincolnton. The *North Carolina Argus* of April 11, 1857, said, "Probably she heard of Thompson; and . . . it may have occurred to her that it was far better to 'push along, keep moving.'"

25. *Western Democrat*, March 17, 1857. The story was quoted from the *Cheraw Gazette*, as was the following legal conundrum, which appeared in the *Western Democrat* on May 5, 1857:

Mr. J. P. Smith, arrived at Cheraw a few weeks ago, from Scotland, with the African twins, of whom some little talk has been made. During her stay in Scotland, their mother gave birth to another child, whom she brought home with her. Now the question arises, if that child, born on the soil of Scotland, is bond or free? If born free, how can it be held in slavery here? And was not its introduction in this country a violation of the law prohibiting the foreign slave trade? The mother became free when she entered Scotland, but returning here she returns to her owners. The remaining question is, can she enslave her child in her own return to servitude!

Chapter 9. Circus Africans

1. Debrunner, *Presence and Prestige*, 145.

2. *New York Times*, September 9–30, 1906, quoted in Bradford and Blume, *Ota Benga*. See also Buckner, "Ota the Other," 154–75.

3. In addition to those already discussed, there were representatives from these three ethnicities exhibited in the 1880s at London's Royal Aquarium by G. A. Farini, an enterprising Canadian impresario who also mounted sensational shows at several American circuses. For details, see Peacock, *The Great Farini*, and "Africa Meets the Great Farini," 81–106.

4. Handbill from Barnum's American Museum reproduced in Harris, *Humbug*, 177.

5. See Alpern, *Amazons of Black Sparta*; Rydell, "'Darkest Africa,'" 135–55.

6. See Bradford and Blume, *Ota Benga*; J. Green, "A Revelation in Strange Humanity," 156–87; Blume, "Ota Benga," 188–202; see also Buckner, "Ota the Other," 154–75.

7. *The Life History of Clicko*, 2. For a biography of this performer, see Parsons, *Clicko*, and his earlier chapter, "'Clicko,'" 203–27.

8. *Saucerlips/Ubangi Savages*, 1–2.

9. Ibid.

10. Lewiston, *Freak Show Man*, 13. Bradna and Spence, *The Big Top*, 243–51, contains discussion of the Ubangis. See also Teel, *Sideshow Freaks and Features*, 1. Davis, *The Circus Age*, 135, notes, "The women's lips also served as a metaphor for engorged labia, a visual image surely not lost on Euroamerican audiences steeped in stereotypes about black women's supposed sexual availability."

11. Vinson and Edgar, in "Zulus Abroad," describe a large number of authentic and "faux" Zulus performing in the United States between 1880 and 1945. For a more comprehensive view of "Zuluness" in colonial and postcolonial contexts, see the essays collected in Carton, Laban, and Sithole, *Zulu Identities*, especially Carton's "Awaken Nkulunkulu," 133–52, which discusses the difficulties early missionaries in South Africa encountered when attempting to understand traditional Zulu beliefs and practices and relate them to Christian concepts.

12. Wallace, *The Fabulous Showman*, 111.

13. A poster for W. C. Coup's United Monster Shows at the Great Paris Hippodrome in Chicago in 1881 advertises "Princess Amazulu, King Cetewayo's Daughter

and Suite." A newspaper advertisement for the same circus the following year bills "Zulu Princess Amadaga, daughter of King Cetewayo, and her maids of honor"; these women were also said to be "the only Female Zulus who ever left Zululand and the only genuine Zulus in America."

14. Coup, *Sawdust and Spangles*, 166.

15. Walker, *From Sawdust to Windsor Castle*, 130.

16. Middleton, *Circus Memoirs*, 69.

17. Program for P. T. Barnum with Great London Circus, Madison Square Garden, April 17, 1888, held in the Dyer Reynolds Circus Collection, Memphis State University.

18. J. Wood, "Dime Museums, 760.

19. McKechnie, *Popular Entertainments*, 210.

20. For this information I am grateful to Robert Parkinson, former research director of the Circus World Museum, Baraboo, Wisconsin. The words are defined in a glossary appended to O'Brien, *Circus*, 260, and in Wilmeth, *The Language of American*, 299.

21. Ibid.

22. Barnes, *Master Showman*, 204.

23. Chipman, *"Hey, Rube!,"* 29.

24. Sherwood, *Hold Yer Hosses!*, 116, 120. Bartra, in *Wild Men* and *The Artificial Savage*, discusses the history of the notion of wild men in Western culture. See also the essays in Dudley and Novak, *The Wild Man Within*, especially H. White, "The Forms of Wildness," 3–38.

25. Wallace, *The Fabulous Showman*, 162. See also Sherwood, *Here We Are Again*, 193. Barnum elaborated on this notion in a book titled *The Humbugs of the World*.

26. As noted by Cook in "Of Men, Missing Links," 143–46, Barnum originally used the term "What-Is-It?" when introducing a crippled acrobat with unusually short legs at London's Egyptian Hall in 1846 as a "liminal creature." For further discussion of this role, see Cook, *The Arts of Deception*, 119–62.

27. From a Currier and Ives lithograph of the "What-Is-It?" held at the Chicago Historical Society and reproduced in Langston Hughes, *Black Magic*, 62, and here as figure 45 (text omitted). The Kunhardts, in *P. T. Barnum*, 149, claim, "The believability of the 'What is it?' was strengthened by an unwitting Barnum ally, the English scientist Charles Darwin, whose *Origin of Species* had sold out in one day just three months before Barnum introduced his new wonder."

28. Stephens, *Illustrated Memoir*, 47. A second Currier and Ives lithograph of the "What-Is-It?," placing him in a friendlier pose amid five spectators, carries a sample of Stephens's puffery.

29. Bryan, *The World's Greatest Showman*, 115.

30. See, e.g., Conklin, *The Ways of the Circus*, 162–63; Fellows and Freeman, *This Way to the Big Top*, 308–9; Sherwood, *Hold Yer Hosses!*, 124–25; and Datas, *Datas*, 97–99.

31. "Zip Claims Sole Right to Name." A copy of this article is held in the "Zip" file in the Hoblitzelle Theatre Arts Library collection held at the Harry Ransom Humanities Research Center at the University of Texas at Austin.

32. Bryan, *The World's Greatest Showman*, 115.

33. Kunhardt, "Barnum and Brady," 21. Conklin, *The Ways of the Circus*, 162, quotes a handbill with this claim.

34. Conklin, *The Ways of the Circus*, 162.

35. Teel, *Sideshow Freaks and Features*, 13.

36. Conklin, *The Ways of the Circus*, 163.

37. "Uncle" Bob Sherwood, quoted in Teel, *Sideshow Freaks and Features*, 15.

38. In her study *The Circus and Victorian Society*, Brenda Assael has an interesting chapter titled "Clown Laughter, Clown Tears" in which she maintains: "One of the circus's key functions was to make its audiences laugh. The clown was integral to this process" (106). It could be argued that Zip, throughout his career, was this kind of performer, an ethnic clown whose primary purpose was to make audiences laugh.

39. McCullough, *Good Old Coney Island*, 270.

40. Odell, *Annals of the New York Stage*, 7:523–24, 13:109.

41. "Zip, Oldest Freak, Is Ill in Hospital."

42. Pilat and Ranson, *Sodom by the Sea*, 187. For a fuller account of Zip's career, see Cook, "Of Men, Missing Links," 139–57, and *The Art of Deception*, 119–62.

43. "Zip, Dean of Freak Folk, Is Better."

44. Sanger, *Seventy Years a Showman*, 7–8.

45. Ibid., 167–68. For information on British circus performers and managers, see John M. Turner's two-volume *Victorian Arena*.

46. Thompson, *On the Road*, 70. For more on circus wild men, see Adams, *Sideshow U.S.A.*, 164–69.

47. Quoted in Vinson and Edgar, "Zulus Abroad," 48.

48. Mayer, *The Barnum and Bailey Show*.

49. From the 1885 *Program of the Great Barnum and London Nine United Shows*, held at the Hertzberg Circus Collection, San Antonio.

50. Leland, *Memoirs*, 209.

Chapter 10. Africa's First Olympians

1. Johnson, *All That Glitters*, 121. This may be a generous estimate; the Associated Press and Grolier's *The Olympic Story*, 49, states that "even the most exciting events in the St. Louis Games failed to attract more than 2,000 spectators."

2. *New York Times*, August 31, 1904, 5; *New York Daily Tribune*, August 31, 1904, 5; Kieran and Daley, *The Story of the Olympic Games*, 47; Lucas, *The Olympic Games*, 67. In most of these reports, the two "Kaffir" runners were identified as Lentauw and Yamasani. The photograph of them in Martin and Gynn, *The Olympic Marathon*, 41, identifies No. 36 as Jan Mashaini and No. 35 as Len Tau, the numbers and names ascribed to them by van der Merwe in "Africa's First Encounter," 32.

3. *St. Louis Post-Dispatch*, August 28, 1904, 7B. van der Merwe, "Africa's First Encounter, 31, believes that they "had been messengers for the Boers during the war."

4. *St. Louis Daily Globe-Democrat*, August 21, 1904, 13.

5. *St. Louis Post-Dispatch*, August 30, 1904, 4.

6. *St. Louis Daily Globe-Democrat*, August 21, 1904, 13; *St. Louis Post-Dispatch*, August 28, 1904, 7B.

7. *St. Louis Daily Globe-Democrat*, August 8, 1904, 4; *St. Louis Post-Dispatch*, August 30, 1904, 4.

8. *St. Louis Daily Globe-Democrat*, August 21, 1904, 13; *St. Louis Post-Dispatch*, August 28, 1904, 7B.

9. Reported in Schaap, *An Illustrated History*, 70.

10. Lucas, *The Olympic Games*, 50.

11. Martin and Gynn, *The Marathon Footrace*, 21.

12. *St. Louis Daily Globe-Democrat*, August 31, 1904, 6; Scher, "Zulus and the Olympic Games," 12–13; Lucas, *The Olympic Games*, 57–58; Chester, *The Olympic Games Handbook*, 24; Kieran and Daley, *The Story of the Olympic Games*, 47; Matthews, *America's First Olympics*, 137. Tibballs, *The Olympics' Strangest Moments*, 21, claims "the unlucky Len Tau lost valuable ground when he was chased off the road and through a cornfield by two wild dogs!" Van der Merwe, "Africa's First Encounter," 32, citing evidence in a study by Bill Mallon, *A Statistical Summary of the 1904 Olympic Games*, 12–13, suggests that Jan Mashaini "seems the more likely candidate to have been chased by a dog."

13. *St. Louis Daily Globe-Democrat*, August 7, 1904, 15. For recent analyses of significant cultural, political, and pseudo-scientific aspects of these games, see the essays in Brownell, *The 1904 Anthropology Days*, especially Brownell, introduction, 1–58; Eichberg, "Olympic Anthropology Days," 348–82; Knott, "Germans and Others," 278–300; and Parezo, "A 'Special Olympics,'" 59–126.

14. Buel, *Louisiana and the Fair*, 5:1852.

15. Francis, *The Universal Exposition*, 527. This same individual was later placed in a cage with a monkey at the Bronx Zoo. For details, see Bradford and Blume, *Ota Benga*.

16. Lane, "The World's Fair," 3.

17. Stevens, *The Forest City*, n.p. The anecdote appears under a photo titled "The Pygmies at Home."

18. Sullivan, "Anthropology Days at the Stadium," in *Spalding's Official Athletic Almanach*, 257, quoted by Brownell, introduction, 4. Eichberg, in "Olympic Anthropology Days" and "Forward Race," offers an interesting analysis of the festive, "carnavalesque" behavior of these performers. Also, Carlson, "Giant Patagonians and Hairy Ainu," 24, reports:

> The St. Louis Pygmies initially refused to participate in the athletic contests or even to have their picture taken, but, according to the account printed in the *St. Louis Republican*, chief anthropologist Dr. S.C. Simms successfully intervened by promising the little men that after the competition they would be given all the watermelon they could eat. Whatever the inducement, the next day the pygmies agreed to a pole climbing exhibition and a mud fight. They even tried the shop [*sic*] put, but their best effort reached only 13 feet, 7 inches.

19. *St. Louis Post-Dispatch*, quoted by Stanaland, "Pre-Olympic 'Anthropology Days,'" 104.

20. *St. Louis Republic*, August 13, 1904, 5.

21. Ibid.

22. van der Merwe, "Africa's First Encounter," citing linguistic, geographical, and historical evidence, maintains that they were "more likely Tswanas," but Neil Parsons informs me that while Tau is a Tswana or Sotho name, Mashinini (probably the correct spelling of Mashaini) can be identified as a Zulu name.

23. *St. Louis Daily Globe-Democrat*, August 13, 1904, 14.

24. Quoted in Johnson, *All That Glitters*, 125.

25. *St. Louis Republic*, August 13, 1904, 5. For a discussion of world's fairs as an exercise in Western imperialistic self-affirmation, see Rydell, *All the World's a Fair*.

26. Corbey, "Ethnographic Showcases," 341.

27. Associated Press and Grolier, *The Olympic Story*, 53.

Conclusion

1. Affidavit signed by S. Solly and Geo. Moojen (Public Record Office No. KB1/36, pt. 2), and quoted by Strother, "Display of the Body Hottentot," 41.

2. Abrahams, "Disempowered to Consent," 107–9.

3. A Constant Reader, "The Female Hottentot," *Examiner*, October 14, 1810, 653.

4. *Birmingham Advertiser*, May 18, 1847, 3. Also, according to the *Cork Southern Reporter*, February 17, 1848, 2, in a theater in Cork "a ruffian . . . flung an orange from the gallery with great violence, at one of these poor wretches and apparently hurt him considerably."

5. *Curtain, or English Entr'acte*, August 4, 1847, 4.

6. *Era*, May 12, 1850, 10.

7. Scott, *Domination and the Arts of Resistance*, 113.

8. *Globe*, September 29, 1853, 4. Accounts of this hearing can be found in many other London papers of the day. Caldecott sent a letter to the editor of the *Morning Post*, published on September 30, 1853, correcting the name of the defendant to Mangos. *John Bull*, October 1, 1853, said: "we shall not be sorry if [the case] directs public attention to the manifest impropriety of allowing human beings to be exhibited like wild beasts in a civilized and a Christian country. . . . The truth is, that London is not the place for savages; they cannot live in it as free men, nor can the law render any assistance in treating them as *feræ naturæ*."

9. Qureshi, *Peoples on Parade*, 140.

10. A similar conflict between German managers and African performers occurred at a "Wild African" exhibition in Berlin in 1907 when eighteen North Africans, "agitated by the unfamiliar consumption of prohibited alcohol," left their compound and roamed around in the neighboring streets, enjoying the local nightlife. For German reactions to this "uprising," see Bruckner, "Spectacles of (Human) Nature," 144–55.

11. *Liverpool Mercury*, July 27, 1855.

12. *Era*, May 15, 1853, 11.

13. *Morning Chronicle*, May 17, 1853, 3.

14. *Court Journal*, May 7, 1853, 300.

15. For a description of this relationship, see Parsons, *Clicko*.

16. "Manager of Zip Dying from Grief," *New York Times*, June 28, 1926.

17. Bogdan, *Freak Show*, 141.

18. Gene Cohn, "And Just What Was Zip, the Famed 'What Is It?,'" a cutting from an unidentified Chattanooga paper dated April 17, 1926, included in the Hertzberg circus collection at the Witte Museum in San Antonio.

19. Erlmann, *Music, Modernity*.

20. Parsons, "'Clicko,'" 214.

21. "Ota Benga, Pygmy Tired of America," *New York Times*, July 16, 1916, reprinted in Bradford and Blume, *Ota Benga*, 275–76.

22. Miller, "Surely His Mother Mourns," 86–88.

23. "A South African Native's Picture," 137.

24. Miller, "Surely His Mother Mourns," 86–88. One of Wyman's articles, adapted from the *Proceedings of the Boston Society of Natural History*, April 2, 1862, and December 16, 1863, was "Observations on the Skeleton of a Hottentot."

25. Flower and Murie, "Account of the Dissection," 207. For a response to this report, see Devis, "Flower and Murie." For further discussion, see Fauvelle-Aymar, *L'invention du Hottentot*, 342–47.

26. Holmes, *The Hottentot Venus*, 115, found her in Limerick in 1812, and a series of articles about her in Dublin publications, *The Monthly Panorama* (1811) and *Milesian Magazine, or Irish Monthly Gleaner* (1812), suggest she performed there as well.

27. The French scholarship on Hottentot anatomy continued long after Cuvier's pioneering work. See, for instance, the articles by Raphaël Blanchard; Péron and Lesueur; Topinard; and Deniker.

28. See the poster at Aberdeen University Library (Circus bills 54) featuring a "Hottentot Venus from the Cape of Good Hope," who was being exhibited alongside other unusual people and animals. This was Miss Kaitus Vessula, who had also appeared in London in June 1836.

29. See, e.g., the studies of Hottentot physiology by Blumenbach; Fritsch; Luschka; and Schultze. Luschka had dissected a South African woman named Afandy, who had died at age thirty in Ulm.

30. See the undated handbill for "De Wilden of Bosjesmannen" in the Toneel Museum at the University of Amsterdam. This appears to have been the same troupe that appeared in London, but no child appeared with them in the Netherlands. Corbey, "Ethnographic Showcases," 347, quotes a Rotterdam brochure stating that the performers "show more similarity to Apes than to people. . . . Notwithstanding their ferocity these Bushmen are nearly harmless, and even the most fearful person can approach and feel all over them with the greatest confidence."

31. Topinard, "Étude sur les Hottentots," 658, alludes to three Bosjesmans who appeared at the Folies-Bergères.

32. See Hahn, *Schultze & Müller*. Germany subsequently became a leader in ethnological show business after Carl Hagenbeck Jr., whose father had been a successful dealer and exhibitor of exotic animals, took over his father's business in 1866 and eight

years later imported a group of six Sami from Norway's Lapland, putting them on display with a herd of thirty-one reindeer. Thereafter he began to regularly recruit picturesque ethnographic performance troupes to add to his zoological garden in Hamburg. Ames, in *Carl Hagenbeck's Empire of Entertainments*, 3, reveals that "over the course of his career, which ran nearly six decades, he exhibited troupes from Australia, Burma, Cameroon, Canada, Chile, Egypt, Ethiopia, Greenland, India, Labrador, Mongolia, Norway, Russia, Samoa, Somalia, Sri Lanka, the Sudan, the United States, and elsewhere." This came to be known in Germany as the *Völkerschau* (or foreign peoples show). For further discussion of this phenomenon, see the dissertations by Rothfels, "Bring 'em Back Alive"; Bruckner, "The Tingle-Tangle of Modernity"; and Penny, "Cosmopolitan Visions and Municipal Displays"; as well as the book by Zimmerman titled *Anthropology and Anti-humanism in Imperial Germany*. See also Poignant's *Professional Savages* for an in-depth account of touring Australian Aborigines.

33. Toll has discussed the satirical dimension of black minstrelsy in *Blacking Up*.

Bibliography

Newspapers and Magazines

Age (London)
Albion (Liverpool)
Aris's Birmingham Gazette (UK)
Atheneaum (London)
Atlas (London)
Baldwin's London Weekly Journal (London)
Bell's Life in London
Bell's Weekly Messenger (London)
Birmingham Advertiser (UK)
Birmingham Daily Press (UK)
Birmingham Journal (UK)
Birmingham Mercury (UK)
Blackwood's Magazine (London)
Brighton Examiner (UK)
Brighton Guardian (UK)
Bristol Mirror (UK)
British and London Recorder (London)
British Liberator (London)
British Press (London)
British Traveller (London)
Censor (London)

Cerebus; or, the Hell Post (London)
Cheraw Gazette (Cheraw, SC)
Christian Remembrancer (London)
Comic Magazine (London)
Cork Southern Reporter (Ireland)
Courier (London)
Court Journal (London)
Critic, London Literary Journal
Curtain, or English Entr'acte (London)
Douglas Jerrold's Weekly Newspaper (London)
Dramatic Mirror (London)
Dumfries Courier (Scotland)
Dundee Courier (Scotland)
Dundee and Perth Saturday Post (Scotland)
Dundee, Perth and Cupar Advertiser (Scotland)
Edinburgh Evening Post (Scotland)
Edinburgh Observer and New North Briton (Scotland)
English Chronicle (London)
English Gentleman (London)
Era (London)
Evans and Ruffy's Farmer's Journal (London)
Evening Packet (Dublin)
Examiner (London)
Figaro in London
Gentleman's Magazine of Fashion, Fancy Costumes, and the Regimentals of the Army (London)
Ghost (London)
Glasgow Courier (Scotland)
Glasgow Examiner (Scotland)
Globe (London)
Globe and Traveller (London)
Guardian and Public Ledger (London)
Illustrated London News
Illustrated Magazine of Art (London)
John Bull (London)
Johnson's Sunday Monitor (London)
Ladies' Penny Gazette (London)
Lancet (London)
Literary Beacon (London)
Literary Gazette, and Journal of Science and Art (London)
Literary Gazette, and Journal of the Belles Lettres (London)
Literary Panorama: A Review of Books, Magazine of Varieties, and Annual Register (London)
Literary Test (London)
Liverpool Chronicle (UK)

Liverpool Courier (UK)
Liverpool Mail (UK)
Liverpool Mercury (UK)
London Journal and Weekly Record of Literature, Science and Art
London Packet and Chronicle
Manchester Courier (UK)
Manchester Express (UK)
Manchester Guardian (UK)
Midland Counties Herald, Birmingham and General Advertiser (UK)
Milesian Magazine, or Irish Monthly Gleaner (Dublin)
Monthly Panorama (Dublin)
Morning Advertiser (London)
Morning Chronicle (London)
Morning Herald (London)
Morning Post (London)
National Omnibus and General Advertiser (London)
National Register (London)
National Standard, and Journal of Literature, Science, Music, Theatricals and the Fine Arts (London)
New Court Journal and Gazette of the United Services (London)
New Monthly Magazine (London)
New York Daily Tribune
New York Times
News (London)
North Carolina Argus (Wadesboro, NC)
Observer (London)
Old British Spy (London)
Old England (London)
People's Penny Pictures (London)
Pictorial Times (London)
Plymouth Times (UK)
Public Ledger and Daily Advertiser (London)
Representative (London)
Satirist; or Monthly Meteor (London)
Saunders's News-Letter (Dublin)
Solicitor's Journal (London)
South African Commercial Advertiser (Cape Town)
Spectator (London)
Sportsman's Magazine (London)
Standard (London)
St. Louis Daily Globe-Democrat
St. Louis Post-Dispatch
St. Louis Republic
Sun (London)

Sunday Herald (London)
Sunday Times (London)
Tatler (London)
T. Dibdin's Penny Trumpet (London)
Terrific Penny Magazine (London)
Theatrical Observer; and Daily Bills of the Play (London)
Thief (London)
Time (New York)
Times (London)
Wag (London)
Warder (Dublin)
Watchman (London)
Weekly Dispatch (London)
Weekly True Sun (London)
Western Democrat (Charlotte, NC)
Westminster Journal (London)

Books and Articles Cited

à Beckett, Arthur William. *The Becketts of "Punch": Memories of Father and Sons*. New York:
    E. P. Dutton, 1903.
Abrahams, Yvette. "Disempowered to Consent: Sara Bartman and Khoisan Slavery in
    the Nineteenth-Century Cape Colony and Britain." *South African Historical Journal* 35
    (1996): 89–114.
————. "Images of Sara Bartman: Sexuality, Race, and Gender in Early-Nineteenth-
    Century Britain." In *Nation, Empire, Colony: Historicizing Gender and Race*, edited by Ruth
    Roach Pierson and Nupur Chaudhuri, 220–36. Bloomington: Indiana University
    Press, 1998.
Adams, Rachel. *Sideshow U.S.A.: Freaks and the American Cultural Imagination*. Chicago:
    University of Chicago Press, 2001.
Agassiz, Louis, Augustus A. Gould, and Thomas Wright. *Outlines of Comparative Physiology*.
    London, 1851.
Alexander, Elizabeth. *The Venus Hottentot*. Charlottesville: University Press of Virginia,
    1990.
Alpern, Stanley B. *Amazons of Black Sparta: The Women Warriors of Dahomey*. New York:
    New York University Press, 1998.
Altick, Richard D. "Borrioboola-Gha, Bushmen, and Brickmakers." *Dickensian* 74 (1978):
    157–59.
————. *The Shows of London*. Cambridge, MA: Belknap Press of Harvard University
    Press, 1978.
Ames, Eric. *Carl Hagenbeck's Empire of Entertainments*. Seattle: University of Washington
    Press, 2008.
Assael, Brenda. *The Circus and Victorian Society*. Charlottesville: University of Virginia
    Press, 2005.

Associated Press and Grolier. *The Olympic Story: Pursuit of Excellence.* Danbury, CT: Grolier, 1979.

Badou, Gérard. *L'énigma de la Vénus Hottentote.* Paris: Lattès, 2000.

Barnes, Al. *Master Showman.* London: Jonathan Cape, 1938.

Barnum, P. T. *The Humbugs of the World: An Account of Humbugs, Delusions, Impositions, Quackeries, Deceits and Deceivers Generally, in All Ages.* New York: Carleton, 1866.

Bartra, Roger. *The Artificial Savage: Modern Myths of the Wild Man.* Ann Arbor: University of Michigan Press, 1997.

———. *Wild Men in the Looking Glass: The Mythic Origins of European Otherness.* Ann Arbor: University of Michigan Press, 1994.

Baudelaire, Charles. "Some Foreign Caricaturists." [1857]. In Bryant, *The Comic Cruikshank*, 95–96.

Baxter, P. T. W., and Audrey Butt. *The Azande, and Related Peoples of the Anglo-Egyptian Sudan and Belgian Congo.* London: International African Institute, 1953.

Bibliothèque Nationale. *Collection de Vinck: Inventaire Analytique.* Vol. 5. Edited by Marcel Roux. Paris: Maurice Le Garrec, 1938.

Bickerstaff, Isaac. *The Padlock.* 1783. Cambridge: Chadwyck-Healey, 1996.

Blanchard, Pascal, et al., eds. *Human Zoos: Science and Spectacle in the Age of Colonial Empires.* Liverpool: Liverpool University Press, 2008.

Blanchard, Raphaël. "Étude sur la stéatopygie et le tablier des femmes Boschimanes." *Bulletin de la Société Zoologique de France* 8 (1883): 34–75.

Blanckaert, Claude, ed. *La Vénus hottentote: Entre Barnum et Muséum.* Paris: Muséum national d'histoire naturelle, 2013.

Blume, Harvey. "Ota Benga and the Barnum Perplex." In Lindfors, *Africans on Stage*, 188–202.

Blumenbach, I. F. *The Anthropological Treatises of Johan Friederich Blumenbach.* London: Longmans, 1865.

Boëtsch, Gilles, and Pascal Blanchard. "The Hottentot Venus: Birth of a 'Freak.'" In P. Blanchard et al., *Human Zoos*, 62–72.

Bogdan, Robert. *Freak Show: Representing Human Oddities for Amusement and Profit.* Chicago: University of Chicago Press, 1988.

Bolt, Christine. *Victorian Attitudes to Race.* London: Routledge & Kegan Paul, 1971.

Bondeson, Jan. *A Cabinet of Medical Curiosities.* New York: Norton, 1997.

Bradford, Phillips Verner, and Harvey Blume. *Ota Benga: The Pygmy in the Zoo.* New York: St. Martin's Press, 1992.

Bradna, Fred, and Hartzell Spence. *The Big Top: My Forty Years with the Greatest Show on Earth.* New York: Simon and Schuster, 1952.

Brandes, Kerstin. "Hottentot Venus: Re-Considering Saartjie Baartman: Configurations of the 'Hottentot Venus' in Contemporary Cultural Discourse, Politics, and Art." In *Virtual Minds: Congress of Fictitious Figures*, edited by Helene von Oldenburg and Andrea Sick, 40–55. Bremen: Thealit Frauen. Kultur. Labor, 2004.

Brantlinger, Patrick. *Rule of Darkness: British Literature and Imperialism, 1830–1914.* Ithaca, NY: Cornell University Press, 1988.

Brownell, Susan. Introduction to Brownell, *The 1904 Anthropology Days*, 1–58.

————, ed. *The 1904 Anthropology Days and Olympic Games: Sport, Race, and American Imperialism.* Lincoln: University of Nebraska Press, 2008.

Bruckner, Sierra Ann. "Spectacles of (Human) Nature: Commercial Ethnography between Leisure, Learning and *Schaulust.*" In *Worldly Provincialism: German Anthropology in the Age of Empire,* edited by H. Glenn Penny and Matti Bunzl, 220–36. Ann Arbor: University of Michigan Press, 2003.

————. "The Tingle-Tangle of Modernity: Popular Anthropology and the Cultural Politics of Identity in Imperial Germany." PhD diss., University of Iowa, 1999.

Bryan, J., III. *The World's Greatest Showman: The Life of P. T. Barnum.* New York: Random House, 1956.

Bryant, Mark, ed. *The Comic Cruikshank.* London: Bellew, 1992.

Buckner, Jocelyn L. "Ota the Other: An African on Display in America." *Theatre History Studies* 30 (2010): 154–75.

Buel, J. W., ed. *Louisiana and the Fair: An Exposition of the World, Its People and Their Achievements.* 10 vols. St. Louis: World's Progress, 1904.

Burnett, James. *On the Origin and Progress of Language.* 1773. Vol. 1. New York: AMS Press, 1973.

Caldecott, C. H. *Descriptive History of the Zulu Kafirs, Their Customs and Their Country, with Illustrations.* London: John Mitchell, 1853.

Carlson, Lew. "Giant Patagonians and Hairy Ainu: Anthropology Days at the 1904 St. Louis Olympics." *Journal of American Culture* 12 (Fall 1989): 19–26.

Carton, Benedict. "Awaken *Nkulunkulu,* Zulu God of the Old Testament: Pioneering Missionaries during the Early Age of Racial Spectacle." In Carton et al., *Zulu Identities,* 133–52.

Carton, Benedict, John Laband, and Jabulani Sithole, eds. *Zulu Identities: Being Zulu Past and Present.* New York: Columbia University Press, 2009.

Chase-Riboud, Barbara. *Hottentot Venus.* New York: Doubleday, 2003.

Chester, David. *The Olympic Games Handbook.* New York: Scribner's, 1971.

Chipman, Bert Jesse. *"Hey, Rube!"* Hollywood: Hollywood Print Shop, 1933.

Clarke, Monica. *They Call Me Hottentot Venus.* [Raleigh, NC]: Lulu, 2009.

Cloyd, E. L. *James Burnett, Lord Monboddo.* Oxford: Clarendon Press, 1972.

Cole, Arthur Whaley. "'Cape' Sketches." *Household Words* 2, no. 3 (1851): 118–20.

Cole, John William. *The Life and Theatrical Times of Charles Kean, F. S. A.* London: Richard Bentley, 1859.

Coleman, William. *Georges Cuvier, Zoologist: A Study of the History of Evolution Theory.* Cambridge, MA: Harvard University Press, 1964.

Conklin, George. *The Ways of the Circus: Being the Memories and Adventures of George Conklin, Tamer of Lions.* New York: Harper, 1921.

Conolly, John. *The Ethnological Exhibitions of London.* London: John Churchill, 1855.

Cook, James. *The Arts of Deception: Playing with Fraud in the Age of Barnum.* Cambridge, MA: Harvard University Press, 2001.

————. "Of Men, Missing Links, and Nondescripts: The Strange Career of P. T. Barnum's 'What Is It' Exhibition." In Thomson, *Freakery,* 139–57.

Corbey, Raymond. "Ethnographic Showcases, 1870-1930." *Cultural Anthropology* 8, no. 3 (1993): 338-69.

Coup, William Cameron. *Sawdust and Spangles: Stories and Secrets of the Circus.* Chicago: Stone, 1901.

Crais, Clifton, and Pamela Scully. *Sara Baartman and the Hottentot Venus: A Ghost Story and a Biography.* Princeton, NJ: Princeton University Press, 2009.

Crispe, Thomas Edward. *Reminiscences of a K. C.* London: Methuen, 1909.

Crotch, W. Walter. *The Touchstone of Dickens.* London: Chapman and Hall, 1920.

Cugoano, Ottobah. *Thoughts and Sentiments on the Evil and Wicked Traffic of the Slavery and Commerce of the Human Species, Humbly Submitted to the Inhabitants of Great Britain, by Ottobah Cugoano, a Native of Africa.* London: T. Becket, 1787.

Curtin, Philip D. *The Image of Africa: British Ideas and Action, 1780-1850.* Madison: University of Wisconsin Press, 1964.

Cuvier, Georges. "Extrait d'observations faites sur le cadaver d'une femme connue à Paris et à Londres sous le nom de Vénus Hottentote." *Mémoires du Museum d'Histoire Naturelle* 3 (1817): 259-74.

Datas. *Datas: The Memory Man, by Himself.* London: Wright and Brown, n.d.

Davis, Janet M. *The Circus Age: Culture & Society under the American Big Top.* Chapel Hill: University of North Carolina Press, 2002.

Debrunner, Hans Werner. *Presence and Prestige: Africans in Europe.* Basel, Switzerland: Basler Afrika Bibliographien, 1979.

de Castelnau, Frances. *Renseignements sur l'Afrique Centrale et sur un nation d'hommes à queue qui s'y trouverait, d'après le rapport des nègres du Soudan, esclaves à Bahia.* Paris: P. Bertand, 1851.

Dell, Elizabeth Anne. "Museums and the Re-presentation of 'Savage South Africa' to 1910." PhD diss., School of Oriental and African Studies, University of London, 1994.

Deniker, J. "Les Hottentots au Jardin d'Acclimatation." *Revue d'Anthropologie* 3rd series, 4 (1889): 1-27.

Devis, C. W. "Flower and Murie on the Dissection of a Bushwoman." *Anthropological Review* 5 (1867): 319-24.

Dexter, Walter, ed. *The Letters of Charles Dickens.* Vol. 2. Bloomsbury: Nonesuch Press, 1938.

"Diary of Covent Garden Theatre containing the daily receipts and expenditure, the titles of plays performed, etc." London: British Library (Add. ms. 23162).

Dickens, Charles. "The Niger Expedition." In *Miscellaneous Papers*, vol. 1. New York: Chapman & Hall, 1908.

———. "The Noble Savage." *Household Words*, June 11, 1853, 337-39.

———. *Reprinted Pieces and the Lazy Tour of Two Idle Apprentices.* London: Macmillan, 1925.

Drimmer, Frederick. *Body Snatchers, Stiffs and Other Ghoulish Delights.* New York: Fawcett Gold Medal Books, 1981.

———. *Very Special People: The Struggles, Loves, and Triumphs of Human Oddities.* New York: Amjon, 1973.

du Couret, Louis. *Voyage au pays des Niam-Niams*. Paris: Martinon, 1854.

Dudley, Edward, and Maximillian E. Novak, eds. *The Wild Man Within: An Image of Western Thought from the Renaissance to Romanticism*. Pittsburgh: University of Pittsburgh Press, 1972.

Durbach, Nadja. *Spectacle of Deformity: Freak Shows and Modern British Culture*. Berkeley: University of California Press, 2010.

"Earthmen from Port Natal." *Illustrated London News*, November 6, 1852, 371–72.

East, E. H. *Reports of Cases Argued and Determined in the Court of the King's Bench*. London: J. Butterworth, 1811.

Edwards, Paul, and James Walvin. *Black Personalities in the Era of the Slave Trade*. Baton Rouge: Louisiana State University Press, 1983.

Egan, Pierce. *Pierce Egan's Anecdotes (Original and Selected) of the Turf, the Chase, the Ring, and the Stage; the Whole Forming a Critical Panorama of the Sporting World; Uniting with it a Book of Reference and Entertaining Companion to the Lovers of British Sports*. London: Knight & Lacey, 1827.

Eichberg, Henning. "Forward Race and the Laughter of Pygmies: On Olympic Sport." In *Fin de Siècle and Its Legacy*, edited by Mikulás Teich and Roy Porter, 115–31. Cambridge: Cambridge University Press, 1990.

———. "Olympic Anthropology Days and the Progress of Exclusion: Toward an Anthropology of Democracy." In Brownell, *The 1904 Anthropology Days and Olympic Games*, 343–82.

Ellis, Theodore Richard, III. "The Dramatist and the Comic Journal in England, 1830–1870." PhD diss., Northwestern University, 1968.

Equiano, Olaudah. *The Interesting Narrative of Olaudah Equiano, or Gustavus Vassa, the African, Written by Himself*. London: Author, 1789.

Erlmann, Veit. *Music, Modernity, and the Global Imagination: South Africa and the West*. New York: Oxford University Press, 1999.

Evans, Nicholas M. "Ira Aldridge: Shakespeare and Minstrelsy." *American Transcendental Quarterly* 16, no. 3 (2002): 165–87.

Ewen, Elizabeth, and Stuart Ewen. *Typecasting: On the Arts & Sciences of Human Inequality*. New York: Seven Stories Press, 2006.

Fausto-Sterling, Anne. "Gender, Race, and Nation: The Comparative Anatomy of 'Hottentot' Women in Europe, 1815–1817." In *Deviant Bodies: Critical Perspectives on Difference in Science and Popular Culture*, edited by Jennifer Terry and Jacqueline Urla, 220–36. Bloomington: Indiana University Press, 1995.

Fauvelle-Aymar, François-Xavier. *L'invention du Hottentot: Histoire du regard occidental sur les Khoisan (XVe–XIXe siècle)*. Paris: Publications de la Sorbonne, 2002.

Fellows, Dexter W., and Andrew A. Freeman, *This Way to the Big Top: The Life of Dexter Fellows*. New York: Halcyon, 1936.

Fiedler, Leslie. *Freaks: Myths and Images of the Secret Self*. New York: Simon & Schuster, 1978.

Final Close of the St. George's Gallery, Hyde Park Corner, Piccadilly. Zulu Kafirs. Last Few Days in London. London, 1853.

Flower, W. H., and James Murie. "Account of the Dissection of a Bushwoman." *Journal of Anatomy and Physiology* 1, no. 2 (1867): 189–208.

Fox, Celina. "Political Caricature and the Freedom of the Press in Early Nineteenth-Century England." In *Newspaper History from the Seventeenth Century to the Present Day*, edited by George Boyce, James Curran, and Pauline Wingate, 226–46. London: Constable, 1978.

Francis, David R. *The Universal Exposition of 1904.* St. Louis: Louisiana Purchase Exposition, 1913.

Franco, Suzanne. *Exile Child: Based on the Life of Sarah Bartmann.* Cambridge: Vanguard Press, 2005.

Frankel, Freddy. *Hottentot Venus: Poems of Apartheid.* Columbus, OH: Pudding House, 2003.

Fritsch, Gustav. "Die Afrikanischen Buschmanner als Urrasse." *Zeitschrift für Ethnologie* 12 (1880): 289–300.

Frost, Linda, ed. *Conjoined Twins in Black and White: The Lives of Millie-Christine McKoy and Daisy and Violet Hilton.* Madison: University of Wisconsin Press, 2009.

Fryer, Peter. *Staying Power: The History of Black People in Britain.* London: Pluto Press, 1984.

Gardiner, Allen Francis. *Narrative of a Journey to the Zoolu Country in South Africa.* London: W. Crofts, 1836.

Geoffroy-Saint-Hilaire, E., and Frédéric Cuvier. *Histoire naturelle des mammifères avec des figures originales, coloriées, dessinées d'après des animaux vivans.* Paris: Belin, 1824.

George, Mary Dorothy. *Catalogue of Political and Personal Satires in the Department of Prints and Drawings in the British Museum.* Vols. 8–10. London: British Museum, 1978.

Gerzina, Gretchen Holbrook, ed. *Black Victorians/Black Victoriana.* New Brunswick, NJ: Rutgers University Press, 2003.

Gikandi, Simon. *Slavery and the Culture of Taste.* Princeton, NJ: Princeton University Press, 2011.

Gilman, Sander L. "Black Bodies: White Bodies: Toward an Iconography of Female Sexuality in Late Nineteenth-Century Art, Medicine and Literature." *Critical Inquiry* 12, no. 1 (1985): 204–42.

———. *Difference and Pathology: Stereotypes of Sexuality, Race and Madness.* Ithaca, NY: Cornell University Press, 1985.

Golan, Daphna. *Inventing Shaka: Using History in the Construction of Zulu Nationalism.* Boulder, CO: Lynne Rienner, 1994.

Goodall, Jane R. *Performance and Evolution in the Age of Darwin: Out of the Natural Order.* London: Routledge, 2002.

Gordon, Robert J. *Picturing Bushmen: The Denver African Exhibition of 1925.* Athens: Ohio University Press, 1997.

———. "The Venal Hottentot Venus and the Great Chain of Being." *African Studies* 51, no. 2 (1992): 185–201.

Gordon-Chipembere, Natasha, ed. *Representation and Black Womanhood: The Legacy of Sarah Baartman.* New York: Palgrave Macmillan, 2011.

Gould, Stephen Jay. "The Brain Appraisers." *Science Digest*, September 1981, 86.

———. "The Hottentot Venus." *Natural History* 91, no. 10 (1982): 20–27.

————. *The Mismeasure of Man*. New York: Norton, 1981.

Grant, James. *The Metropolitan Weekly and Provincial Press*. London: G. Routledge and Sons, [1872].

Gratiolet, Pierre. *Mémoire sur les plis cérébraux de l'homme et des primates*. Paris: Bertrand, 1854.

Gray, Stephen. *Hottentot Venus and Other Poems*. Cape Town: David Philip, 1979.

Green, Jeffrey. "A Revelation in Strange Humanity: Six Congo Pygmies in Britain, 1905–1907." In Lindfors, *Africans on Stage*, 156–87.

————, ed. *Under the Imperial Carpet: Essays in Black History*. Crawley, UK: Rabbit Press, 1986.

Green, Lawrence G. *Thunder on the Blaauwberg: A Book of Rare, Strange and Curious Episodes Inspired by a Storm; Personal Experiences, Encounters with Unusual Characters, Mysteries and Legends*. Cape Town: Howard Timmins, 1966.

Hahn, Rudolf. *Schultze und Müller unter den Zulu-Kaffern: Schwank in zwei Bildern*. Berlin: A. Hofmann, 1854.

Hamilton, Carolyn. *Terrific Majesty: The Powers of Shaka Zulu and the Limits of Historical Invention*. Cambridge, MA: Harvard University Press, 1998.

Hammond, Dorothy, and Alta Jablow. *The Africa That Never Was: Four Centuries of British Writing about Africa*. New York: Twayne, 1970. Rpt., *The Myth of Africa* (New York: Library of Social Science, 1977).

Harris, Neil. *Humbug: The Art of P. T. Barnum*. Boston: Little, Brown, 1973.

History of the Bosjesmans, or Bush People: The Aborigines of Southern Africa. London: Chapman, Elcoate and Co., 1847.

History of the Earthmen, or Erdmanniges: Discovered in 1851, far up the Orange River, above the Bushmen or Bosjesman, in South Africa: a race of people, 3 ½ feet high, who burrow under ground: the first ever brought to Europe. London: R. S. Francis, [1853].

Hoad, Neville. *African Intimacies: Race, Homosexuality, and Globalization*. Minneapolis: University of Minnesota Press, 2007.

Hobson, Janell. *Venus in the Dark: Blackness and Beauty in Popular Culture*. New York: Routledge, 2005.

Holmes, Rachel. *The Hottentot Venus: The Life and Death of Saartjie Baartman: Born 1789 – Buried 2002*. London: Bloomsbury, 2007. Rpt., *African Queen: The Real Life of the Hottentot Venus* (New York: Random House, 2007).

Honour, Hugh. *The Image of the Black in Western Art: From the American Revolution to World War I*. Vol. 4, pts. 1 and 2. Houston: Menil Foundation, 1989.

Hughes, Langston. *Black Magic: A Pictorial History of Black Entertainers in America*. New York: Bonanza Books, 1967.

Isaacs, Nathaniel. *Travels and Adventures in Eastern Africa, Descriptive of the Zoolus, Their Manners, Customs, with a Sketch of Natal*. 1836. Cape Town: Struik, 1970.

Jahoda, Gustav. *Images of Savages: Ancient Roots of Modern Prejudice in Western Culture*. London: Routledge, 1999.

Johnson, William O. *All That Glitters Is Not Gold: The Olympic Games*. New York: G. P. Putnam's Sons, 1972.

Kahn, Joseph. *Catalogue of Dr. Kahn's Celebrated Anatomical Museum*. London: W. J. Golbourn, n.d.

————. *Men with Tails: Remarks on the Niam-Niams of Central Africa.* London: W. J. Golbourn, 1855.

Karp, Ivan, and Steven D. Lavine, eds. *Exhibiting Cultures: The Poetics and Politics of Human Display.* Washington, DC: Smithsonian Institution Press, 1991.

Kieran, John, and Arthur Daley. *The Story of the Olympic Games, 776 B. C. to 1972.* Philadelphia: J. B. Lippincott, 1973.

Killam, G. D. *Africa in English Fiction, 1874–1939.* Ibadan, Nigeria: Ibadan University Press, 1968.

Kirby, Percival. "A Further Note on the Hottentot Venus." *Africana Notes and News* 11, no. 5 (1954): 165–66.

————. "The Hottentot Venus." *Africana Notes and News* 6 (1949): 55–62.

————. "The 'Hottentot Venus' of the Musée de l'Homme, Paris." *South African Journal of Science* 50, no. 12 (1954): 319–22.

————. "La Vénus Hottentote en Angleterre." *Aesculape* 33, no. 1 (1952): 14–21.

————. "More about the Hottentot Venus." *Africana Notes and News* 10 (1953): 124–34.

Knott, Suzuko Mousel. "Germans and Others at the 'American Games': Problems of National and International Representation at the 1904 Olympics." In Brownell, *The 1904 Anthropology Days,* 278–300.

Knox, Robert. *The Races of Man: A Fragment.* Philadelphia: Lea and Blanchard, 1850.

Kunhardt, Dorothy Meserve. "Barnum and Brady." *Colliers,* April 29, 1944, 21.

Kunhardt, Philip B., Jr., Philip B. Kunhardt III, and Peter W. Kunhardt. *P. T. Barnum: America's Greatest Showman.* New York: Knopf, 1995.

Kunzog, John C. "Millie Christine—The Two-Headed Lady." *Hobby-Bandwagon* 6, no. 4 (1951): 3–7.

Kushner, Tony. "Selling Racism: History, Heritage, Gender and the (Re)production of Prejudice." *Patterns of Prejudice* 33, no. 4 (1999): 67–86.

Lane, Geneva. "The World's Fair as a Woman Sees It." *St. Louis Globe-Democrat,* August 18, 1904.

Latham, R. G. "Ethnological Remarks upon Some of the More Remarkable Varieties of the Human Species, Represented by Individuals Now in London." *Journal of Ethnological Science* 4 (1856): 148–50.

Lawrence, William. *Lectures on Physiology, Zoology and the Natural History of Man.* London: J. Callow, 1819.

Leland, Charles Godfrey. *Memoirs.* New York: Appleton, 1893.

Lemon, Mark. *Mr. Punch: His Origin and Career.* London: Printed by J. Wade, [1870].

Lewiston, Harry. *Freak Show Man: The Autobiography of Harry Lewiston.* Los Angeles: Holloway House, [1968].

Lichtenstein, Heinrich. *Reisen im südlichen Afrika in den Jahren 1803, 1804, 1805 und 1806.* Berlin: Salfeld, 1811–1812.

The Life History of Clicko, the Dancing Bushman of Africa. N.p.: n.d.

Lindfors, Bernth, ed. *Africans on Stage: Studies in Ethnological Show Business.* Bloomington: Indiana University Press, 1999.

————, ed. *Ira Aldridge: The African Roscius.* Rochester, NY: University of Rochester Press, 2007.

———. *Ira Aldridge: The Early Years, 1807–1833*. Rochester, NY: University of Rochester Press, 2011.

———. *Ira Aldridge: The Vagabond Years, 1833–1852*. Rochester, NY: University of Rochester Press, 2011.

Livingstone, David. *A Popular Account of Missionary Travels and Researches in South Africa*. London: John Murray, 1875.

Lucas, Charles J. P. *The Olympic Games, 1904*. St. Louis: Woodward and Tiernan, 1905.

Luschka, Hubert von. "Sur les organs génitaux externes d'une femme de race Bosjeman." *Journal de l'Anatomie et de la Physiologie* 7 (1870–71): 164–70.

Lyons, Charles H. *To Wash an Aethiop White: British Ideas about Black African Educability, 1530–1960*. New York: Teachers College Press, 1975.

Lysons, Daniel. "Collectanea; or a Collection of Advertisements and Paragraphs from the Newspapers, Relating to Various Subjects." Vols. 1 and 2, unpublished scrapbook held at the British Library (1881.b.6).

MacDonald, Joyce Green. "Acting Black: *Othello*, *Othello* Burlesques, and the Performance of Blackness." *Theater Journal* 46 (1994): 231–49.

Magubane, Zine. "Which Bodies Matter? Feminism, Poststructuralism, Race, and the Curious Theoretical Odyssey of the 'Hottentot Venus.'" *Gender and Society* 15 (2001): 816–34.

Mallon, Bill. *A Statistical Study of the 1904 Olympic Games*. Durham, NC: [Bill Mallon], 1981.

Marsh, Jan, ed. *Black Victorians: Black People in British Art, 1800–1900*. Aldershot, UK: Lund Humphries, 2005.

Marshall, Herbert, and Mildred Stock. *Ira Aldridge: The Negro Tragedian*. London: Rockliff, 1958.

Marshall, John. "On the Brain of a Bushwoman; and on the Brains of Two Idiots of European Descent." *Philosophical Transactions of the Royal Society in London* 154 (1864): 500–58.

Martell, Joanne. *Millie-Christine: Fearfully and Wonderfully Made*. Winston-Salem: John F. Blair, 2000.

Martin, David E., and Roger W. H. Gynn. *The Marathon Footrace: Performers and Performances*. Springfield, IL: Charles C. Thomas, 1979.

———. *The Olympic Marathon: The History and Drama of Sport's Most Challenging Event*. Champaign, IL: Human Kinetics, 2000.

Maseko, Zola. *The Life and Times of Sarah Baartman: "The Hottentot Venus."* New York: First Run/Icarus Films, [1998].

———. *The Return of Sara Baartman*. New York: First Run/Icarus Films, 2003.

Master, Sharad. "Sarah, Sarah: More on Sarah Bartmann and Her Equally Tragic Namesake." *Quarterly Bulletin of the National Library of South Africa* 58, no. 2 (2004): 76–86.

Mathews, Mrs. [Anne]. *Memoirs of Charles Mathews, Comedian*. Vol. 4. London: Richard Bently, 1839.

Matthews, George R. *America's First Olympics: The St. Louis Games of 1904*. Columbia: University of Missouri Press, 2005.

Mayer, Joe. *The Barnum and Bailey Show Routebook of the Season of 1888.* N.p.: n.d.

Mayhew, Athol. *A Jorum of "Punch" with Those who Helped to Brew it: Being the Early History of "The London Charivari."* London: Downey, 1895.

McCullough, Edo. *Good Old Coney Island.* New York: Charles Scribner's Sons, 1957.

McKechnie, Samuel. *Popular Entertainments through the Ages.* London: Sampson, Low, Marston, n.d.

Middleton, George. *Circus Memoirs, as Told to and Written by His Wife.* Los Angeles: George Middleton, 1913.

Miller, Mathew Smith. "Surely His Mother Mourns for Him: Africans on Exhibition in Boston and New York, 1860–61." BA Honors Thesis, Harvard College, 2011.

Millie-Christine. *The Greatest Wonder of the World: Millie Christine, The Two-Headed Lady, The Most Wonderfully Made of God's Creatures. Complete History, Together with Reports of Medical Examinations of This Marvel of Mankind. With Compliments of The Great Inter-Ocean Largest and Best Show On Earth. John B. Doris, —Proprietor. Wherein Millie Christine will hold Semi-Daily Receptions Without Charge!* N.p.: John B. Doris, [1883].

————. *History and Medical Description of the Two-Headed Girl Sold by Her Agents for Her Special Benefit, Told in "Her Own Peculiar Way" by "One of Them."* 1869. Stratford, CT: Alton Vixierbild, 1976.

Mitter, Partha. "The Hottentot Venus and Western Man: Reflections on the Construction of Beauty in the West." In *Cultural Encounters: Representing "Otherness,"* edited by Elizabeth Hallam and Brian V. Street, 35–50. London: Routledge, 2000.

Molineux, Catherine. *Faces of Perfect Ebony: Encountering Atlantic Slavery in Imperial Britain.* Cambridge, MA: Cambridge University Press, 2012.

Moore, Grace. "Reappraising Dickens's 'Noble Savage.'" *Dickensian* 98 (2002): 236–43.

Mortimer, Owen. *Speak of Me as I Am: The Story of Ira Aldridge.* Wangaratta, Australia: Owen Mortimer, 1995.

Morton, Thomas. *The Slave.* 1816. Cambridge: Chadwyck-Healey, 1996.

Netto, Priscilla. "Reclaiming the Body of the 'Hottentot': The Vision and Visuality of the Body Speaking with Vengeance in *Venus Hottentot 2002.*" *European Journal of Women's Studies* 12, no. 2 (2005): 149–63.

Nicholson, Watson. *The Struggle for a Free Stage in London.* Boston: Houghton Mifflin, 1906.

Nicoll, Allardyce. *A History of Early Nineteenth Century Drama, 1800–1850.* Cambridge: Cambridge University Press, 1930.

North, John S. *The Waterloo Directory of English Newspapers and Periodicals, 1800–1900.* Waterloo, Canada: North Waterloo Academic Press, 1997.

O'Brien, Esse Forrester. *Circus: Cinders to Sawdust.* San Antonio: Naylor, 1959.

Odell, George C. D. *Annals of the New York Stage.* New York: Columbia University Press, 1931–1942.

Parezo, Nancy J. "A 'Special Olympics': Testing Racial Strength and Endurance at the 1904 Louisiana Purchase Exposition." In Brownell, *The 1904 Anthropology Days,* 59–126.

Parks, Suzan-Lori. *Venus*. New York: Theatre Communications Group, 1990.

Parsons, Neil. "'Clicko': Franz Taaibosch, South African Bushman Entertainer in England, France, Cuba, and the United States, 1908–1940." In Lindfors, *Africans on Stage*, 203–27.

————. *Clicko: The Wild Dancing Bushman*. Auckland Park, South Africa: Jacana Media, 2009.

Patten, Robert L. *George Cruikshank's Life, Times, and Art*. Vol. 1, *1792–1835*. London: Lutterworth Press, 1992.

Peacock, Shane. "Africa Meets the Great Farini." In Lindfors, *Africans on Stage*, 85–106.

————. *The Great Farini: The High-Wire Life of William Hunt*. Toronto: Viking, 1995.

Penel, Jean Dominique. *Homo Caudatus: L'hommes à queue d'Afrique Centrale; Un avatar de l'imaginaire occidental*. Paris: SELAF, 1982.

Penny, H. Glenn, III. "Cosmopolitan Visions and Municipal Displays: Museums, Markets, and the Ethnographic Project in Germany, 1868–1914." PhD diss., University of Illinois at Urbana-Champaign, 1999.

Péron, F., and C. A. Lesueur. "Observations sur le tablier des femmes Hottentots." *Bulletin de la Société Zoologique de France* 8 (1883): 15–33.

Pickering, Michael. *Stereotyping: The Politics of Representation*. New York: Palgrave, 2001.

Pieterse, Jan Nederveen. *White on Black: Images of Africa and Blacks in Western Popular Culture*. New Haven, CT: Yale University Press, 1992.

Pilat, Oliver, and Jo Ranson. *Sodom by the Sea: An Affectionate History of Coney Island*. Garden City, NY: Garden City, 1943.

Poignant, Roslyn. *Professional Savages: Captive Lives and Western Spectacle*. New Haven, CT: Yale University Press, 2004.

"Political Periscope." *Literary Panorama: Being a Review of Books, Magazines of Variety, and Annual Register* 9 (1811): 192.

Prestney, Susie. "Inscribing the Hottentot Venus: Generating Data for Difference." In *At the Edge of International Relations: Postcolonialism, Gender and Dependency*, edited by Phillip Darby, 86–105. London: Pinter, 1997.

Prichard, James Cowles. *The Natural History of Man*. 4th ed. London: H. Baillière, 1855.

Program of the Great Barnum and London Nine United Shows. N.p.: n.p., 1885.

Qureshi, Sadiah. "Displaying Sara Baartman, the 'Hottentot Venus.'" *History of Science* 42 (2004): 233–57.

————. *Peoples on Parade: Exhibitions, Empire, and Anthropology in Nineteenth-Century Britain*. Chicago: University of Chicago Press, 2011.

Racinet, Auguste. *Le Costume Historique*. Vol. 2. Paris: Firmin-Didot, 1876.

Ragatz, Lowell Joseph. *The Fall of the Planter Class in the British Caribbean, 1763–1833: A Study in Social and Economic History*. New York: Century, 1928.

Rigby, Peter. *African Images: Racism and the End of Anthropology*. Oxford: Berg, 1996.

Ritter, Sabine. *Facetten der Sarah Baartman: Repräsentationen und Rekonstruktionen der "Hottentottenvenus."* Berlin: Lit Verlag Dr. W. Hopf, 2010.

Roberts, M. *The Whig Party, 1807–1812*. London: Macmillan, 1939.

Rothfels, Nigel T. "Bring 'em Back Alive: Carl Hagenbeck and Exotic Animal and People Trades in Germany, 1848–1914." PhD diss., Harvard University, 1994.

Ryan, James R. *Picturing Empire: Photography and the Visualization of the British Empire.* Chicago: University of Chicago Press, 1997.

Rydell, Robert W. *All the World's a Fair: Visions of Empire at American International Expositions, 1876–1916.* Chicago: University of Chicago Press, 1984.

———. "'Darkest Africa': African Shows at America's World Fairs, 1893–1940." In Lindfors, *Africans on Stage,* 135–55.

Samuelson, Meg. *Remembering the Nation, Dismembering Women? Stories of the South African Transition.* Scottsville, South Africa: University of KwaZulu-Natal Press, 2007.

Sancho, Ignatius. *Letters of the late Ignatius Sancho, an African.* Edited by Joseph Jekyll. London: J. Nichols, 1782.

Sanger, "Lord" George. *Seventy Years a Showman.* London: MacGibbon and Kie, 1910.

Saucerlips / Ubangi Savages / French Equatorial Africa / Historical Sketch — Origins — Habits and Customs. Paris: Catalogues Industriels Touly, n.d.

Schaap, Richard. *An Illustrated History of the Olympics.* New York: Knopf, 1963.

Scher, David. "Zulus and the Olympic Games." *Janus,* 1975, 12–13.

Schiebinger, Londa. *Nature's Body: Gender in the Making of Modern Science.* Boston: Beacon Press, 1993.

Schlicke, Paul. "À Beckett, Gilbert Abbott (1811–1856)." *Oxford Dictionary of National Biography.* Oxford: Oxford University Press, 2004. 1: 58–59.

Schultze, Leonhard. *Zur Kenntnis des Körpers der Hottentots und Buschmänner.* Jena: Gustav Fischer, 1928.

Scobie, Edward. *Black Britannia: A History of Blacks in Britain.* Chicago: Johnson, 1972.

Scott, James C. *Domination and the Arts of Resistance: Hidden Transcripts.* New Haven, CT: Yale University Press, 1990.

Scully, Pamela. "Peripheral Visions: Heterography and Writing the Transnational Life of Sara Baartman." In *Transnational Lives: Biographies of Global Modernity, 1700–Present,* edited by Desley Deacon, Penny Russell, and Angela Woollacott, 27–40. New York: Palgrave Macmillan, 2010.

Sexton, George. "Anatomical View of the Question of Men with Tails." In Kahn, *Men with Tails,* 5–10.

Sharpley-Whiting, T. Denean. *Black Venus: Sexualized Savages, Primal Fears, and Primitive Narratives in French.* Durham, NC: Duke University Press, 1999.

Sherwood, Robert Edmund. *Here We Are Again: Recollections of an Old Circus Clown.* Indianapolis: Bobbs-Merrill, 1926.

———. *Hold Yer Hosses!: The Elephants Are Coming.* New York: Macmillan, 1932.

Schiebinger, Londa. *Nature's Body: Gender in the Making of Modern Science.* Boston: Beacon Press, 1993.

"Show Girl — Old Style." *Solicitor's Journal* 98 (1954): 545.

Shyllon, Folarin. *Black People in Britain, 1555–1833.* London: Oxford University Press for the Institute of Race Relations, 1977.

Skotnes, Pippa, ed. *Miscast: Negotiating the Presence of the Bushmen.* Cape Town: University of Cape Town Press, 1996.

Smith, Anna H. (with additions by H. Bruce). "Still More about the Hottentot Venus." *Africana Notes and News* 26, no. 3 (1984): 95–98.

Smith, Sheila. *The Other Nation: The Poor in English Novels of the 1840s and 1850s.* Oxford: Clarendon Press, 1980.

Sòrgoni, Barbara. "'Defending the Race': The Italian Reinvention of the Hottentot Venus during Fascism." *Journal of Modern Italian Studies* 8, no. 3 (2003): 411–24.

"A South African Native's Picture of England." *Natal Journal* 2, no. 7 (1858): 126–38.

Spielmann, M. H. *The History of "Punch."* London: Cassell, 1895.

Stanaland, Peggy. "Pre-Olympic 'Anthropology Days,' 1904: An Aborted Effort to Bridge Some Cultural Gaps." In *Play as Context: 1979 Proceedings of the Association for the Study of Play*, edited by Alyce Taylor Cheska, 101–6. West Point, NY: Leisure Press, 1981.

Stanton, William. *The Leopard's Spots: Scientific Attitudes toward Race in America, 1815–59.* Chicago: University of Chicago Press, 1960.

Stepan, Nancy. *The Idea of Race in Science: Great Britain, 1800–1860.* London: Macmillan, 1982.

Stephens, John L. *Illustrated Memoir of an Eventful Expedition into Central America Resulting in the Discovery of the Idolatrous City of Iximaya, in an Unexplored Region; and the Possession of Two Remarkable Aztec Children Maximo (the boy) and Bartola (the girl). Descendants and Specimens of the Sacerdotal Caste (now nearly extinct) of the Ancient Aztec Founders of the Ruined Temple of that Country.* New York: Wyn Koop, Hallenbeck and Thomas, 1860.

Stevens, Walter B. *The Forest City: Comprising Official Photographic Views of the Universal Exposition Held in St. Louis, 1904.* St. Louis: N. D. Thompson, 1904.

Strother, Z. S. "Display of the Body Hottentot." In Lindfors, *Africans on Stage*, 1–61.

Sullivan, James E., comp. *Spalding's Official Athletic Almanach for 1905.* New York: American Sports, 1905.

Swinburne, Algernon Charles. *Studies in Prose and Poetry.* London: Chatto and Windus, 1894.

Taub, Myer, and Retnev Siocnarf. "The Hottentot Venus: An Historical Tragicomedy." Unpublished typescript workshopped for a B.A. Honours degree, School of Dramatic Art, University of the Witwatersrand, 1993.

Teel, Jay. *Sideshow Freaks and Features.* Ansted, WV: Petland Press, n.d.

Thackeray, William Makepeace. *Vanity Fair.* London: Bradbury & Evans, 1848.

Theal, George McCall, ed. *Records of the Cape Colony from May 1809 to March 1811.* Vol. 7. Cape Town: Government of the Cape Colony, 1900.

Thompson, W. C. *On the Road with a Circus.* New York: Goldman, 1903.

Thomson, Rosemarie Garland. *Extraordinary Bodies: Figuring Physical Disability in American Culture and Literature.* New York: Columbia University Press, 1997.

———, ed. *Freakery: Cultural Spectacles of the Extraordinary Body.* New York: New York University Press, 1996.

Tibballs, Geoff. *The Olympics' Strangest Moments: Extraordinary but True Stories.* London: Robson Books, 2008.

Tobias, P. V. "Saartje Baartman: Her Life, Her Remains, and the Negotiations for Their Repatriation from France to South Africa." *South African Journal of Science* 98, no. 3/4 (2002): 107–10.

Toll, Robert C. *Blacking Up: The Minstrel Show in Nineteenth-Century America.* New York: Oxford University Press, 1974.

Toole-Stott, R. *Circus and Allied Arts: A World Bibliography, 1500–1962.* Vol. 3. Derby, UK: Harpur, 1962.

Topinard, M. "Étude sur les Hottentots observés au Jardin d'Acclimatation." *Bulletin de la Sociéte de Médecine Pratique de Paris* (1888): 657–63.

Traill, Anthony. "The Languages of the Bushmen." In *The Bushmen: San Hunters and Herders of Southern Africa*, edited by Phillip V. Tobias, 137–47. Cape Town: Human and Rousseau, 1978.

Tromp, Marlene, ed. *Victorian Freaks: The Social Context of Freakery in Britain.* Columbus: Ohio State University Press, 1996.

Turner, John M. *Victorian Arena: The Performers: A Dictionary of British Circus Biography.* 2 vols. Formby, UK: Lingdales Press, 1995 and 2000.

Tyler, J. S. *The Bosjesmans. A Lecture on the Mental, Moral, and Physical Attributes of the Bush Men. With Anecdotes by Their Guardian.* Leeds: C. A. Wilson, [1847].

Upham, Mansell. "From the Venus Sickness to the Hottentot Venus: Saartje Baartman and the Three Men in Her Life: Alexander Dunlop, Hendrik Caesar and Jean Riaux." *Quarterly Bulletin of the National Library of South Africa* 61, no. 1 (2007): 9–22.

van der Merwe, Floris J. G. "Africa's First Encounter with the Olympic Games in . . . 1904." *Journal of Olympic History* 7, no. 2 (1999): 29–34.

Verneau, R. "Le centième anniversaire de la mort de Sarah Bartmann." *L'Anthropologie* 27 (1916): 178.

Vinson, Robert Trent, and Robert Edgar. "Zulus Abroad: Cultural Representations and Educational Experiences of Zulus in America, 1880–1945." *Journal of Southern African Studies* 33, no. 1 (2007): 43–62.

Vlasopolos, Anca. "Venus Live! Sarah Bartmann, the Hottentot Venus, Re-Membered." *Mosaic* 33, no. 4 (2000): 129–43.

von Luschka, Hubert. *Die Anatomie des Menschen in Rücksicht auf die Bedürfnisse der praktischen Heilkunde: 2,2 Die Anatomie des menschlichen Beckens.* Tübingen: Laupp, 1864.

Walker, Thomas (Whimsical). *From Sawdust to Windsor Castle.* London: Stanley Paul, 1922.

Wallace, Irving. *The Fabulous Showman: The Life and Times of P. T. Barnum.* New York: Knopf, 1959.

Walvin, James. *Black and White: The Negro and English Society, 1555–1945.* London: Allen Lane, Penguin Press, 1973.

Waters, Hazel. "Ira Aldridge and the Battlefield of Race." *Race & Class* 45, no. 1 (2003): 5.

———. *Racism on the Victorian Stage: Representation of Slavery and the British Character.* Cambridge: Cambridge University Press, 2007.

White, Charles. *An Account of the Regular Gradation in Man and in Different Animals and Vegetables.* London: C. Dilly, 1799.

White, Hayden, "The Forms of Wildness: Archaeology of an Idea." In Dudley and Novak, *The Wild Man Within*, 3–38.

Willis, Deborah, ed. *Black Venus 2010: They Called Her "Hottentot."* Philadelphia: Temple University Press, 2010.

Wilmeth, Don B. *The Language of American Popular Entertainment: A Glossary of Argot, Slang, and Terminology.* Westport, CT: Greenwood, 1981.

Wiss, Rosemary. "Lipreading: Remembering Saartjie Baartman." *Australian Journal of Anthropology* 5, nos. 1–2 (1994): 11–40.

Wood, J. G. "Dime Museums as Seen from a Naturalist's Standpoint." *Atlantic Monthly* 55 (June 1885): 759–65.

Wood, Marcus. *Radical Satire and Print Culture, 1790–1822.* Oxford: Clarendon Press, 1994.

Wylie, Dan. *Savage Delight: White Myths of Shaka.* Pietermaritzburg, South Africa: University of Natal Press, 2000.

Wymans, Jeffries. "Observations on the Skeleton of a Hottentot." *Anthropological Review* 3 (1865): 333.

Youé, Chris. "Sara Baartman: Inspection/Dissection/Resurrection." *Canadian Journal of African Studies* 41, no. 3 (2007): 559–67.

Young, Jean. "The Re-Objectification and Re-Commodification of Saartjie Baartman in Suzan-Lori Parks's *Venus.*" *African American Review* 31, no. 4 (1997): 699–708.

Yunge, E. F. *Memoirs, 1843–1863.* St. Petersburg: Sphinx 1913. In Russian.

Zimmerman, Andrew. *Anthropology and Antihumanism in Imperial Germany.* Chicago: University of Chicago Press, 2001.

"Zip Claims Sole Right to Name: Circus Man seeks Legal Authority to Halt Use of Cognomen for Pet Monkey." *Sun* (London), April 7, 1926.

"Zip, Oldest Freak, Is Ill in Hospital." *New York Times*, April 8, 1926.

"Zip, Dean of Freak Folk, Is Better." *New York Times*, April 11, 1926.

Index

Page numbers in italics indicate illustrations.

Abbott, Mr., 66
à Beckett, Gilbert Abbott, 49–52, 56–57, 72, 202n7
Aberdeen, 52, 55; Aberdeen University Library, 199n27, 218n28
abolition, 17, 35, 73, 152
abolitionists, 6, 42, 150; campaign of, 73; exhibitors as, 132, 144, 151; leaders of, 17, 21, 23, 212n24; propaganda of, 36; satire on, 201n19
Aborigines, 28
Abrahams, Yvette, 185
Abyssinia, 125
Academy of Sciences, Paris, 125
Act for the Abolition of Slavery throughout the British Empire, 73
actors, 8, 47–74, 95–96, 196, 202n6
Afghans, 175
African Americans, 8, 47–74, 88, 169, 174, 180
African Institution, 17, 20–23, 25, 27
African National Congress, 31
African Roscius, 49–50, 53–55, 57, *59*, 63–64, 68, 70–74

African Theatre, 48
African Tragedian, 48–49, 72
African Twins, 131–57, *136*, *139*, *145*, *153*
Agassiz, Louis, 126
Ahmee, Tamee, 171, 174
Ainus, 170, 182
Alabam, 164
albinos, 146, 175
Alcatraz Island, 211n17
Aldridge, Ira, 8, 47–74, *54*, *59*, *69*
Al G. Barnes circus, 159, 164, 211n17
Algerian Arab, 175
Alighieri, Dante, 71
Aliwal South, 177
Amazons, 158
Amazulu Princess, *165*, 213–14n13
America, 142, 146–49, 152, 167; circus in, 163–65, 174; civil war in, 132; fairs in, 132; geography of, 144; imagination in, 171; music in, 88, 103; racism in, 7, 176, 210n28; show business in, 157
American Indians, 97, 180–81
American Museum, 158, 167, 192

239

Ames, Eric, 219n32
Anson County, North Carolina, 151
Anthropological Games, 180–84
Anthropology Department, St. Louis World's
   Fair, 180, 183
anthropophagi, 125
antiapartheid, 109
antislavery, 34
apes: chattering of, 208n30; considered human
   ancestors, 28, 75; resemblance of Africans
   to, 3–4, 159, 169, 180, 218n30
Aquarial and Zoölogical Gardens, Boston, 192
Arabs, 124, 127, 130, 175
Arada, 175
Athens, 177, 180
Atlantic Ocean, 135
Attorney General, 20, 23
audience: behavior of, 15, 186–87, 189; British,
   78, 88, 135–38, 195–96; circus, 159, 162,
   166, 175; at Covent Garden Theatre, 47,
   49, 57–72; London, 55, 91–109; provincial,
   56, 88, 137–38, 146; at Royal Coburg
   Theatre, 58; Shakespearean, 8, 57–72
Australia, 28, 175, 219n32
Azande. *See* Niam-Niams
Aztec Lilliputians, 5, 91, *105*, 138, 175, 212n6
Aztecs, 175

Baartman, Sartjee ("The Hottentot Venus"), 5,
   11–46, *12, 13, 18, 29, 30, 32, 38, 39, 41, 43,*
   83, 158–59, 185–87, 189, 192, 196, 198n1
Babington, Thomas Gisborne, 17, 19, 198–99n13
baboons, 11, 82–83, 88
ballad of "the Hottentot Ladie and her lawful
   Knight," 24–26, 199n24
Baltimore, 174
Barnes, Al G., 159, 164, 211n17
Barnum, P. T., 159–62, 165–67, 169–71, 174–75,
   190, 192
Barnum's American Museum, 192, 208–9n39
Bartholomew Fair, 68
Basutos, 177
Bath, 55
Batwa, 158
Bedford Hotel, London, 140, 144
Belfast, 52
Belgian Congo, 159, 176

Belgium, 5, 93, 192
Benga, Ota, 158, 180, 182, 190, *191*
Bengal, 124
Berlin, 119, 121, 174, 192, 217n10
Bickersteth, B., 137
Birmingham, 78, 81, 146, 148–49, 154, 186
Bishop, J. G. R., 76
Blackburn, Thomas, 137
Blackmar, Luke, 146
black minstrels, 195
Blood River, South Africa, 90
Boers, 18, 85, 90, 177
Boer War Exhibition, 177, 190
Bogdan, Robert, 190
Bonaparte, Napoleon, 83
Borneo, 124, 164–65, 175
Bosjesmans ("Bushmen"), 5, 76–88, *77, 79, 80,*
   84, 158, 186–87, 189, 192, 195, 207n8
Boston, 135, 192; Society of Natural History, 192
Boswell, James, 125
Botocudoes, 175
Bound Brook, New Jersey, 190
Bow-knuckle, 165
Bow Street Police Court, 143
Brighton, 55
Bristol, 171
Britain: British Isles, 5, 76, 83, 111, 132, 143, 146;
   empire of, 22, 73, 142; government of, 6,
   34, 63, 73, 89–90, 164; justice in, 26–27,
   152, 189; people of, 6, 24, 44, 46, 51, 75,
   78, 81, 88, 90, 111, 128, 130, 162, 177; press
   in, 73–74, 125, 135, 144; racism in, 18–20,
   76–88; territories of, 27, 34, 73; theater in,
   47, 53, 62, 93
Broad Bottoms, 36–37, 40
Broadway, 171
Broca, Paul, 28
Broderip, Mr., 188–89
Bronx, 165; Bronx Zoo, 158, 190, 216n15
Brower, Mr., 132–35
brutes, 3, 46, 78, 82
Bryan, J., 169
Buckingham Palace, 91
Buddhist priests, 175
Bullock, William, 12, 19–20
Bullock's Museum, 12, 42
bunk, 165–66

Burke and Hare scandal, 207n8
Burma, 175, 219n32
Burnett, James (Lord Monboddo), 125
Bushmen, 28, 76–88, 97–98, 186

Caffre. *See* Kaffir/Kafir
Caldecott, A. T., 89–93, 97
Caldecott, Charles Henry, 89–90, 92–93, 98–104, 187–89
Caledon, Lord, 16, 19, 198–99n13
Camberwell, 186
Camden, 163
Cameroon, 219n32
Canada, 60, 219n32
cannibals, 124, 127–28, 130, 159, 176, 210n28, 211n16
Cape Colony, 76, 177
Cape of Good Hope, 16, 18
Caribbean, 34, 138
caricatures, 7, 12, 34–46, *45*, 50, *195*
Carlyle, Thomas, 209–10n16
cartoons, 24, 35–36
Carvajal, Felix, 177
Catlin, George, 83
Caucasians, 4
Central America, 91
Cetshwayo/Cetewayo, 162, 164, 213–14n13
Cezar, Hendric, 12, 14–16, 18–20, 23, 27, 185–86, 189, 200–201n7
Chaka. *See* Shaka
Charlotte, North Carolina, 150–51, 212n24
Cheraw, South Carolina, 212–13n25
Chicago, 158
Chile, 219n32
chimpanzees, 82, 88
Chinese, 124
Chinese Museum, 91, 93
choirs, South African, 190
Church Missionary Society, 17
Circassians, 124
circus, 158–75, *161*
Circus World Museum, 214n20
civil war, American, 132, 154, 157
Clicko. *See* Taaibosch, Franz
clicks, 81–85
Colonial Office, Natal, 90
colonization, 34

Colored Orphan Asylum, New York, 158
Columbus County, North Carolina, 131
comparative anatomy, 5
Coney Island, 170–71, 190
Congo, 159, 183
Congo River, 138
Congress of Curious People, 171, 175
Conolly, John, 86, 130
Constantinople, 125–26
Cook, Frank, 190
Cook, James, 214n26
Copts, 124
Corbey, Raymond, 183, 218n30
counterfeits, 83, 174
Court of Admiralty, 147
Covent Garden Theatre, 47–74, *54*, *59*, 202n23
Crais, Clifton, 33, 199n21, 200–201n7
Crito, 55
Croker, John Wilson, 50
Cronje, Piet, 177
Croydon, 88
Cruikshank, George, 42, 44, 195, *195*, 201n19
Cuba, 137–38, 140, 142, 177, 190
Currier and Ives, 214n27
customs, 91–92, 98–99, 106, 124, 188
Cutting, James, 192
Cuvier, Baron Georges, 4–5, 11, 28, 46, 159, 192
Cyprus, 61

Dahomey, 158, 165
dancers, 35, 41, 108, 175, 190
Dark Continent, 5, 107, 171
Darwin, Charles Robert, 3, 159
Davis, Janet, 213n10
Debrunner, Hans Werner, 158
de Castelneau, Francis, 128, 211n15
de Coubertin, Baron Pierre, 184
Delagoa Bay, 116
Denver African Expedition, 207n7
despotism, 99
Devizes, 186
Dickens, Charles, 83–84, 89–111, 208n30, 209–10n16; *Bleak House*, 97, 208n30; *A Child's History of England*, 97; *Household Words*, 97, 208n30
Diddear, Charles Bannister, 61
dime museums, 132, 164

Dingane, 90, 93

Disney, Walt, 171

Djelabs, 127

Doris, John B., 132–35, 146, 149, 152, 211–12n1

Dowton, William, 62

Dr. Kahn's Celebrated Anatomical Museum, 123–30

drummer, 22, 25, 110

Drury Lane Theatre, 48–49, 52–53, 57, 67–68, 143–44

Du Barry, Captain, 159

Dublin, 55, 82

du Couret, Louis, 125, 127–28, 211n15

Duke of Clarence, 40–42, *41*

Dundee, 140–44

Dunlop, Alexander, 12, 14, 19–23, 27

Durban, 89–90, 115

Dutch, 18–22, 26, 85, 185, 187

dwarfs, 16, 22, 91, 195

Earl of Liverpool, 198–99n13

Earls Court, 190

Earthmen, 5, 85–88, *86*, *87*, 91, 102, *105*, 158, 189–90, 195, 208–9n39

East India Nautch Dancing Girls, 175

Edgar, Robert, 210n28, 213n11

Edinburgh, 52, 55

Egan, Pierce, 48

Egypt, 53, 124

Egyptian Hall, 77, *80*, 144, *145*, 214n26

Eldon, Lord Chancellor, 40

elephant, 103, 110, 119, 127

Elias, 150

Ellenborough, Lord, 21, 23, 198–99n13

emancipation, 35–36, 148, 151, 153; Emancipation Act, 6; Emancipation Proclamation, 157

England: black population in, 4–5; caricatures in, 34–46, 56; court cases in, 17–26, 147–49, 185–89; exhibitions in, 10–28, 75–130, 135–40, 144–49, 171, 174; Georgian, 12; press in, 14–17, 137–38; theater in, 47–74

English language: fluency in, 88; foreign accent in, 48, 138; King's, 48; performance in, 88; phonology, 81; translation, 22, 111–22, 187

Enlightenment, 6

Eskimos, 28

Estevano, Don Pedro, 137

Ethiopia, 124, 219n32

ethnocentrism, 71

ethnology, 6, 31, 91, 192; exhibitions, 7–8, 93, 164, 175, 218–19n32; science of, 73, 78, 124, 127; and Society of London, 86, 91, 130

Europe: attitudes in, 78, 83, 85–86, 107, 130, 162; capitals of, 91; civilization of, 106, 110, 184; colonial policy of, 85; exhibitions in, 124, 131, 152, 158, 192; norms in, 107

Eve, 28

exploration, 6–7, 125–26, 130

expositions, 120

fairs, 5, 132, 158, 183

Faku, 118

Far East, 175

Farini, G. A., 213n3

Fenelon, François de Salignac de la Mothe, 83

Ferguson's Extraordinary Exhibition of Nature and Art and Grand Promenade, 199n27

Figaro (Paris), 50

Figaro in London, 49–51, 53, 55–56, 66, 70–73, 202n7

Fiji, 164

Flora, 85, 88, 190, 192, 208–9n39

Flower, W. H., 192

flu, 67–68, 72, 205n91

folksong, 49

Fores (publisher), 39

Formosa, 124

France, 5, 11, 28, 31, 93, 113, 119, 125, 144, 167, 192; actors in, 51–52; anatomical scholarship in, 218n27; artists in, 46; attitudes in, 27; caricatures in, 44, *45*, 46; and Equatorial Africa, 159; government of, 125; language of, 60, 81; media in, 125–26, 128, 130; money in, 121; National Assembly of, 31; Olympiad in, 176; performers in, 51; spectators in, 44, 46; theater in, 28

fraud, 16, 48, 149–50, 162, 166, 174, 212n6

freaks, 5, 8, 39, 94–95, 140, 158, *160*, 174, 195

Freetown, Sierra Leone, 17

Gallery of all Nations, 124, 128
Gambia, 169
Gambia River, 167
Gamtoos River, 10, 33
Garcia, Mr., 179
Gardiner, Captain Allen Francis, 100
Garrick, David, 55
Garrick Club, 54, 66
Gasalee, Mr., 23
George, Mary Dorothy, 37, 39, 41, 44
Georgian era, 34–36, 46
Germany, 5, 93, 113, 192, 217n10, 218–19n32
Ghilanes, 127
giants, 16, 23, 165, 175, 180, 195
Gikandi, Simon, 8
Glasgow, 52, 82, 146
Gordon, Robert J., 207n7
Gordon-Chipembere, Natasha, 33
gorillas, 167
Gould, Augustus A., 126
Gratiolet, Louis Pierre, 28
Great Barnum and London Nine United Shows, 175
Great Chain of Being, 3–4, 46
Greatest Show on Earth, 159
Great Inter-Ocean Largest and Best Show on Earth (John B. Doris), 132
Great Paris Hippodrome, Chicago, 213–14n13
Great Trek, 90
Greece, 177
Greenland, 219n32
Grenville, Lord William Wyndham, 36–40, *38*, 46
Guatemalans, 175
Guitard, Arend Jacob, 22
Gulf of Bengal, 124
Gulf of Benin, 126
Gulliver, Captain, 127
Gynn, Roger W. H., 179

habeas corpus, 20, 25, 142, 147
Hagenbeck, Carl, Jr., 218–19n32
Hammond, Dorothy, 6
Handel, George Frideric, 203n24
Hankey, 33
Hans, Yousouf, 183

Harris, R. W., 177, 179
Harvey, Miss, 39, *39*
Haymarket Theatre, 67–68
Heath, William, 37, 39–40, 42
Hertzberg circus collection, 218n18
Hicks, Thomas J., 179
Hindoos, 124, 175
Holland, 19
Holmes, Rachel, 33
homo sapiens, 3, 46, 76
Honour, Hugh, 8
Hottentots, 11, 75, 190, 192–93, *193*
Hottentot Venus. *See* Baartman, Sartjee
"The Hottentot Venus, or Harlequin in Africa," 27
Humanitas, 16–17, 198n8
human rights, 7, 75, 148, 189
humbug, 56, 98, 166–67, 174–75
Hyde Park, 28
Hyde Park Corner, 91, 93–94, 98, 103, 109, 187

India, 124, 219n32
Indians, American, 97, 174–75, 180–81, 184
Indian Venus, 175
Inman, Thomas, 137
Ipi-Tombi, 109
Ireland, 5, 16–17, 164, 171, 192; election in, 106; House of Commons, 106
Isaacs, Nathaniel, 99–100
Isandlwana, 164
Islam, 128, 159
"The Israelites in Egypt; or the Passage of the Red Sea," 53
Italian Opera House, 51, 67

Jablow, Alta, 6
Jackson, Bill, 162
Jamaica, 142
Jantjes, Steaurma, 190, 192–93, *193*
jazz opera, 107
Jerrold, Douglas: *Nell Gwynne*, 52
Johannesburg, 107
John Bull, 78
Johnson, William Henry (Zip, the "What-Is-It?") 167–76, *168*, *169*, *172*, *173*, 190, 196
jokes, 24, 35, 50, 167

Kaffir/Kafir, 89–110, 166, *166*, 175, 180, 183, 187–89, 192, 195

Kaffraria, 10

Kahn, Dr. Joseph, 123–30

Kean, Charles, 52–53, 202n19

Kean, Edmund, 48, 52–53, 55, 62, 64

Keene, Mr. (Ira Aldridge), 48, 55, 63–64, 70, 72

Kemble, John Philip, 55, 62, 64

Kemble, Stephen, 55, 62, 64

Khoi/Khoisan, 36, 83

kidnapping, 133–34, 140–43, 152

kid show, 159

"Kie" show, 165

King George III, 36

King Kong, 107–9

Knightsbridge, 187

Knox, Robert, 95, 207n8

Kwa Zulu, 109

Labrador, 219n32

Lacy, Michael Rophino, 203n24

Lake Chad, 159

Lambert, Mr., 16

Lambry (kingdom), 124

Lancaster, 49, 56

Lapland, 124, 219n32

Laporte, Pierre, 51–53, 57, 67, 70, 202n19, 203n27

Larcher, Chief, 189

Lawrence, Sir William, 4

Le Blanc, Justice, 20

Leech, John, 97

Leeds, 135

Lentauw. *See* Tau, Len

Leopard Children, 175

leopards, 102–4

Lewis, Frederick Christian, 37, 40, 42, 200–201n7

Lewis, Thomas, 137

Lichtenstein, Dr. Heinrich, 78

Lincolnton, North Carolina, 212n24

Linnaeus, Carolus, 124

Liverpool, 76, 81, 135, 137–40, 146, 148, 174

Liverpool Museum, 19

Livingstone, David, 83

Lloyd, James, 164

London, 8, 35–39, 44, 47–74, 89–130, 138, 162, 175, 187, 192, 196; black population in, 4–5; court cases in, 10–28, 187–89; exhibitions in, 85–86, 135, 140, 143–44; media, 79–80, 82–83, 140

Lord Temple, 40

Louisiana Purchase, 176

Lucas, Charles J. P., 179

lusus naturae, 131

Macaulay, Zachary, 17, 19–20, 42, 198n8, 199n21

Macintyre, P., 137

Macready, William Charles, 62

Madagascar, 158

Madison Square Garden, 162

Maginley, Dr., 137

Mandela, Nelson, 31

Mangos/Manyos, 187–89, 217n8

Manifold, W. Wright, 137

man monkey, 167, 195

Mansfield, Lord William Murray, 142

Mansion House, Charlotte, North Carolina, 150

manumission, 138, 144, 148, 151, 154, 157

marathon, 176–84, *178*

Marquis of Buckingham, 40

Marsh, Jan, 8

Marshall, Charles, 91, 93, 95

Marshall, Herbert, 201n3

Marshall, John, 28

Martell, Joanna, 212n1

Martin, David E., 179

Martinus, 85–88

Masaniello, 52

Mashaini, Jan, *178*, 215n2

Massachusetts, 179

Mathews, Charles, the Elder, 48–49, 72

Mbeki, Thabo, 33

McCoy/McKoy, Alexander, 131–34

McCoy/[McKoy], Jacob, 131, 134

McCoy/[McKoy], Monemia, 131–35, 146–49, 151–54

McGee, W. F., 183

Mecca, 125, 128, 130

melodrama, 48, 52, 62

midgets, 175

Millar, William, 135, 137–38, 140–44, 149–50

Millie-Christine, 131–57, *155*, *156*, 175, 189, 211–12n1

Milton, John, 83

missing link, 3, 46, 75, 159, 165, 167, 170, 195

missionaries, 111
Missionary Society, 16–17
Mohammedans, 175
Molineux, Catherine, 8
Mongolia, 219n32
Monkey House, Bronx Zoo, 158
monkeys, 11, 61, 83, 88, 119, 126
Montague, Lady, 50
Moojen, George, 22
Moore, Grace, 208n30, 209–10n16
Moors, 47, 53, 55, 57–58, 60–61, 72, 175
Mortimer, Owen, 201n3
Moung-Bok, 175
Mpande, 90, 93, 118
mud fight, 183, 216n18
mulattos, 28, 58, 171
Müller, Mr., 193–94
Mungo, 57, 67, 69–70
Murie, James, 192
Museé de l'Homme, 11, 31, 158
Museum of Natural History, Vienna, 158
musicians, 35, 42

Natal, 85, 89–91, 95, 99, 111–12, 114, 120, 122, 187–88
Negritos, 181
Neptune, 40–41
New Amsterdam Theatre, 171
Newark, New Jersey, 135
New City Theatre, 72
New Jersey, 135, 171
New Orleans, 133, 135, 140, 152
Newton, Isaac, 83
New World, 5, 34, 47, 132
New York, 134–35, 137, 140, 148, 158, 171, 192, 196; exhibitions in, 158; performances in, 107, 109, 171, 196; theater in, 48–49
New Zealand, 57
Niam-Niams (Azande), 123–30, *129*, 211n16
Nicobar Islands, 124
Niger, 49, 55–56, 66, 70
"Nig show," 159
noble savage, 83, 97–107, 208n30
non-Western peoples, 3, 7–8, 33, 107, 175, 180, 184
North Africans, 217n10
North America, 34, 90, 124, 132, 138, 144, 190

North Carolina, 131, 133, 135, 137, 148, 150, 152–53, 157
Norway, 219n32
Nova Scotia, 17
Nubians, 175

Oceania, 175
O'Donnell, John, 137
"Ojibbeways," 83, 98, 174
Olympic Games, 176–84, *178*
Oriental Society and Geographical Society, Paris, 125
Orphan Court, Philadelphia, 144, 149

Padlock, The, 67, *69*
Paganini, Niccolò, 51
Panda. *See* Mpande
pantomime, 17, 52, 95, 98
paradoxes, 7, 175
Paris: exhibitions in, 5, 27–28, 158; media in, 50; Olympiad in, 176; performances in, 27–28; scientists in, 11, 125–26, 192; Scots guards in, 44; size of, 119
Parkinson, Robert, 214n20
Parliament, 37, 40, 73
parody, 9, 183
Parsons, Neil, 213n7, 217n22
Patagonians, 124, 175, 180–81
Peabody Museum of Archaeology and Ethnology, 192–93
Pennsylvania, 138, 142–44
Perceval, Spencer, 36, 40
Philadelphia, 134–35, 138, 144, 146, 148–50
Philippines, 124, 180–81
photography, 7
Piccadilly, 10, 17, 36, 123, 144, 146
Pickering, Michael, 4, 107
Pietermaritzburg, 89, 111, 116
Pieterse, Jan Nederveen, 8
pinheads, 195
Planché, James Robinson: "Reputation; or the State Secret," 52
poet-laureate, 103
Polhill, Captain, 49, 52
Polo, Marco, 124
popular literature, 6
Port Elizabeth, 76

Port Natal, 85, 95, 187–88
Portugal, 171
"Possum Up a Gum Tree," 49
prejudice, 35, 63, 66, 68, 81, 102, 209–10n16
Prichard, James Cowles, 81
Prince of Wales, 36
Prince Regent, 36, 42
Princess's Theatre, 52
Princes Theatre, 107
prodigies, 164, 175
propaganda, 36
prostitution, 27
providence, 63, 68
Prussia, 5, 93, 113, 119, 192
pseudo-Africans, 8, *163*
pseudo-Zulus, *163*, 164, 195
Ptolemy, 124
Pygmies, 85, 158, 175, 180–84, *181*, *182*, *191*, 196, 216n18
pygopagus symmetros, 131–32

Quebec, 137, 140
Queen Elizabeth, 143
Queen's Hall, Liverpool, 138
Queen Victoria, 28, 91, 118, 162

race: characteristics of, 28; experts on, 28, 106, 110, 124, 126–27, 130; human, 57; individuals representing, 10, 31, 36, 46, 78, 82, 85–86, 112, 121, 167, 177; theories of, 4–5, 184
racism, 5–6, 72, 106, 110
Ragatz, Lowell Joseph, 73–74
Red Sea, 130
Retief, Piet, 90
Ridsdale, Miss, 39, *39*
Rigby, Peter, 197n1
Ringling Bros. and Barnum & Bailey Circus, 159, *160*, 190
Rio, Orio, 171, 174
Romantic age, 6, 12; thought, 106
romantic myth, 83, 97
Rossini, Gioacchino Antonio, 203n24
Rowlandson, Thomas, 42
Royal Aquarium, 213n3
Royal Coburg Theatre, 36, 58
Royal College of Surgeons Museum, 192

royal family, 42, 49, 99–100, 118, 200–201n7
Royal Olympic Theatre, 36
Royal Pavilion Theatre, 36, 72
Royal Society, 28
Royalty Theatre, 36, 204n71
Russia, 42, 117, 219n32
Ryder, Richard, 40

Sadler's Wells Theatre, 48, 68
Sahara, 46, 85, 175
Sami, 219n32
Samoa, 219n32
San, 5, 76–88. *See also* Bosjesmans; Earthmen
Sanger, George, 171, 174
satire, 35, 37, 39, 42, 50, 56
"savages": as athletes, 183–84; behavior of, 186–89; caricatures of, 37, 78, 128; dish-lipped, 159; fraudulent, 162, 164, 167–71, 174–75, 190; ignobility of, 97–110; language of, 81–82; place of, 7, 106; scientific examinations of, 192
Savage South Africa spectacle, 190
scandal, 27
Schultze, Mr., 93–94
Scotland, 5, 17, 44, *45*, 52, 125, 140, 143–44, 146–47, 192, 212–13n25
Scott, Freeman, 149
Scott, James C., 187
Scully, Pamela, 33, 199n21, 200–201n7
Secretary of State for the Colonies, 90
Selma, 134
Senegal, 47–48, 53, 57–58, 67, 73
Senzangakhona, 93
servants, 4, 35, 76
settlers, 34, 90
Sexton, George, 124–26, 128
Seymour, Richard, 50
Shaka, 90, 93, 97, 118–19, 209n2
Shakespeare, 8, 47, 49, 60, 62–63, 138; *Hamlet*, 49; *King Lear*, 65; *King Richard III*, 49; *Macbeth*, 109; *Merchant of Venice*, 53, 202n23; *Othello*, 8, 47, 49, 52–54, 57–59, 61–65, 67–70, 72–73, 108, 112, 202n23
Sheffield, 146
Shepstone, J., 180
Sheridan, Richard Brinsley, 37, 40
Sherwood, Bob, 165

Siamese, 175; twins, 131–57
sideshows, 159, 162, 164, 174, 180, 195
Sierra Leone, 17
Singhalese, 175
Sioux, 175
slavers, 113, 127, 146, 148, 151, 154, 206n108, 212–13n25
slavery: abolition of, 15, 34, 73–74; in New World, 34–35, 135, 137, 212–13n25; responses to, 11, 6, 8, 35, 143–44, 152, 189
slaves: attitudes toward, 6, 34–36, 128, 130, 141–44; manumission of, 138, 144, 148, 151, 154, 157; as performers, 15, 185–86; trafficking in, 90; in United States, 131–32, 135, 148–52, 154, 157
Smith, E. T., 143–44
Smith, G. B., 204n71
Smith, Joseph P., 133–35, 143, 146–49, 151–52, 154, 212–13n25
Smith, Mrs. Joseph P., 154, 157
Smith, Sheila, 209–10n16
snakes, 78, 110, 119–20
Society of Friends, 104
Society of West India Planters and Merchants, 74, 206n108
soldiers, 4, 117–18
Solly, S., 22
Somalia, 219n32
Somersett, James, 142–43
sorcery, 102
soul, 75, 165
South Africa: performers from, 10–46, 75–122, 162–66, 169, 176–96
South America, 175
speech, 66, 75–88, 104, 171
Spring Gardens, 34
Sri Lanka, 219n32
St. George's Gallery, 91, 94, 98, 104, 187
St. Louis, 176–84, 181, 182, 191
Stamford, 146
Stepan, Nancy, 5
stereotypes, 4, 6, 8, 35, 48, 72, 107, 175
Stock, Mildred, 201n3
Stowe, Harriet Beecher, 141, 209–10n16; *Uncle Tom's Cabin*, 141
Sudan, 219n32
Sumatra, 124

Surrey Theatre, 72
Swazis, 177
Swinburne, Algernon Charles, 28
Syrians, 175, 180

Taaibosch, Franz ("Clicko"), 159, 160, 190, 196
Table Bay, 90
Tamboo, Africa, 148
Tau, Len, 178, 215n2
taxes, 101, 113
Taylor, Samuel, 150
Texas, 133
Thackeray, William Makepeace, 28
Thames tunnel, 114
Théâtre de Vaudeville, Paris, 16
Theatre Royal, Liverpool, 138, 139
Thistle Hall, Dundee, 140
Thompson, William, 135, 137–38, 140–52, 212n24
Tibbals, Howard, 212n1
Timbuktoo, 40, 44
Todars, 175
Tom Thumb, 5
Toneel Museum, Amsterdam, 218n30
Tree, Ellen, 63–65
Tripoli, 124
troglodytes, 5, 85
Tshabalala, Junior, 110
Tshandalas, 175
Tugela River, South Africa, 90
Two-Headed Nightingale. *See* Millie-Christine
Tyler, J. S., 186–87, 207n8
Tylney-Long, Miss, 40

Ubangis, 159, 161, 213n10
Uj-Magr Gypsies, 175
Umabatha, 109
Underhill, Mr., 146–49, 152
United African Twins. *See* Millie-Christine
United States of America, 131–35, 137–38, 140–42, 150–57; abolition in, 35; black theater in, 48–49; circus in, 158–75; kidnapping in, 133–34, 140, 152; Olympics in, 176–84
University of Amsterdam, 218n30

Van Wageninge, Peter, 17, 19, 198–99n13
Venice, 53

Venus de Medici, 30–31, *30*
La Vénus hottentote, ou haine aux Françaises, 28
Vessula, Kaitus, 199n27, 218n28
Vestal, T. A., 134–35, 146
Viljoen, Ben, 177
Vinson, Robert Trent, 210n28, 213n11
Virginia, 142
Völkerschau, 219n32
vulgarity, 36, 60, 71–72, 124

Wadesboro, North Carolina, 133
Wales, 5, 36
Wallack, Henry, 62–66
Wallack, James, 57
Walvin, James, 197n11
warriors, 5, 99, 104, 109, 159, 162
Waterloo, 42, 44
W. C. Coup's United Monster Show, 213–14n13
Wellesley, Richard Colley, 40
West Africa, 95
West End, London, 67, 72
Western world, 7–9, 27, 33, 110, 170, 183–84, 189, 196
West Indies, 28, 35, 58, 74, 90, 206n108
"What-Is-It?." *See* Johnson, William Henry
Whig, 36, 50
White, Captain O. K., 190
White, Charles, 3

Whiteville, North Carolina, 131
Whitman, Walt, 28
Wigley's Rooms, 39
"wild man," 164–65, 170, 174, 195, 214n24
Williams, Charles, 40, 42
witchcraft, 95, 102, 120
Witte Museum, San Antonio, 218n18
World's Fair, 176–77, 180–83, *181, 182, 191,* 196
Wright, Thomas, 126
Wyman, Jeffries, 192

Yahoos, 127
Yamasani. *See* Mashaini, Jan
Yankees, 138, 151
Yonkers, 165
Yucatan Peninsula, 164

Zanga, 55, 67, 70
Zip. *See* Johnson, William Henry
zoos, 91, 158, 175, 190
zoological gardens, 104, 192, 218–19n32
Zulu Kaffirs, 89–110, *92, 94, 96, 105, 108,* 175, 187–89, 192, *194,* 195
Zululand, 5, 83, 89–122, 158–59, 162–65, 175, 177, 183, 187–89, 192, 195
Zulu musicals, 109–10
Zulu ticket, 164

AFRICA AND THE DIASPORA

History, Politics, Culture

SERIES EDITORS

Thomas Spear
Neil Kodesh
Tejumola Olaniyan
Michael G. Schatzberg
James H. Sweet

Spirit, Structure, and Flesh:
Gendered Experiences in African Instituted Churches among the Yoruba of Nigeria
Deidre Helen Crumbley

A Hill among a Thousand: Transformations and Ruptures in Rural Rwanda
Danielle de Lame

Defeat Is the Only Bad News: Rwanda under Musinga, 1896–1931
Alison Liebhafsky Des Forges; edited by David Newbury

Power in Colonial Africa: Conflict and Discourse in Lesotho, 1870–1960
Elizabeth A. Eldredge

Nachituti's Gift: Economy, Society, and Environment in Central Africa
David M. Gordon

Intermediaries, Interpreters, and Clerks:
African Employees in the Making of Colonial Africa
Edited by Benjamin N. Lawrance, Emily Lynn Osborn, and
Richard L. Roberts

Naming Colonialism: History and Collective Memory in the Congo, 1870–1960
Osumaka Likaka

Early African Entertainments Abroad:
From the Hottentot Venus to Africa's First Olympians
Bernth Lindfors

Mau Mau's Children: The Making of Kenya's Postcolonial Elite
David P. Sandgren

Whispering Truth to Power:
Everyday Resistance to Reconciliation in Postgenocide Rwanda
Susan Thomson

Antecedents to Modern Rwanda: The Nyiginya Kingdom
Jan Vansina

Being Colonized: The Kuba Experience in Rural Congo, 1880–1960
Jan Vansina

The Postcolonial State in Africa: Fifty Years of Independence, 1960–2010
Crawford Young